"I Know It's Dangerous"

Y0-BDX-490

"I Know It's Dangerous"

Why Mexicans Risk Their Lives to Cross the Border

Lynnaire M. Sheridan

The University of Arizona Press   Tucson

JV 6483 .S538 2009 $24.95
Sheridan, Lynnaire M.
"I know it's dangerous"

3235500364150058

The University of Arizona Press
© 2009 The Arizona Board of Regents
All rights reserved

www.uapress.arizona.edu

Library of Congress Cataloging-in-Publication Data

Sheridan, Lynnaire M. (Lynnaire Maria)
    I know it's dangerous: why Mexicans risk their lives to cross
the border / Lynnaire M. Sheridan.
        p.   cm.
    Includes bibliographical references and index.
    ISBN 978-0-8165-2790-8 (hard cover : alk. paper) —
ISBN 978-0-8165-2857-8 (pbk. : alk. paper)
    1. United States—Emigration and immigration—
Government policy.   2. Mexicans—United States.   3. Illegal
aliens—United States.   4. Mexico—Emigration and
immigration.   I. Title.
    JV6483.S538   2009
    304.8'73072—dc22   2009030065

Publication of this book is made possible in part by the proceeds
of a permanent endowment created with the assistance of a
Challenge Grant from the National Endowment for the
Humanities, a federal agency.

♻

Manufactured in the United States of America on acid-free,
archival-quality paper containing a minimum of 30%
post-consumer waste and processed chlorine free.

14   13   12   11   10   09   6   5   4   3   2   1

One [U.S. Border Patrol] agent asked me why I was crossing. "Necessity," I said. "Do you think I'd be here if I didn't need to be? I know it's dangerous."

—*Rosa Hernández Cruz*

This book is dedicated to all the unauthorized migrants who have died trying to cross the U.S.–Mexico border.

Contents

Figures

Note: Unless otherwise specified, all photographs are by author.

Table

Preface

As I flew into Tijuana, the rooftops of its hundreds of factories gave me a chill. They reminded me of the killings of young female factory workers in Ciudad Juárez. To my mind, Tijuana was equally dangerous; documentaries had told me about its high crime, drug trafficking, and people smuggling. As I drove through downtown, I took mental snapshots of the beggars at its traffic lights, the dilapidated shacks on its hills, and the large steel wall downtown that divided it from the United States. Tijuana seemed like a quicksand pit, poised to trap you and slowly pull you under. Life was a battle played out on its mean streets and winning was merely surviving another day.

Getting to know Tijuana is a long process. Now that I can perceive its subtleties, I have begun to relish the city's unique character. With time comes the morbid satisfaction that you are somehow more alive when you experience the grittiness of life. There is a certain intrigue and pleasure that comes from living on the edge—between safe and dangerous, wealth and poverty, Mexico and the United States. Tijuana is a place where the usual conventions of culture and language do not apply, where there is not one but many realities, many experiences and many representations of everyday life.

I spent almost two years in the field picking through messages, signs, and experiences to get at one of the most problematic issues playing out in and around Tijuana: the migration of Mexicans to the United States. Migration is both an overt and covert activity that is deeply embedded in this city's daily life.

Initiating my research in 2003, I went into the field determined to gain new insights into the social impacts of large-scale tourism on Mexican communities. As I settled into my fieldwork, however, the border caught my attention. I recognized that tourist numbers were directly related to border policies. When the United States increased security measures at the border, its citizens stayed home rather than cross into Mexico and have to endure long waits on their return home.

Being from Australia, an island continent, I was fascinated by this land border and its influence on many aspects of everyday life on either side. I was constantly observing how life in the United States and Mexico was at once different and the same along the border. I lived the border life, shopping in San Diego while paying rent in Mexican pesos, picking the best of both sides. For me, the border hardly existed: I could cross and move freely between the two worlds. For many of my Mexican friends, however, the border was an impenetrable barrier and the United States inaccessible.

I would learn that different individuals perceive and understand the U.S.–Mexico border according to their particular beliefs and experiences. Some believe it is a physical barrier, while others believe it is a political illusion. For some, such as local residents, the border is a reality; for others, such as politicians in faraway cities or potential migrants in their Mexican villages, it is merely imagined. An arbitrary line on a map, the border is recognized by some and ignored by others, namely, the migrants who choose to cross it. In global economic terms, as evidenced by the North American Free Trade Agreement, the border may not exist at all, whereas in U.S. policy it is fixed and firm. That the border could mean something different to each person, according to his or her experiences or perceptions, was far beyond what I had expected to find. It left me with more questions than answers.

As a social researcher, when the façade of an integrated transborder life fell away, I could see the political, economic, and sociocultural role of the divide in everyday life, in particular, the interplay between border policy and migration. From popular songs on the radio, from graffiti around Tijuana, and from people in the street, I discovered that migration was dangerous. People were dying; not just a few Mexicans but the thousands trying to cross into the United States each day were affected. In ordinary discussions, I soon found out that "migrants," past and present, were not strangers but people I had come to know. More shocking, human traffickers were not mysterious figures from the underworld but friends of my acquaintances.

By this time, the large-scale tourism I was investigating had been much reduced by substantial delays at the border, and my research hampered by political barriers. I decided to focus on a topic that everyone wanted to talk to me about: the migration of Mexicans to the United States. I was immediately struck by the dehumanizing language of most publications and political reports on border management: they referred to migrants and, most often, to their experiences only in terms of statistics: numbers of detainees, numbers of deportations, numbers of deaths. Research that centered on the migrants as people could, I felt, make an important contribution to understanding an issue crucial to Mexicans and Americans alike.

My background both drew me to and uniquely suited me for this research. I speak both English and Spanish but am neither Mexican nor American and thus could ask questions without being labeled either a "gringa" or a "beaner." I have lived for equal periods of time in Mexico and the United States. I have special insights into migration, having had to obtain work and tourist visas in both countries. Indeed, migration became part of my life. I met and migrated with my Mexican fiancé (now husband) to Australia in the course of my research. Thus my analytical nature was matched with empathy, which enabled me to establish rapport with timid migrants, bold human traffickers, government officials, and antimigration spokespeople.

This book presents the human side of migration, a highly complex issue dominated by economic and legal arguments, with racial and cultural insecurities seldom far below the surface. In particular, it seeks to distill out the migrant voice, to discover, clarify, and analyze the Mexican response to the risks migrants face in crossing the border.

Acknowledgments

First and foremost, I would like to thank my research participants for their time, trust, and honesty. Many thanks also to the organizations that assisted me, including the American Friends Service Committee, Border Angels, Casa del Migrante en Tijuana, Centro Binacional de Derechos Humanos, Comisión Nacional de Derechos Humanos, Grupo Beta, Instituto Nacional de Migración, Raza Rights Coalition, and the Secretaría de Relaciones Exteriores.

I thank the University of Western Sydney and, in particular, my doctoral supervisors, Gregory Teal and Gabriela Coronado, for supporting this research project. Many thanks also to my friends and colleagues in Mexico, particularly to Arturo Lopez and his family, and to Patti Hartmann, Kristen Buckles, Jeffrey Lockridge, and the team at University of Arizona Press for all their assistance. And, finally, special thanks to my family, to my parents for their constant encouragement, and to my husband for all his support.

"I Know It's Dangerous"

1
Mexican Experiences, Responses, and Management of Migration Risks

The unauthorized migration of Mexicans to the United States—without formal U.S. permission or contrary to the terms of such permission—is undoubtedly one of the most crucial economic, social, political, and humanitarian issues facing these two countries. The sensitivity of this topic means that, on an official level, it has been strategically overlooked for most of recent history. So long as there were benefits for both countries, such as labor for U.S. employers and income for Mexican families, and the negative consequences of migration were minimal, it was relatively easy to sustain the status quo.

Since the early 1990s, however, the level of U.S. border security has intensified, dramatically so since the terrorist attacks of September 11, 2001. The result has been increased levels of risk to unauthorized migrants crossing into the United States from Mexico, the majority of whom are Mexicans. Nevertheless, despite increasing risk—on average, one migrant dies every day while attempting to cross the border unauthorized—Mexicans continue to migrate to the United States in growing numbers.

Delving into the social and cultural processes of migration, this study explores how Mexicans experience, respond to, and manage the risks of unauthorized migration. It is the fruit of two years of ethnographic fieldwork undertaken at the border in 2003–2004 and is based on two key premises: (1) Mexicans experience, but can only respond to, rather than proactively alter, the intrinsic risks of unauthorized migration to the United States; and (2) the risks facing unauthorized migrants crossing into the United States are escalating due to deliberate changes to the U.S. border policies.

As we will see, implementation of stricter border policies by the United States has not dissuaded unauthorized migration from Mexico but has, instead, increased the risks facing migrants as they seek to avoid detection, detention, and deportation back to Mexico. Although the policies have been effective in channeling migrants away from urban centers and into remote areas, contrary to the expectations of the U.S. government, neither the harsh climatic conditions nor the difficult terrain of these areas has deterred migration. Instead, relying on a variety of strategies, and especially on their social and family networks to select human traffickers who have good knowledge of the current situation at the border, a growing number of migrants have achieved safe and successful crossings under these more dangerous circumstances.

Moreover, as policies have changed and border crossings have become more dangerous, migrants have reduced the frequency of their crossings. They are now more willing to expose their women and children to the risks of these fewer crossings to ensure that, in the longer term, their families remain intact. This response suggests that the population of unauthorized migrants in the United States is most likely increasing rather than decreasing. Thus stricter U.S. border measures appear to have raised the risks to unauthorized migrants without materially benefiting the United States.

Meaningful responses by the Mexican government, civil society, and the news media to such heightened risks have been stifled by the difficult politics of migration. The result has been scare campaigns at one end of the spectrum and rescue campaigns at the other. Both may have been more effective in educating the U.S. public on the plight of the unauthorized migrants than in dissuading the migrants from crossing. The ironies of such campaigns are not lost on the migrants. For example, posters and press releases warn of the risks of dealing with human traffickers, yet these same traffickers are responsible for the estimated 10,000 safe and successful crossings each day.

Mexican popular culture, expressed in both art and music, has moved beyond political barriers to openly present the complexities of unauthorized migration, the interwoven realities of the border crossing, where migration can be the best or worst decision a family can make, and where the migrants' fate is decided by the interaction of particular people and policies. Drawing on real-life stories, artists and musicians more closely depict actual migrant experiences of risk, which helps explain the popularity of their pictures and songs among both migrants and the broader Mexican community.

To reach these conclusions required, on the one hand, carefully analyzing the historical, economic, political, and cultural context of unauthorized migration from Mexico to the United States and, on the other, gathering insights from those who were willing to take the risks, the unauthorized migrants. The journey toward understanding risk and unauthorized migration from Mexico begins with an overview of why unauthorized migrants worldwide are subject to risk, background on unauthorized migration from Mexico to the United States, and a brief presentation of my research methodology.

From Global Migration Trends to the Personal Risks Encountered by Mexican Migrants

In 2000, approximately 3 percent of the world's people lived outside their country of origin. That equates to around 150 million people, 12 million of whom were refugees. Although relatively few when compared to the world's total population of more than 6 billion at the time, migrants continue to generate considerable controversy. According to Peter Stalker, this is because

> to ask about the rights of immigrants is to reopen many awkward questions. Migrants, for example, typically do many of the "3-Ds" dirty, dangerous and difficult jobs and work for desperately low pay. But why should those who do the least desirable jobs get paid less, when they deserve to get paid more? Migrants also require us to think about international solidarity. Should the accident of being born in France rather than Morocco, say, entitle you to be seven times richer? When French and Moroccans live apart, the question scarcely arises, but once they start to rub shoulders there can be uncomfortable and sometimes violent friction.[1]

The controversy surrounding migrants is not limited to just work and pay. Migrants spoil the perfect image of the modern nation-state, revealing inconsistencies in the underlying social beliefs and practices that sustain everyday life and national ideologies. Migration puts in question an individual's identity as well as the basis for his or her particular social and economic status. The strongest reactions to migration are typically felt in the receiving countries, where migrants are perceived as not sharing in a receiving country's national identity.[2]

Although migration is not a new practice, the proportionally high numbers of migrants after World War II have heightened awareness of migration issues and exacerbated the consequences of both inbound and outbound migration. Until then, migration control measures, such as passports and visas, were largely unknown. Indeed, Joseph Nevins

contends, to reinforce its nationhood as it becomes ever more intercon-
nected with the global economy, the modern nation-state has required
ever stricter controls for the movement of workers in and out of its
national borders.[3] "People are not only legal citizens of a nation," Stuart
Hall tells us; "they participate in the idea of the nation as represented
in its national culture. A nation is a symbolic community and it is this
which accounts for its 'power to generate a sense of identity' [to use Bill
Schwarz's term]."[4]

As globalization cuts across national boundaries to integrate and
connect communities outside of the nation-state, domestic policy is
used to strengthen boundaries and the sense of belonging within the
country.[5] When nationalism gives rise to violent antimigrant sentiment,
the already vulnerable migrants are subject to physical threats as well as
poor working conditions.[6] Under these difficult conditions, one might
ask why migrants continue to work in foreign countries rather than stay
within their own communities. Two popular theories attempt to explain
current migration patterns.

The individual theory of migration assumes that the potential migrant
carefully evaluates the different options and determines the destination
that would best suit his or her circumstances, ideally a place where there
are good work prospects and the migrant can attain the highest wage.
Thus, Stalker suggests, a Thai laborer who could earn $100 a month in
nearby Malaysia would, ideally, travel to Israel, where the minimum
monthly wage is $650.[7]

The structuralist theory of migration, in contrast, deems the potential migrant as vulnerable and subject to forces beyond his or her control. The migrant merely reacts to these forces, commonly referred to as
"push and pull" factors: "these forces could be economic, or social, or
political pushing people out of one country and pulling them towards
another. In the sending country, the structural forces pushing emigrants
out could be population pressure, or land shortage, or gender discrimination. In the receiving country, the structural forces attracting the
immigrant could be a shrinking population, or a shortage of people to
work on the land, or the demand for domestic servants."[8]

One key concept espoused by the structuralist theory is that the
global economy and labor markets are established on wage imbalances
both within and between nations. In one country, the dual labor market
creates one layer of workers with stable, secure, and high-paying jobs,
while another group of people are limited to dirty, difficult, dangerous,

and low-paying tasks. So long as there are wage differentials between countries, migrants are prepared to travel to other countries to undertake the low-paying jobs because these are higher paying than the same type of work in their own country. Regulating migration sustains the domestic and global wage imbalance by controlling the flow of migrant workers. If this were not the case, theoretically, the imbalance would be smoothed out and migration would fall off.[9]

Although the individual and structuralist theories explain some instances of migration, they do not explain many others. Stalker highlights two such instances. A developed country with wages well above those of its developing counterparts, New Zealand should, theoretically, attract rather than lose migrants, but it does not. And because Greece belongs to the European Union, Greeks could legally migrate to Luxembourg or any other member-state where the average per capita income is substantially higher, but they do not. Although the same external forces may apply, individual responses appear to differ for reasons indiscernible by economic migration models.[10]

Everette Lee, a structural theorist, nevertheless believes that it is possible to model migration patterns by identifying all the factors driving migration and thus come to understand its complexities. He proposes four key factors that act on a person's predisposition to migrate. These are the conditions in the country of origin (push), the state of affairs in the receiving country (pull), intervening obstacles (barriers), and the personal context (societal and individual beliefs or perceptions and the material circumstances). Lee's model incorporates the challenges of migration as perceived by potential migrants and their personal situations; it does not assume that people respond only to economic stimuli. The nuances of human decision making, in his opinion, substantially affect the migration outcome.[11]

Although most people migrate to improve their economic situation, their decisions may not always be strictly in accord with labor market models, which narrowly define migrants as workers. So long as migration research is dominated by economic or political studies, understanding the underlying sociocultural rationales for migration will be limited. If there is to be informed migration policy debate, however, sociocultural research must investigate intervening obstacles to migration and aspects of personal circumstances that affect migration decision making.

There are numerous economic studies of the unauthorized migration of Mexicans to the United States, including seminal works by academics such as Jorge Bustamente and Wayne Cornelius, but there are few social or cultural studies. Works such as David Maciel and María Herrera Sobek's *Culture across Borders: Mexican Immigration and Popular Culture*, José Manuel Valenzuela Arce's *Nuestros piensos: Culturas populares en la frontera México–Estados Unidos*, Claire Fox's *The Fence and the River: Culture and Politics at the U.S.–Mexico Border*, Pablo Vila's *Crossing Borders, Reinforcing Borders* and Susan Mains's *Contested Spaces: Representing Borders and Immigrant Identities between the United States and Mexico* are all important exceptions.[12] That said, most of these studies focus on the cultural products and practices emerging at the U.S.–Mexico border, rather than on the culture of migration itself, and even fewer studies consider the culture of risk inherent in unauthorized migration practices despite the often fatal consequences of taking that risk.[13]

According to U.S. border policy analyst Joseph Nevins, the United States currently uses risk as a tool to discourage unauthorized crossings, but, even with increasing migrant deaths, there appears to be no actual decrease in unauthorized crossings. Under these circumstances, an investigation into the social factors that affect migrant decisions to cross the border is vital to formulating sound U.S. migration policy.[14]

"Risk" implies a degree of predictability and an opportunity to avert negative outcomes through the management of risk factors. Risk provides those who subject themselves to it with a tool by which to demand compensation for negative consequences. Thus, despite efforts to scientifically define and calculate it, risk is highly politicized. Governments are responsible for protecting the public from risk by legislation but are also held responsible, or blamed, for the consequences of their policies, as constituents demand effective policies that maximize positive and minimize negative outcomes. In light of the deaths of unauthorized Mexican migrants, this accountability has serious implications for both the U.S. and Mexican governments.[15]

In theoretical terms, if all the potential sources of risk are identified, then the probability of an event occurring may be calculated. In real life, however, a poor understanding of how people perceive risk and how they decide to act where risk is involved hampers risk management. Perceptions of risk may be affected by age, education, socioeconomic status, culture, and gender. Personal attitudes are integral to the decision-making process and, according to Mary Thompson et al., the final decision is affected by "the degree of dread the person feels toward the risk in question, the extent to which the risk is known to the individual, and the likely consequences if the risk in question should occur."[16]

Michael Siegrist, Carmen Keller, and Henk Kiers discovered that cultural differences affected risk perception. They identified that people in cultures with generally high levels of trust and confidence (a feeling that everything is under control and uncertainty is low) have reduced perceptions of risk. In contrast, those who have low general confidence and general trust have heightened perceptions of risk, even of old or familiar risks. Furthermore, although a weak trend, according to a 1996 review of the literature, women tended to express higher levels of concern about potential risks than did men.[17]

Society and the people around the decision maker therefore heavily influence that person's understanding of the risks and the potential outcomes. Risk management research on individual decision making has, however, overlooked social influences and the general societal consensus regarding the risk involved. This is a serious oversight because, according to Mary Douglas, "anger, hope, and fear are part of most risky situations. No one takes a decision that involves costs without consulting neighbors, family, work friends. These are the support group that will help if things go wrong."[18]

The greater the risk, the more an individual craves input from family and friends. This social network provides valuable insights into the situation, based on either experience or perceptions of the risk. In the case of migration, participants in decision making become stakeholders in the process, sometimes receiving dividends (remittances) or suffering loss of income depending on the outcome of the decision. According to Chris Martin, this is particularly the case with unauthorized migration since "migration decisions are rarely taken by individuals alone: they are more likely to be coordinated household decisions, in which the support of wider kith and kin networks is expected. For this reason, migrants may be particularly able to withstand the risks of migration and unconducive working conditions." Martin suggests that suffering may be accepted and accommodated if the migrant believes that the longer-term gain, for the individual or the family, outweighs any shorter-term loss.[19] In the case of unauthorized migration from Mexico to the United States, the border is a threshold that, once passed, leads to a relatively safe and stable existence.[20] If the migrant can endure the risks of the crossing, the long-term benefits are considerably greater than can be achieved in Mexico.[21] Moreover, most potential migrants are already "at risk," being particularly vulnerable to economic instability. In the eyes of the migrants, the peril of crossing the border may be less than the peril of their current circumstances and thus justify their undertaking the migration journey.

On another level, social networks provide vital information that helps individuals avoid the pitfalls of unauthorized migration. "What often happens," explains Stalker, "is that one adventurous, or desperate, person or family settles arbitrarily in a new place. If these pioneers are successful, they then send the word back to others, triggering a sequence of 'chain migration.' In fact few migrants travel without overseas contacts—people who can help them find accommodation and employment. In this case, individuals making their own choices eventually build up a migration structure all of their own."[22] Essentially, the information provided and the very existence of these linkages give the next wave of migrants the confidence to leave home and settle in another country.[23]

Extensive and close-knit networks of Mexican families and friends stretch across the border and provide potential migrants with up-to-date information about the status of migration at the border and employment in the United States. It is the strength of these cross-border linkages, David Lorey contends, that has allowed Mexicans to migrate despite stricter border security measures. Although the input by family and friends is widely acknowledged, the role of social networks in risk-centered decision making is yet to be investigated in any meaningful way.[24]

In a more general sense, the role of society in decision making also needs to be considered. The sheer number of Mexicans migrating to the United States may have established a culture of acceptance. If this is so, it may have lessened the perceptions of risk and increased a false sense of security. After the death of her migrant husband, Brazilian Nilce Aparecida Moreira da Silva explained that her husband "knew there was some risk [in crossing the border from Mexico], but he wasn't nervous, because he saw that so many other people from around here had gone and done well in the United States."[25]

The number of migrants who successfully reach the United States may appear to compensate for those who are less fortunate. That "everybody" is migrating may reinforce and justify the decision to migrate but lessen consideration by individuals and their families of the actual risks that each individual might face.

Having defined risk in the context of unauthorized migration from Mexico, let us now examine Mexico's economic dependency on the United States, its consequent limited capacity to reduce the risks faced by Mexicans crossing the border, and the patterns of risk associated with changes to U.S. border policies.

U.S. Border Policies and the Changing Risks to Mexican Migrants

Estimates of the overall number of unauthorized migrants in the United States vary considerably: in 2008, the American Immigration Lawyers Association estimated it to be 12 million, for example, whereas the Federation for American Immigration Reform (FAIR) suggested that the number exceeded 13 million.[26]

From 1990 to 2003, an estimated 300,000 unauthorized Mexican migrants were crossing the border each year. In 1996, the INS estimated that 54 percent of all unauthorized migrants in the United States were Mexican. That said, unauthorized crossings accounted for 1 percent of all border crossings from Mexico in 1996.[27] The overwhelming majority of Mexicans crossed the border legally, with some 40,000 people crossing from Tijuana each day to work in San Diego, and with Mexican shoppers crossing the border some 250 million times to spend an estimated 25 billion dollars in the United States every year.[28]

According to Mexican figures, in 2003, 8 million Mexican-born people resided in the United States; this is equivalent to 9 percent of Mexico's population at the time. Mexico estimated that 3.4 million of the 8 million Mexican residents were unauthorized, and another half million temporary seasonal workers came and went without permission.[29]

Since the 1970s, there has been a rapid increase in unauthorized migration from Mexico. This has been attributed to the post–World War II population explosion in Mexico, an increase of 30 million people in just twenty years. Although the Mexican economy was arguably able to keep pace until the late 1970s, a fall in oil prices increased foreign debt. This resulted in an economic crisis, with some 10 million Mexicans sliding into poverty. The economic crisis created a strong push factor and encouraged Mexicans to consider migration, authorized or otherwise, as a poverty reduction strategy.[30] The crisis also exacerbated the already significant level of income disparity between Mexico and the United States; higher wages in the United States have always acted as a strong migrant pull factor. For example, an average factory worker in the United States earns four times as much as a Mexican factory worker and thirty times as much as a Mexican agricultural worker.[31]

A 2002 estimate suggests that remittances from unauthorized Mexican migrants residing in the United States supported 1.2 million Mexican families at the time, contributing to both individual and regional economic development.[32] A record $23 billion was sent from the United States to Mexico in 2006. Remittances are second only to petroleum in generating foreign exchange for Mexico.[33] The reliance on remittances from unauthorized workers is so widely accepted that even municipal governments solicit funds from their Mexican constituents now living in the United States. For example, Mayor Alberto Ruiz Flores of Valparaiso toured the United States trying to convince the town's migrants, who wire $100,000 to family members each month, to share some funds with local government to develop shared community infrastructure.[34]

At no time in history has the Mexican federal government attempted to stop the unauthorized migration of its citizens to the United States, basing this stance on the Mexican constitution, which entitles all Mexican citizens to freedom of movement throughout the entirety of Mexican territory—they are free to move up to the border and untouchable to their government once they cross.[35] It is only in the last quarter of the twentieth century, according to David Heer, that the Mexican government has demanded some protection of unauthorized migrants, or at least some consideration of their human rights.[36]

The turnaround is attributed to recognition of unauthorized migration as Mexico's economic safety valve. Suddenly, the national government began referring to citizens working in the United States as "heroes" who battle against racial injustice in the United States. Skeptics claim that these comments, made under the pretense of defending migrant rights, may actually be part of a strategy to encourage further unauthorized migration or, at the very least, to justify the current levels of remittance funds.[37]

With the implementation of U.S. unauthorized migration strategies, such as California's Operation Gatekeeper (discussed later in this chapter), the situation has become more complicated for the Mexican government. As Mexican citizens become exposed to ever-greater levels of physical and psychological risk, there is a call by both Mexicans and Mexican Americans for greater political accountability. Although most of the blame is cast upon the U.S. government, the Mexican government is increasingly being held responsible. Human rights advocates, such as Claudia Smith, state that, although the United States may be blamed for its deadly border policies, Mexico is also to blame so long as the government fails to bring ideas to the negotiating table and to demand that the rights of its migrant citizens be respected.[38]

The Mexican government is now expected to speak out and act against the potentially lethal border protection strategies of the United States. In part, this may be because of a genuine sense of concern, but it is also likely to be a response to domestic discontent and concern over the death of migrants who left in search of an income to support their families. Moreover, Mexicans legally residing in the United States, an important source of Mexico's revenue, have secured the right to vote in Mexico and want to have a say in the development associated with their economic contribution. Those in government, who wish to remain in office, need to satisfy these two migrant-related constituent groups.[39]

Ironically, when the Mexican government did appear to make a serious effort to establish a migration accord with the United States, it was sidetracked by the terrorist attacks of September 11, 2001, which sparked tighter and tougher regulation of the borders against those who were "invading" the United States.[40] Tensions built up between the United States and Mexico as the more security conscious United States perceived all unauthorized migrants as potential terrorists escaping border controls.[41] Evaluating the diplomatic situation between Mexico and the United States, Jerry Kammer reported that "at an international economic summit in Mexico, [President Vicente] Fox tried again to engage Bush on the undocumented immigrants Fox calls heroes and vows to protect. Bush wasn't buying. He wanted to talk about the war on terrorism and the dangers of Saddam Hussein. The confab was called a flop on both sides of the border. Mexico's hopes on immigration have fallen victim not only to Bush's focus on terrorism since the Sept. 11 attacks, but also to the inflated expectations of the two presidents."[42]

Although Mexican President Vicente Fox and U.S. President George W. Bush continued to discuss seasonal worker programs, political analysts in the regional news media stated that, even with presidential momentum, there was little support for immigration reform in the U.S. Congress.[43]

In the likelihood that immigration reform will not be seriously considered by Congress anytime soon and that the United States will continue to formulate and enforce unilateral border and migration policies, there is not much the Mexican government can do to reduce risk to its unauthorized migrant citizens. U.S. border policy decisions are pivotal to the exposure of unauthorized Mexican migrants to physical and psychological risk.

In the meantime, Mexican migrants have responded to the tense political situation and the tightening of border security measures by moving away from short-term toward long-term or more permanent migration to the United States. In the first half of the 1970s, Wayne Cornelius found that only 19 percent of male migrants wanted to live permanently in the United States, and thus only 1 percent had brought their wives (and potentially their children) with them. By 1976, David North and Marion Houstoun found that 11 percent of unauthorized male migrants were now bringing their wives, in preparation for a longer-term stay.[44] According to Leigh Binford, because of the greater risks of the border crossing, it is now preferable to remain in the United States for the long term. "The tightened border strengthened and enriched immigrant smugglers and raised the cost of migration both in monetary and human terms, as migrants bypassed heavily patrolled urban areas for treacherous desert and mountain terrain. The policy also converted a previously circular migration into a more permanent one, as many of those who had succeeded in entering the United States prolonged their stays in order to avoid the hazards of another crossing following a visit home."[45]

The longer stay is also encouraged by the shift in the U.S. economy from seasonal work toward service industries. Sheldon Maram's study found that, by 1980, 70 percent of unauthorized migrants were service industry workers based in the factories and restaurants of Los Angeles. They crossed and never returned to Mexico.[46] Service industry jobs provide regular, rather than seasonal, employment, making it more attractive to remain for the long term in the United States.[47]

Spending long periods of time in the United States, for whatever reason, means that Mexicans are now both economically and culturally dependent on U.S. society. The United States not only pays migrant workers wages so they can support their families but now also educates their children, many of whom are not even Mexican citizens but are U.S. citizens by birth. With families stretching across the border, migration has seeped into everyday life and family culture.

Beyond economic necessity, migration to the United States has now taken on a role in the routines and rituals of Mexican life. In some communities, young boys reach a certain age and then migrate to the United States as though it were a rite of passage into adulthood. According to Graciela Orozco, Esther González, and Roger Díaz de Cossio, in "some Mexican towns, particularly those with a strong history of migration, going to the United States for a season is like a rite of passage for young men, even when their family is well off. That's what has been found in many communities in Jalisco, Michoacán, and Guanajuato."[48]

Challenge, risk taking, and adventure serve as vital tests of manhood in a variety of cultures. They are most commonly associated with rites of passage for adolescent males. Even in Western society, many teenagers see taking risks as fundamental to personal growth and the creation of self.[49]

In Pegueros, unauthorized migration is a tradition, with grandfathers, fathers, and sons all sharing this experience. Males who do not migrate may be stigmatized and, at the very least, may suffer the anguish of seeing the local girls swarm around successful migrants who return with cars and money. To the men of Pegueros, migration is integral to their status and identity as men.[50] Indeed, border researcher Pablo Vila emphasizes that migration economics, culture, and identity are all closely entwined and "most of those problems have their origins in complex issues of culture and identity."[51]

According to Eric Hobsbawm, tradition is a process of formalization and ritualization of past actions, if only through repetition. Thus the sheer number of Mexicans migrating to the United States generation after generation has created a tradition. The migration journey has changed over time to become, for many Mexicans, as much cultural as it is economic.[52]

Thus, too, even though migration patterns were originally forged by economic necessity (the need for Mexican workers to move elsewhere to secure an income), today established cultural processes, social networks, and even rites of passage reinforce the traditional migration patterns. The intertwining of economics and culture means that it would be impossible to change, that is, to slow or stop, this culture of migration without resolving the economic issues facing Mexico. But even if economic circumstances were to change, unauthorized migration would continue, at least to some extent, for several years thanks to its sociocultural momentum, fueled by family reunion, and to its rite-of-passage appeal. This would be particularly the case if no legal alternative to unauthorized migration were provided. Research focusing only on economic factors thus overlooks the important contribution of culture to migration. Maciel and Herrera Sobek make the point that "the cultural elements of Mexican immigration, and the cultural/artistic manifestations that this immigration process has inspired, have not received the academic inquiry that they merit. . . . In spite of the critical importance of the cultural dimension of Mexican immigration, until recently, and with very few exceptions, the subject had remained neglected by the scholars of both countries."[53]

Even within the area of cultural research, the emphasis has been on the cultural products and the role these play in the creation of a sense of meaning, sociopolitical awareness, and the aesthetics of border life—products such as the literature, photography, and graffiti discussed in Luis Humberto Crosthwaite's *Puro Border: Dispatches, Snapshots and Graffiti from La Frontera*, or the blending of cultural traditions as featured in Maciel and Herrera Sobek's *Culture Across Borders: Mexican Immigration and Popular Culture*. In *Ethnography at the Border* and *Crossing Borders, Reinforcing Borders*, Pablo Vila has moved the debate forward by examining the social processes of border crossing, both authorized and unauthorized.[54] Still, the majority of sociocultural studies have not looked at the often fatal risks taken by Mexican migrants, despite the impact that increasing numbers of migrant deaths have on Mexican and U.S. society.

Thus, even though data at the fringes suggest migration is a cultural phenomenon existing not just within but often beyond economics, relatively few studies have stepped outside of economic, or even policy-based, research approaches to investigate the cultural nature of migration. Having established the economic and cultural dependence of Mexicans on unauthorized migration to the United States, the current study will strive to understand the way in which culture is important in developing migration strategies and risk management.

Because the Mexican government has a limited capacity to influence the United States, we need to closely examine U.S. border management strategies over time to determine the implications of the interplay between risk and these strategies for the well-being of unauthorized Mexican migrants.

Indeed, the United States has not always followed clear and consistent policies for managing its southern border. Instead, the pendulum has swung from tight regulation of the border during economic downturns to loose regulation during upturns, to encourage unauthorized migrants to fill labor shortages.[55]

According to Philip Martin and Michael Teitelbaum: "Choices about immigration have long been controlled less by logic than by unorthodox coalitions that bring together antagonistic regional, ideological, economic and ethnic interest groups."[56]

In a traditional political process, governments create policy from consensus. In the case of migration and border management, the general public of the United States has been politically apathetic, perhaps because it is not part of the migration process, thus the debate is left to the nationalistic antimigration groups and predominantly Mexican American, pro-migration lobby groups. The antagonism between these two groups is extreme and may be traced back to the Treaty of Guadalupe Hidalgo and the controversial establishment of the current divide between the United States and Mexico.

The United States–Mexico War, 1846 to 1848, was settled with the Treaty of Guadalupe Hidalgo, signed February 2, 1848. With U.S. forces occupying Mexico City, General Antonio López de Santa Anna, Mexico's commanding officer, sold one-third of Mexican territory to the United States, thus establishing a new international boundary.[57] Together with land sold under the Gadsden Purchase in 1854, Mexico ceded, in all, one-half of its territory to the United States. For their part, the Mexican people accepted neither the Treaty of Guadalupe Hidalgo nor the "loss" of their national territory.[58]

The Treaty of Guadalupe Hidalgo is still relevant to the unauthorized migration of Mexicans to the United States today because, according to Daniel James, for most migrants, the border is not a moral barrier:

> Mexico had left behind in the conquered territories many thousands of people, including both Indians and Mexican settlers. An estimated 75,000 Mexicans chose to become U.S. citizens[, and] their presence north of the Rio Grande, which finally became the borderline between Mexico and the United States, had the effect of rendering the new "border" basically unreal. As they always had, people on both sides traveled back and forth, exchanged goods and services, intermarried, shared the same religious, cultural, and linguistic traditions, in utter freedom. Even after formal customhouses and immigration checkpoints were established, nothing really interfered with the human intercourse that had been going on for centuries. In time, the border seemed to behave like a "third nation," its inhabitants equally remote in many ways from their respective central governments.[59]

For Mexicans and Mexican Americans interacting as a part of everyday life, the treaty created a legal divide but did not establish an effective physical or even symbolic barrier. Mexicans residing in the United States continued to see the land as their own despite changing political circumstances. Mexico-based Mexicans felt historical rights to the land, considered the treaty unjust, and tended to ignore the new divide.

The treaty failed to make "illegality" a moral barrier to unauthorized migration. Even today perceptions of the treaty as unjust and therefore not binding are used, particularly by Mexican Americans, to justify unauthorized migration.[60] Because the illegality of their crossing the border unauthorized is not perceived as an intervening moral obstacle, migrants have no moral sense of doing wrong. Instead, they view the border not as a legal or moral barrier, but as a physical one.

To understand the history of physical barriers and the heightening of physical and psychological risk at the border, we need to examine U.S. migration laws, policy, and practices. Technically, the first-ever migration law, banning the immigration of convicts and prostitutes into the United States, was enacted by the United States in 1875. But it was the Immigration Act of 1917, requiring an $8 fee for migration, and the 1924 amendment, requiring a $10 fee for a tourist visa, that first defined U.S. migration policy, a policy based essentially on economic restrictions rather than on clear, character-based selection protocols.[61]

The United States has been historically reliant on Mexican labor. In the early 1900s, U.S. farmers and railway owners actively recruited Mexicans. Between 1910 and 1919, some 200,000 Mexican migrants headed for Texas, Arizona, and California.[62] In 1925, the U.S. Congress passed legislation to establish the U.S. Border Patrol to prevent both the smuggling of contraband and the unauthorized immigration of Chinese from Mexico and Canada into the United States.[63]

The beginning of the Great Depression in 1929 led to significant changes in U.S. migration policies, and, for the first time, it became a crime to cross from Mexico into the United States without official documents. A backlash to the economic crisis was accompanied by the mass expulsion of unauthorized Mexican migrants known as "Operation Wetback," so named because the migrants arrived wet (*mojados*) into the United States after crossing the Rio Grande. Despite this and other anti-migration initiatives, there were still, according to some reports, about 750,000 unauthorized Mexican migrants living in the United States in 1954.[64]

During the 1940s, partly as a result of World War II, U.S. demand for labor increased. The Bracero Program was established between the United States and Mexico to enable a set number of Mexicans to enter the United States as legitimate seasonal laborers. Its bureaucratic requirements, however, led many workers to shun the program. With jobs being enthusiastically offered to Mexicans, independent of their migration status, more Mexican migrants than ever were arriving, unauthorized, into the United States.[65] The hiring of such migrants, under the guise of the Bracero Program, was further encouraged by a provision in the 1952 amended Immigration Act that made it lawful. For the first time, the influence of employers on migration legislation made itself felt.[66]

In 1964, the Bracero Program ceased and the United States developed a principally unilateral migration policy.[67] Legislation in 1965 established a quota system, with 120,000 migrants allowed to enter from the Western Hemisphere (the Americas). Then, in 1976, the quota was changed to 20,000 per Western Hemisphere nation, substantially reducing the number of Mexicans who could legally enter the United States. This legislation coincided with the growing public awareness of unauthorized migration, in part generated by the INS itself. As Heer explains, "The existence of undocumented migrants was not considered a major social problem until the early 1970s when the Commissioner of the U.S. Immigration and Naturalization Service set the probable number of undocumented immigrants in the United States at from 6 to 8 million persons. He later characterized the inflow as a 'silent invasion of the United States.'"[68]

The commissioner's estimated unauthorized migrant figures sparked broad public awareness of the unauthorized migration of Mexicans to the United States. Because most alternate estimates at the time were substantially lower—3 to 4 million—leading commentators suspected that the commissioner's figures were politically motivated.[69]

With increasing public scrutiny, a watershed for U.S. migration management was the 1986 Immigration Reform and Control Act. Approved by the U.S. Senate on October 17, 1986, the act contained five principal components: sanctions for employers of unauthorized workers, legalization of many unauthorized workers (through an amnesty), a limited agricultural guest worker program, the requirement that the INS obtain warrants before conducting open-field raids, and, finally, the authorization of more funds to the INS to implement more stringent border security measures.[70]

The reforms were designed to dramatically reduce the unauthorized migrant population by legalizing approximately 50 percent of the migrants. Employer sanctions were put in place to keep the remaining unauthorized migrants from finding work, with the expectation that most would voluntarily return to Mexico; over time, the others would be discovered and deported.[71] Some 3 million unauthorized immigrants sought to be legalized through the Immigration Reform and Control Act's amnesty provision and some 2.4 million were actually granted legal status.[72] This was of great benefit to Mexicans, who made up six out of every ten unauthorized migrants living in the United States at the time.[73]

Unauthorized migration from Mexico to the United States did appear to slow for a three-year period after the 1986 reforms but then returned to previous levels.[74] Some claim that the reforms became ineffective when employer sanctions were weakened and then poorly implemented.[75] In particular, criticism centered on the limited number of government migration agents allocated to employer sanctions, 350 agents being responsible for 7 million employers. Furthermore, fewer than half of the 12,714 cases reported from 1989 to 1994 resulted in fines. For many employers, the possible sanctions were not an obstacle to receiving the benefits of cheap labor. Thus the easy availability of jobs in the United States continued to be a magnet for unauthorized migrants. By 1990, U.S. Border Patrol statistics reported a return to pre-1986 levels, with 1.5 million unauthorized migrants being detained each year and many more achieving successful entry to the United States.[76]

The inability of the 1986 federal reforms to control unauthorized migration provoked stricter state government reforms in California, Texas, Arizona, and Florida. The atmosphere was particularly tense in California during the 1990s. As Alberto Ledesma explained at the time: "Mexican undocumented migration has recently become a significant issue in the political arena, especially in California. The growing population of Mexican immigrants with their perceived 'need' for social services, education, and cultural space has created a backlash against all immigrants—documented and undocumented—a backlash that has manifested itself in such varied forms as the Federal Immigration Reform and Control Act of 1986, California's English-Only movement of the late 1980s and 1994's Proposition 187."[77]

The most controversial anti–unauthorized migration measure was California's Proposition 187, which would prevent "illegal aliens" from receiving the benefits of public services in California. On November 8, 1994, it was approved by 59 percent of the voters.[78] Proposition 187 was designed to reduce the popularity of California as a migrant destination and to address the costs of providing services to an unauthorized migrant population.[79] When the proposition was found to be unconstitutional, there were public protests in California; the state legislature tabled every proposed new migration reform. "The failure of immigration laws to stem the tide," explains Manuel González, "once again resurrected xenophobic sentiments, particularly vis-à-vis Mexicans. The fears were most pronounced in California, where denunciations of illegals reached a fever pitch. Violence was common. The backlash created by border problems was so intense that a whole series of measures was introduced in the state assembly to combat Mexican immigration. The drive, spearheaded by Republican assemblymen in Southern California, enjoyed popular success."[80]

Anti-Mexican sentiment led to vigilantism, including "beaner" raids (*beaner* being a derogatory term used by antimigrant and racist groups when referring to Mexicans) on Mexican migrant workers, including a gun attack led by local teenagers in Encinitas, California. The White Aryan Resistance and Light Up the Border led border protests to endorse any proposal for the militarization of the United States' southern border. These protest groups were founded, or at least supported, by employees of the Immigration and Naturalization Service to foster antimigration sentiment, perhaps to attract more funding for their service or merely to uphold their personal beliefs.[81]

One force behind the backlash was a rapid and obvious demographic change in California. In 1990, an estimated 4.3 million Mexican-born people lived in the United States; the number reached 8.7 million in the year 2000. More than three-quarters of these migrants were concentrated in just four states: California (42.6 percent), Texas (21.4 percent), Illinois (6.5 percent), and Arizona (5.2 percent).[82] Forty-four percent of all unauthorized Mexican migrants were living in Los Angeles County.[83] In the past, unauthorized migrants undertook seasonal work in rural areas and were out of sight to most U.S. citizens, but, with a shift in the U.S. economy, these workers were doing service jobs and were now highly visible to urban voters.[84]

In San Diego, antimigrant sentiments were exacerbated by the city's transition from being predominantly Anglo to more noticeably Hispanic and by the fact that, during the early 1990s, one-third of all unauthorized entries into the United States took place there.[85] Protests increased awareness of unauthorized migration; to satisfy voters, policies began to incorporate stronger enforcement measures with reinforcement of border structures. Not surprisingly, most efforts were concentrated on the San Ysidro–Tijuana border divide.[86]

As a first measure, in September of 1989, floodlights were installed along the boundary at San Ysidro and, within the period of a year, the number of U.S. agents was increased by almost a hundred. This was followed by the construction of the border wall at San Ysidro–Tijuana, the first of eight raised between 1990 and 2003 in California and Arizona. This measure assuaged antimigration sentiment to some extent but gave rise to other community concerns. The wall, built by the U.S military from corrugated steel once used as landing mats in the Vietnam War, was perceived as a symbol of violence between two supposedly peaceful neighbors.[87] The campaign to erect physical barriers at the border has continued to the present day, with regular proposals for border walls, or reinforcements of current walls, being considered by Congress.[88]

In Mexico, the border wall was likened to the Berlin Wall; critics in the United States recalled earlier proposals for a "Tortilla Curtain" and a "Carter Curtain." When originally proposed by the Carter administration, the concept of a border wall sparked protests culminating in a march at San Ysidro in January 1979, attended by over 1,300 Mexican Americans. At the time, the San Diego City Council opposed a fence, claiming it would be ineffective for border control and would only serve to hurt relations with Mexico.[89]

Soon after the border wall was completed in 1990, the U.S. Border Patrol declared it to be effective. There were fewer attacks on migrants in the no-man's land (a vacant zone) on the U.S. side of the border and a decrease in human traffickers driving into the United States. Limited evidence suggested that migrant traffic had shifted eastward to the outskirts of the urban areas.[90] There was no consideration of the potentially greater risks for migrants on the Mexican side of the border.

In the context of increasing structural and symbolic measures to reinforce the border, in September 1993 El Paso U.S. Border Patrol Chief Silvestre Reyes implemented Operation Hold the Line. In a proactive strategy designed to prevent unauthorized migration at the border, as distinct from the usual reactive practice of rounding up unauthorized migrants during raids in urban El Paso, 400 U.S. Border Patrol agents were situated at equal distances apart along the Rio Grande River, 24 hours a day and 7 days a week.[91]

By first accounts, Operation Hold the Line appeared to deter unauthorized migration. In its first week, the number of U.S. Border Patrol apprehensions dropped from 800 to 150 per day.[92] On the other hand, as David Spener discovered through observation and interviews, migrants were still crossing the border by avoiding areas under surveillance. Migrants came more and more to rely on *coyotes* or human traffickers, who increased their fees in response to the greater difficulty in crossing migrants and the higher demand for their services. Fewer workplace raids in El Paso meant that migrants, once across the border, would remain undetected and that it was now safer to stay in El Paso. Ironically, the risk of being caught and the rising cost of crossings encouraged long-term migration to the United States. In any case, based on broad public and political perceptions, variations of Operation Hold the Line were adopted by other urban areas along the border, the most notable being Operation Gatekeeper, implemented in California in October 1994.[93]

Operation Gatekeeper also coincided with, and perhaps responded to, the signing of the North American Free Trade Agreement (NAFTA), which established a free trade zone between the United States, Mexico, and Canada.[94] U.S. policy makers, according to Jorge Durand, Nolan Malone, and Douglas Massey, "sought to restrict the movement of workers across the Mexico–U.S. border; U.S. authorities were constructing a framework to integrate North American markets to facilitate cross-border movement of goods, capital, commodities, and information, a vision that became a reality with the implementation of the North American Free Trade Agreement."[95]

Indeed, some political analysts suggest that Operation Gatekeeper served both those ends.[96] At the time NAFTA was put in place, it was argued that U.S. business interests in Mexico would promote economic development and create jobs for Mexicans in Mexico, thus alleviating the need for unauthorized migration. Instead, the economic downturn in rural Mexico caused by the importation of cheap U.S. agricultural goods raised the level of unemployment in Mexico and stimulated the flow of migrants to the United States.[97] The official rationale for Operation Gatekeeper presented by the U.S. government was, however, "to restore integrity and safety to the nation's busiest border."[98]

Order has been achieved at some points along the border. With fewer migrant crossings in urban areas, the border appears to be "secure" and unauthorized migration "under control." By 2002 in San Diego, for example, attempted crossings had fallen off and the U.S. Border Patrol's migrant apprehensions had dropped from 46 percent to 16 percent of the number registered nationally. By contrast, migrant crossings have been increasing in the remote desert areas of California's neighbor, Arizona. Overall, there has not been a drop in actual migration crossing attempts.[99]

Operation Gatekeeper deliberately aimed to channel migrants from urban to remote areas so that natural features, such as mountains and rivers, would act as a physical challenge to unauthorized migration. Thus Operation Gatekeeper was based on the assumption that increased physical barriers would discourage migration and reduce the actual numbers of unauthorized migrants attempting to cross into the United States.[100] According to Leslie Berestein, however, this has not been the case:

> Architects of Gatekeeper anticipated that human traffic would shift but relied on the inhospitable terrain of the mountains and desert to deter most would-be border crossers. It didn't. Today the U.S. government spends millions to rescue people who risk their lives attempting to slip through the fortified border.... Thousands of migrants have been rescued, some on the brink of death. But more than 300 still die each year, leading critics to question the wisdom of a border strategy that requires rescues in the first place.[101]

When migrants cross where there are fewer U.S. Border Patrol agents, they are less likely to be rescued should things go wrong, and, indeed, migrant deaths in Arizona's desert areas have quadrupled since the inauguration of Operation Gatekeeper.[102] Between 1994 and 2003, the number of deaths in the U.S. Border Patrol sectors from San Diego to Yuma increased by 500 percent.[103] A total of 23 migrants died in 1994, 61 in 1995, 59 in 1996, 89 in 1997, 145 in 1998, and 110 in 1999.[104] Six years later, the death rate would climb sharply: in the nine months from October 2004 to August 2005, 366 migrant deaths were recorded.[105]

Despite the growing number of migrant deaths, Mark Krikorian of the Center for Immigration Studies suggests that death is not a deterrent to Mexican migrants because the United States has "created an incentive to take foolish risks . . . we're saying if you run this gauntlet and can get over here, you're home free."[106]

The increase in migrant deaths does imply that migrants find the physical terrain much more difficult than previous urban sites of unauthorized crossing, such as Tijuana. Although exposure to the elements (resulting in heat prostration or hyperthermia) claims most lives, Operation Gatekeeper has also exacerbated human-caused risk. The increased levels of border security mean greater reliance on professional traffickers to get migrants to the United States but, to avoid detection, trafficking operations are more sophisticated and attract higher fees. As the cost of reaching the United States increases, the lure of fast money attracts

novice traffickers, but their inexperience can have serious consequences.[107] In the case of one novice coyote, who was responsible for the
death of 19 people when 75 migrants were locked into his airtight trailer,
inexperience was considered a major contributor to the deadly outcome:
"Defense attorney Craig Washington contends that more experienced
[traffickers would] have known the risk of packing so many people into
a sealed trailer."[108]

Novice traffickers are renowned for abandoning migrants. For example, in the *Ottawa Sun* it was reported that "searchers have found two
more dead men in the scorched south-western Arizona desert, bringing
to 14 the number of would-be illegal immigrants who died after being
abandoned by a [trafficker] while attempting to sneak across the border,
authorities said yesterday."[109]

As the profitability of human trafficking increases, it has become attractive to organized crime. These crime networks can coordinate trafficking, lend money to migrants for the crossing and then charge exorbitant
interest rates, have migrants indentured for low pay in the United States
or, as an increasingly popular alternative, use migrants as drug mules in
return for automatic release from debt.[110] According to U.S. Border Patrol
agent Keith Stitt: "Most migrants use smugglers, who charge anywhere
from $150 to $500 for assistance as footpath guides or as chauffeurs of
trucks that carry as many as 40 migrants at a time. Often, smugglers rob
their clients, force them to serve as drug runners or collect their fees and
then tell the Border Patrol in exchange for a $150 informant's fee."[111]

Thus, rather than making the border safer, Operation Gatekeeper
seems to have made it more dangerous, increasing both the physical and
the human-caused risk of death. Moreover, U.S. Border Patrol detention figures suggest that unauthorized migration is just as prevalent as
it was prior to Operation Gatekeeper.[112] Although it has not made the
border safer, at least not for Mexicans, Operation Gatekeeper has successfully moved unauthorized migration to rural areas, making it less
visible to urban populations.

The 2001 terrorist attacks on the United States have significantly
increased the vigor with which the United States undertakes border
regulation and implements Operation Gatekeeper. Essentially, terrorism has fueled suspicion of all foreigners entering the United States and
particularly those entering without authorization. Mexican migrants are
no longer considered simply an economic problem; they are now considered to be a potential terrorist threat to U.S. society.[113]

To respond to the terrorist threat, an array of government agencies, including the INS and the U.S. Border Patrol, were amalgamated and placed under the authority of the Department of Homeland Security, which was then granted extensive powers of inspection, arrest, and detention together with considerable autonomy. Human rights advocates fear that the aggressive, even abusive behavior of U.S. law enforcement officers toward Mexican migrants will go unchecked, deemed acceptable in the name of national security.[114] More generally, it has been predicted that Mexican migrant deaths will rise as migrants take even greater risks to avoid intensified border security.[115]

From this review of U.S. border and migration policies, it can be seen that the risks facing unauthorized migrants crossing into the United States have escalated because of deliberate policy changes, changes that have failed to consider both the full implications of risk as a tool to dissuade migration and the cultural nature of risk, thus unauthorized migration from Mexico to the United States has continued without any measurable letup.

Although this discussion has clarified why there are increasing levels of risk, it has not addressed why potential unauthorized Mexican migrants fail to perceive risk as an intervening obstacle. In part, the increasing number of migrants may reflect greater economic push factors from Mexico. The North American Free Trade Agreement may have resulted in more unemployed Mexicans and thus more potential migrants willing to take the risk of crossing unauthorized. Alternatively, it may be that migrants, relying on old information provided by successful migrants now established in the United States, are unaware or ignorant of increasing levels of risk at the border. The conditions were very different for those who went before them; the very nature of risk at the border has changed with Operation Gatekeeper. Although it might appear contrary to economic models, it seems likely that some migrants will continue to migrate because of tradition, migration being quintessential to identity formation and becoming an adult male. Despite the growing risk, the number of such migrants is likely to increase with Mexico's population. In considering all these possibilities, this study asked unauthorized migrants to explain how they experienced and then managed risk to reduce this obstacle (or at least their perceptions of it) to the point where they could cross unauthorized from Mexico to the United States.

Documenting Personal Experiences and Societal Responses to the Risks Encountered by Mexican Migrants

My investigation into Mexican experiences, responses, and management of the risks encountered by unauthorized Mexican migrants in crossing over to the United States is based on extensive sociocultural fieldwork that sought to interpret patterns emerging from the complex, interacting social systems surrounding the process of unauthorized migration. My research methodology combined four principal data-gathering and analytic procedures:

1. In-depth interviews: To document individual migration journeys and the perspectives of community stakeholders including the Mexican government, nongovernmental organizations, artists, and songwriters on migrant experiences, responses, and management of risk, I conducted twenty in-depth interviews: nine of migrants, six of government officials, six of civil society organizations, two of academic researchers, two of artists, and one of a songwriter.

2. Analysis of newspaper articles: To identify the risks encountered by unauthorized Mexican migrants and, as recommended by anthropologist Mary Douglas, to determine the assignment of blame by journalists as they explained the causes of risk,[116] I read, classified, and analyzed articles in Tijuana's *El Mexicano*, Sunday editions of Tijuana's *Frontera*, and pertinent editions of Ensenada's *El Vigía* between March 2003 and October 2004.

3. Analysis of Mexican border art: I sampled artworks with messages about migration and risk along some 17.4 kilometers (10.8 miles) of the border wall on the Mexican side at Tijuana, beginning at Playa Tijuana (32° 32′ 03.5″ N, 117° 07′ 21.9″ W) and ending at the eastern end of Cuauhtemoc Boulevard (32° 32′ 50.4″ N; 116° 58′ 05.0″ W), adjacent to Tijuana's international airport, and subjected these works to ethnographic analysis. I interpreted their symbols according to meanings determined by the research participants or from references to the artwork in the media or literature. Some of the artists, interviewed in depth, themselves explained the symbolic meaning of their art.

4. Analysis of Mexican popular song: Having selected Los Tigres del Norte's album *Pacto de sangre* (Blood Pact) and Molotov's song "Frijolero" (Beaner) for their popularity as reflected in album sales, I analyzed them by interpreting their lyrics within the context of comments by the

artists or songwriters either during in-depth interviews or as reported in the news media. In my analysis, to determine the origin of the songs, to identify where the concepts came from, to explore the blurry area where personal experience can be converted into myth, and, in particular, to understand the message about risk and unauthorized migration the musicians were trying to express in their music, I followed the approach of Simon Frith in *Performing Rites: On the Value of Popular Music*. Frith tried to "hear three things at once: words, which appear to give songs an independent source of semantic meaning; rhetoric, words being used in a special, musical way, a way which draws attention to features and problems of speech; and voices, words being spoken or sung in human tones which are themselves 'meaningful,' sing of persons and person-alities."[117] Although I considered the words, rhetoric, and voices in the popular songs separately, my analysis, like Frith's, is integrated.

I undertook this multipronged approach to data collection to attain a holistic understanding of risk and the culture of unauthorized migra-tion in Mexico and to contribute to the growing body of ethnographic research on the border. I found the ethnographic research techniques used by Vila in *Ethnography at the Border* a useful guide on how to obtain different types of data that would reveal the complexities of life at the border. They inspired me to use several different types of data collection but ensured that the common thread was a focus on the unauthorized migrant experience and perspective.[118]

Miriam Davidson's *Lives on the Line: Dispatches from the U.S.–Mex-ico border*, a series of biographies, helped me design a technique both to record and to present the complex migrant interview data.[119] Oscar Lewis's *Five Families* provided a useful example of how to weave and link migrant stories together to reveal their commonalities and to iden-tify emerging trends.[120]

The rapid data capture techniques of Dana Taplin, Suzanne Scheld, and Setha Low in their "Rapid Ethnographic Assessment in Urban Parks: A Case Study of Independence National Historic Park" provided me with plenty of ideas on how to capture packets of information from many dif-ferent data sources in a short amount of time. Reading this article moti-vated me to systematically collect information with attention to detail throughout my study, even if the actual event encountered was random or only lasted for a short period of time. It led me to always carry a voice recorder, camera, and notebooks in the course of my research so that I was ready to interview whenever the occasion arose, whether it was a chance encounter with a human trafficker or a border Mass lasting only an hour.[121]

Mariangeles Rodríguez's *Mito, identidad y rito* and Eileen Oktavec's *Answered Prayers: Miracles and Milagros along the Border* provided insights into how to capture the cultural nuances of Mexicans and Mexican Americans, my study's target group.[122] In particular, Oktavec's approach to data collection during site visits helped me document the spaces and places characteristic of unauthorized migration in this study: Tijuana, Santa Ana, and Irapuato. Her technique for detailed documentation of religious artifacts informed my careful documentation of the art installations on the border wall at Tijuana.[123] Joseph Nevins's detailed analysis of the effects of the United States border management policy Operation Gatekeeper inspired my analysis of the response of Mexican institutions (government, civil society and the news media) to the escalating risks of unauthorized Mexican migration to the United States.[124]

As noted before, even within the area of ethnographic and cultural research, the emphasis to date has been on researching cultural products and the role these play in creating a sense of meaning, sociopolitical awareness, and the aesthetics of border life, such as the literature, photography, and graffiti discussed in Crosthwaite, Williams, and Byrd's *Puro Border: Dispatches, Snapshots and Graffiti from La Frontera* or the blending of cultural traditions featured in Maciel and Herrera Sobek's *Culture across Borders: Mexican Immigration and Popular Culture*.[125] In *Ethnography at the Border* and *Crossing Borders, Reinforcing Borders*, Pablo Vila has moved the debate forward by examining the social processes of border crossing, both authorized and unauthorized.[126] Most sociocultural studies have not looked at risk and the death of Mexican migrants, despite the impact increasing numbers of migrant deaths have had on Mexican and U.S. society. I used the pioneering work of anthropologist Mary Douglas, and particularly her *Risk and Blame: Essays in Cultural Theory*, to guide my analysis of risk within the cultural context of unauthorized migration from Mexico.[127]

The challenge of such ethnographic research, according to George Marcus and Michael Fischer, is "how to represent the embedding of richly described local cultural worlds in larger impersonal systems of political economy."[128] To meet this challenge, my research gives preference to the firsthand testimony of unauthorized Mexican migrants because they have personally experienced the migration journey and its attendant risks. Moreover, because of their "illegal" status, these

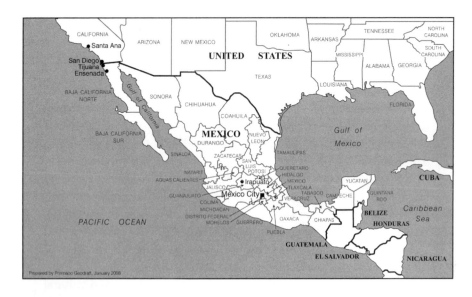

Figure 1.1 The U.S.–Mexico border, showing the research study sites. (Map by Promaco Geodraft)

migrants have had little opportunity to express their views to broader society. Howard Becker, cited in Steven Taylor and Robert Bogdan, suggests that researchers choosing to present "reality" from the point of view of those experiencing it would do well to interview the powerless, who have few avenues for exposing their views.[129] Anselm Strauss and Juliet Corbin concur: researchers need to present the perspectives and voices of the groups they are studying rather than the assumptions made by others.[130]

To capture a range of different stakeholders and to trace migrant social networks, I took several different research approaches, collecting data in Tijuana, Ensenada (some 50 miles south of Tijuana), Mexico City, and Irapuato (some 200 miles northwest of Mexico City) on the Mexican side of the border and in San Diego and Santa Ana (some 80 miles northwest of San Diego) on the U.S. side (see fig. 1.1). All these sites are relatively close to the San Diego–Tijuana border, except Mexico City and Irapuato, both situated in central Mexico; Irapuato is renowned for its high levels of migration to the United States.[131] I selected the sites as focal points in a particular unauthorized migration network, with Irapuato being an important sending community, Santa Ana a popular receiving community, and Tijuana–Ensenada the border zone through which many migrants pass.

I conducted my site research largely in the Californias, even though much of the unauthorized migration today is taking place farther east, with greater rates of entry into Arizona than into California. That said, most Mexican migrants crossing into Arizona still have California as their destination and most of the organizations (government and civil society) are still based either in California or Baja California. Moreover, until recently, California was the site of most·unauthorized crossings into the United States.[132] Within this region and sociocultural setting, I was able to examine a representative section of the border, what happens there, and why migrants cross it. The fieldwork component of my research took place between March 2003 and October 2004 while I was living in Ensenada, Baja California. From the very beginning, I attempted to secure interviews with the U.S. Department of Homeland Security and the U.S. Border Patrol, seeing these organizations as pivotal to presenting a U.S. perspective in my research. Despite amiable telephone conversations with staff in both these organizations and a personal visit to the Border Patrol area headquarters in Chula Vista, I was unable to secure personal interviews with representatives of these organizations, which appeared reluctant to provide local information, instead referring me back to their central offices in Washington, D.C. It was at this point that I decided to focus my study only on Mexican responses, experiences, and informal management of the U.S. border policy.

My book does not consider the morality of unauthorized migration from Mexico but, instead, analyzes Mexican responses to this phenomenon, which occurs whether or not it is sanctioned. To avoid moral connotations, and following the suggestion of Joseph Nevins, I refer to migration from Mexico to the United States undertaken without the formal permission of the U.S. government or contrary to the terms of such permission as "unauthorized migration" and to those who undertake it as "unauthorized migrants."[133]

Within unauthorized migration, migration via an official port of entry using false, stolen, borrowed, or no longer valid documents is known as "documented unauthorized migration." The alternative, "undocumented unauthorized migration," refers to migration without documents, whether via a port of entry or across other, usually less secure, parts of the border.[134]

I have provided a glossary to clarify these and a variety of other terms used in this book. Some Spanish terms are used as such, particularly where English speakers living in the border region have adopted them. Please note that all translations of comments by research participants and, unless otherwise noted, quotations from Spanish-language sources are my own. Chapter 2 presents the personal stories of unauthorized migrants and analyzes their encounters with risk at the border. Chapter 3 examines the roles played by the Mexican government, nongovernmental organizations, and the news media, potential advocates for Mexican citizens at risk, to determine the crucial official response to unauthorized migration. Chapters 4 and 5 then investigate Mexican cultural responses to the increasing risks of unauthorized migration by analyzing art on the border wall at Tijuana and critiques of migration and the migrant experiences of risk in Mexican popular music. And the book's conclusion draws together the different components of my study to outline the implications of this research for U.S. migration policy on unauthorized Mexican migrants.

2
Delving into the Migrant's World

The narratives in this chapter describe the social, logistical, and emotional processes that a migrant undergoes during the unauthorized migration journey, a powerful, transformative experience with long-term consequences not only for the migrant but for the migrant's family and community as well. While recognizing that each migrant's journey is unique, this chapter shows how U.S. migration policy has affected individual migration experiences of risk at the border, how individual reactions form a common pattern across the unauthorized migrant population, and how critical aspects of migration decision making exacerbate or reduce risk. It presents a series of four individual migration stories, from the most to the least recent crossing, before closely examining the experiences of the Hernández Cruz family, a family that has managed the risks of unauthorized migration to the United States for more than 25 years.

The narratives were compiled by threading together the details of events as recollected by the migrant participants and then putting these into chronological order. During each interview, I clarified inconsistencies and discrepancies as they arose. Taking into account that their memories were inevitably affected by subsequent recollections and discussions, I asked all participants to link the times in their accounts to those of world events or of family milestones such as births, deaths, and marriages. In the Hernández Cruz family case study, I carefully cross-checked different family member accounts to arrive at the most accurate composite narrative possible.

Four Individual Experiences of Migration

Presenting both the male and female perspective, these individual narratives look at four very different experiences of unauthorized migration occurring at different periods of time within the last 25 years.

Diana: Migrating to Keep Her Family Together

"¿Bueno?" I asked the unfamiliar female voice on the other end of the telephone line. "This is Diana," the voice replied, "the girl from the bus. Do you remember me?" It took me a few seconds to recall her; it must have been at least three months since I had met her on the bus to Tijuana. We were both traveling from Ensenada to cross the border at Tijuana. She had sat down next to me and we had chatted a little. I had given her my number, but had forgotten all about it. I wondered why, after so much time, she had decided to give me a call.

I remembered that Diana was studying to become a beautician, and I asked her how her course was going. "I've had to let it go for a while. I've been away a lot lately," she replied. She asked about my research project, and I explained that my original tourism project disintegrated when the government cancelled development funding, but that I was really "into" my new project. I was now investigating the risks of unauthorized migration to the United States. She paused, and then her voice lit up, "Can you keep a secret?" she asked. "My husband is working illegally in the United States." She then told me that the day we met she was not going shopping in San Diego, as she had said, but was going to visit her husband in Los Angeles instead. To me, this was a timely coincidence: I was looking for migrants to interview for my study. I immediately invited Diana to participate in my study, and she agreed to give a confidential interview.

Just two days after our phone conversation, we met at a café. I was struggling to recall her features when I spotted her: a young woman, average height, with shoulder-length dark brown hair, jeans, and a T-shirt. Her simple, makeup-free presentation seemed to belie her training as a beautician. At her side stood her well-dressed three-year-old son. When we sat down and ordered coffee, I could tell that Diana was keen to talk, eager to share her perspective. She treated me like an old friend but, at the same time, seemed to enjoy sharing her story with someone who did not really know her, better still, with someone who did not know her family.

Diana and her husband, she explained, were from a rural community with only a hundred houses, near Culiacán, Sinaloa. She had some schooling and had worked as a teacher for a while, but her husband had no formal education and could not find work. In May 2003, five months before I interviewed Diana, her husband crossed, unauthorized, into the United States to find work. Diana was now using her U.S. tourist visa, obtained while she was a teacher, to visit her husband.

Although she had worried about the crossing, her husband was not too concerned: he was crossing at the river and knew how to swim. Diana knew that documents were out of the question: her husband did not have stable work; in any case, she believed that they would have lost more money trying to arrange a visa than paying a coyote.

To Diana, the benefits of migration were almost immediate; her husband was now earning about $700 every two weeks, compared to $100 in Mexico, and he had already paid off the $1,500 his coyote charged to cross him. Diana was careful with the money he gave her and had saved enough to put down a deposit on some land in Ensenada. If she could just convince him to stay in the United States for two years, they would be able to buy the land free and clear, but this seemed increasingly unlikely because her husband wanted to return to Mexico to see his son.

Although Diana could visit the United States as often as she liked, her son, lacking a visa, could not. Instead, he stayed with his grandmother (Diana's mother-in-law) in Ensenada when Diana went north to visit her husband. Consequently, the father and child had not seen each other for five months. In August 2003, the Friday before our interview, the U.S. Consulate in Tijuana turned down her tourist visa application for the boy. It was a difficult situation, with her husband desperate to see their son and Diana wanting to save money for a better future together in Mexico.

After our interview, we chatted about life in general before saying good-bye. Later that evening, I got a call from Diana. Her husband had arranged to smuggle their son to the United States that Saturday. A lady with a son of similar age would arrive in Tijuana and, for $1,000, Diana's son would cross with the stranger using her son's documents. Diana was scared; she feared she would never see her child again. I asked her to call me to let me know how things went.

Saturday came and went with no phone call. In fact, I did not hear anything from Diana until I called her on January 19, 2004. Fortunately, she had trusted me enough to give me her phone number in Los Angeles. Somewhat hesitantly (there were others in the room), she let me know everyone was all right; she had settled in with her husband and son. She had not called because she had not returned to Ensenada. She hoped to be back there soon to put down a deposit on the land. I did not hear from her again.

A Mother's Sacrifice. Diana's husband left for the United States to improve their economic situation: they had a young son to raise. "My husband migrated," she explained, "because there are more work opportunities in the United States than in Culiacán. Honestly, my husband doesn't have any education. He doesn't know how to read or write. . . . He couldn't get work, and when he did, the most he could earn here is 450 to 500 pesos (45 to 50 dollars) a week. My husband doesn't want to be [in the United States] but we need to save some money to build a house [in Mexico]."

Diana did not like it that her husband had to travel as an unauthorized migrant: "Mexicans and others crossing into the United States without a visa face many risks, including death. They die because they don't know how to swim, yet they try to cross the river. Or the migration officials shoot them. The American police [U.S. Border Patrol] are another death threat, they mistreat them, capture them, and they don't send them straight back to Mexico. Instead, they go to jail."

According to Diana, getting a tourist visa was a fundamental way to reduce the risks of unauthorized migration. She has one herself because "at least you don't go as an illegal. They can't detain you because you have permission to be there. . . . The benefit of a tourist visa is that you don't cross as an illegal and then you can keep renewing your stay. . . . I can go and then keep renewing my permit and it costs only $8. The benefit is that I'm not illegal; they can't kick me out."

Diana had tried without success to get a U.S. tourist visa for her young son. She did not even attempt to get one for her husband. Because he had no steady job, the U.S. government was unlikely to grant him one. What was worse, she explained, was that U.S. migration officers

> don't care about the cost of getting a visa. It [cost us] 3,000 pesos [about $300] to get to the consulate from where we lived [in Sinaloa]. It was more expensive and more effort than undocumented migration. To try to get a visa for my husband in Sinaloa, you have to go to the consulate in Hermosillo some twelve hours away. You have to pay the travel costs and you end up spending 5,000 pesos just for them to say no. He doesn't have a steady job, a stable income, and so of course [U.S. migration officials] think he wants to go and live there.

Diana acknowledges that her husband was planning to go to the United States, not as a tourist, but to work, but still she believes that far fewer migrants would get hurt or die in crossing unauthorized if only the U.S. government

> would at least approve [more] visas. The gringo we had only issued two out of the eleven visas requested that hour. I'd at least approve

50 percent of visas to reduce the risks that people face. To me, there aren't people who should or shouldn't get visas, but to the gringos, there are. I ask myself why they refuse visas when people want to cross properly, to cross legally. Yes, they want to work, but perhaps if the consulate turned down fewer visas, Mexicans would come and go and wouldn't spend so much time there. We stay longer because it is expensive to pay a coyote, to save the money. . . . My husband can leave the United States, that's no problem, but you have to pay a coyote to get him back in again.

Diana believed that Mexicans would spend less time overall in the United States if they were given visas that allowed them to freely move between the two countries. She explained, "I spend a week each month with my husband and then I come back. I come back because of my son. My husband is going to cross him, and it makes me think twice because he's a child. . . . Really, if the American Consulate approved more visas, [this could have been avoided]. An American is not going to wash plates. An American is not going to wait on tables. Mexicans are the ones who wait on them, sweep, and mop. What would the gringos do without Mexicans?"

If her husband were able to move freely back and forth across the U.S.–Mexico border, they would not endure family fragmentation, nor would they have to smuggle their child across the border. They could relocate to the United States for one long period of time, just for the time required to purchase a property in Mexico. Although Diana pointed out some of the flaws in the U.S. migration policy, she also blamed the Mexican government for not acting to create more jobs: "The Mexican government should generate more employment and not demand so much education. There are many intelligent people without an education. . . . If there were more job opportunities and they paid better, there wouldn't be the problem of wanting to cross."

With her son's tourist visa application refused, Diana realized that her son might have to be smuggled into the United States and was in the process of undertaking a pretrip risk assessment:

It's a big sacrifice. God willing, my husband can cross my son, but many times, they find out, and they take the children. Gringos are like that. They take the children and put them in an orphanage. They deport the parents but not the child; they adopt out the child. For example, you and your child might use the birth certificate of another child to cross, but if they figure this out . . . they take the children, and the parents can lose their visas, but the child who was being crossed illegally stays there. It is a big risk to cross a child. It is riskier than crossing an adult. Many people are afraid of crossing children since the parents are going to be over there and the children will be over here. People risk a lot [to be together].

Frightened and relying on hearsay, Diana was worried that her child would be harmed during his unauthorized migration. She worried that the U.S. government would intercept the smugglers and adopt out her son to U.S. citizens.

If she and her husband were to smuggle their son across the border, however, they would, at the very least, pick a coyote who was known to their family, a risk reduction strategy because they would not have to pay beforehand. Her husband, Diana explained, "migrated with a friend, and a friend of his friend crossed them for $1,500. If the coyote doesn't know you, then you have to pay up front before crossing, and if you don't make it, you lose the money. Since my husband knows his coyote, he just paid a little each week until he paid off the full $1,500. My husband would go to [the coyote's] house and give him the money. Thirteen days ago, he made his last payment."

Overall, Diana was critical of both U.S. and Mexican governments for putting her husband and son at risk. She felt that, though her U.S. tourist visa afforded her some protection by sparing her the risks and costs of unauthorized migration, U.S. migration officers presented an important risk for her husband and son due to the threat of physical violence and because the officers might even adopt out migrant children.

Arturo: Migrating for Career Advancement

I had not seen Arturo or his brother, Luis, for a few years. I had first met Luis in Canada and then, in 2002, I met Arturo when I went to stay at their family home in an upper-middle-class suburb of Mexico City. So when they were both going to be in San Diego, I took the opportunity to get together with them. As we greeted each other at the San Ysidro trolley station, Arturo told me that they did not have much time because they had to get the car back to their cousin before he finished work in Chula Vista. I agreed to go with them.

When we arrived at the workshop where his cousin installed car stereos, the "guys" (Latino and Middle Eastern men) were joking around out front. Luis handed the keys over to his cousin, and we squished together into the pickup truck to drive back across the border to Tijuana. The trip was fast and frightening. Speed limits and regulations were ignored. I sighed with relief when we reached the cousin's home in Tijuana, but it, too, was a little daunting. The street was dark; filled with old cars, the yard was like a junkyard; inside, the house was only dimly lit. Fortunately, we did not stay long. Since Luis had to fly back to Mexico City, the cousin only stayed long enough to drink a beer before dropping us all at the airport. Afterward, Arturo accompanied me to the bus station, and we arranged for him to visit me in Ensenada.

When Arturo arrived in Ensenada a few weeks later, he seemed nervous and very uptight, which I thought was all about his starting a new life in San Diego. It was not until November 2003, when I met with him again in Mexico City, that he revealed the details of his crossing the border. It was the migration issues he had faced as a young professional trying to get work in the United States and his close encounters with the Tijuana underworld that had put him on edge.

As we began the interview, Arturo explained that he had obtained a ten-year B1/B2 tourist visa in Mexico City in 1994 at the age of 18. He did not use it until 2002, however, when he crossed to go to a conference in San Antonio, Texas. Getting the visa had been easy for him; only later did he realize how hard it is for most people. He spent July to September 2003 in Tijuana, using his visa to cross into the United States some 70 times to interview for jobs, attend professional conferences, and do some freelance work. During this time, he also had an uncensored introduction to the negative aspects of border life: human trafficking and drugs.

In the company of his cousin, Arturo witnessed deals to smuggle people into the United States, and he had even driven a smuggled migrant's car into the United States. He was on the fringes of the drug world; he had met coyotes involved with drugs, the son of a drug lord, and, when staying over in the United States with his cousin, he had been surrounded by drug users. All the while, he was looking for legal sponsorship to the United States so that he could work in the information technology field.

Arturo felt uncomfortable, like an outsider, particularly because he did not want to be an unauthorized migrant in the United States. He had a degree, in contrast to his cousin, who had only finished junior high school. Arturo concluded that, whether unauthorized or authorized, there were still considerable cultural adjustments to be made to integrate into life in the United States. It was always difficult to migrate, but, as an unauthorized migrant, you were more vulnerable generally; at the border, where the two worlds met, you were vulnerable to illegal activities. In the end, Arturo returned to his family in Mexico City, where he continues to seek ways to migrate legally to the United States.

Encounters with the Underworld. Arturo was attempting to migrate to the United States because, even with a higher education, his potential earnings in Mexico would be relatively low compared to his colleagues in other countries around the world: "Salaries are very low and taxes in Mexico are very, very high. The quality of life after 40 is difficult since you can't get work. In contrast, in the United States, even if you work washing dishes, you can get an income and live, something you can't do here. . . . The unemployed turn into delinquents in Mexico, or opt to migrate in search of a better life."

Arturo was hopeful he could develop his career in computer design but was willing to work in low-wage jobs just to make ends meet. Perhaps because he did have more choices and was better educated, Arturo was constantly thinking about the risks of unauthorized migration and was even part of pretrip assessment processes for those around him. When he and his cousin went to arrange the crossing of a friend, they "didn't reach an agreement with the *pollero* [trafficker] because the pollero wanted money before the crossing so we went and picked our friend up. He didn't cross that time."

Arturo was very suspicious of coyotes and their activities. He identified them as a potential source of risk to unauthorized migrants. Selecting a coyote, in Arturo's opinion, depends on

> the trust or distrust you feel for the coyote. · · · We met this guy at eleven at night, he had a gun and we were surrounded by guys who looked like narcos [drug smugglers]. We went to seal the deal for a friend but he didn't cross because he didn't trust the coyote—he made him very nervous. The guy scared us, and we weren't even the ones who were going to cross. In the end, we said, "Don't go with him." . . . When you want to migrate, you're put in touch with all sorts of people. They tell you to go to such and such a ranch, but often it is a very remote place, outside of the city, far from everything. It's very dangerous. When I saw those guys it made me very nervous.

Simply by being involved in human trafficking in remote areas, Arturo believed that migrants were more susceptible to risk. If you were carrying money, this was even worse because your coyote or other bandits might attack you. Experienced unauthorized migrants, Arturo told me, "recommend that you don't take money with you because there are other coyotes, and other people, who might mug you. So they suggest you pay after the crossing, not before or even during the process."

Arturo had a huge advantage in that he could use a tourist visa to cross and work. But he still believed that there was some risk involved. His cousin had developed a system that would help reduce detection of how many visits he made to the United States. Arturo's cousin

> uses different cars with different number plates because [U.S. migration officials] record license plates when you enter and leave. Without a doubt other people are doing the same. I think people will opt for crossing on a weekly basis rather than daily, or go as a passenger rather than driving their car. . . . At the moment, he might use one car for three days in a row, then another for a different day. He has been doing this [working illegally in the United States] for seven years. . . . They never used to check how many times a car crossed the border, but, since September 11, there are stricter controls.

The examples of Arturo and his cousin suggest that, with the implementation of stricter security measures after Operation Gatekeeper and September 11, 2001, even documented unauthorized workers were changing their strategies. In this case, Arturo's cousin was trying to trick the system by entering the United States using different modes of transport, and was reducing the frequency of crossings with longer stays in the United States. Arturo, for his part, preferred to work in Mexico City for less pay than to regularly undertake an unauthorized crossing using his tourist visa, a trip that was much less risky than an undocumented unauthorized migrant crossing.

Lucía: Migrating to Escape Domestic Violence

"Okay, can you please back up your car . . . so I can check the trunk?" the Homeland Security officer asked, then, finding it empty, waved us through. It was Sunday, May 30, 2004. Lucía and I, having met through mutual friends and now well acquainted, had decided to go shopping in San Diego and combine it with a tour of the border divide where she would relive her unauthorized crossing. This seemed like an interesting opportunity since, unlike most of my other informants, Lucía could now legally move between the two countries.

Lucía's unauthorized crossing took place in 1992, when she was 23 years old. She had a two-year-old daughter and she was running away from her husband. Her father, a U.S. resident, arranged her coyotes. Acting as a husband-and-wife team, the woman coyote would cross Lucía's daughter with her daughter's documents by car via an official port of entry, while the man would cross Lucía on foot near Playa Tijuana. Lucía said good-bye to her daughter before spending two days right at the border with the coyote, just waiting to make a run for it into the United States. They were an hour into their journey when they were detained and deported back to Mexico.

Driving with me through Border Field State Park, next to Playa Tijuana, Lucía recalled the eroded tracks she had run down and the spiky bushes she had hidden in. Although the migration attempt was made at night, and she could not pick out specific landmarks, the landscape seemed altogether familiar to her and everywhere were reminders of her crossing.

Lucía was released from detention at 3 a.m. and dropped off in Tijuana. Alone and frightened, she immediately rang her father to find out about her young daughter. When her father told her he had no news and had assumed the daughter was with Lucía, she became panic stricken. It turned out her daughter was safe after all, but, because these coyotes did not hand children to anyone other than the parents, they did not think to contact the grandfather.

Lucía was now desperate to get into the United States and be reunited with her child. Her father arranged for another coyote (the first had not yet been released from detention) and, that same morning, Lucía walked across the hills beside the San Ysidro U.S. Port of Entry. She rested at a nearby hotel until her father drove down to collect her, and then they picked up her daughter from the coyote's house in San Diego.

Soon after Lucía's safe arrival in the United States, her husband threatened to report Lucía's father to the migration authorities. To keep her father out of trouble, Lucía returned home, swearing that she would get a visa and never take the risk of losing her daughter again. Eventually, she was issued a tourist visa and later legally migrated to the United States under the family reunion provision of U.S. immigration law. Lucía is now divorced.

Desperation. "I crossed to visit my father and see what it was like," Lucía told me. "I was having marriage problems so that's my main reason for wanting to go." Indeed, because she was fleeing from domestic violence, Lucía did not undertake any pretrip risk assessment:

> Honestly, I didn't plan it. I went home and had a fight with my husband. I said, "I'm going to the other side [United States]." I called my dad because he'd been trying to convince me to go there for some time. I never imagined the potential consequences. He told me to meet him in Tijuana in a couple of hours but he did not tell me what clothes to bring or anything so I only took light clothes. Later my dad lent me his jacket and the coyote gave me another shirt. I spent two nights in the cold. . . . It was November.

Because a close friend had been attacked and robbed by coyotes, Lucía believed they were the greatest source of risk at the border. She recommended paying coyotes only on safe arrival in the United States. "If you take the money with you, the coyotes will just take the money. That's why many people say, 'I will pay you on arrival because a family member is going to give me the money' or something like that. It's always a risk to cross. [Lucía's coyote] was going to cross me without being paid a cent [beforehand]—if he wanted to be paid, he had to get me across the border."

In hindsight, Lucía did not think that unauthorized migration was worth the risk: "I was scared. I wouldn't do it again. What hurt me most was the incident with my daughter. I spent time worrying about if I would get her back and if they'd stolen her because I didn't know anything about these coyotes, not even their phone number or address." (The coyote who crossed Diana was expected to contact the other coyotes who crossed her child.) "I thought they were going to steal her and that's why I promised myself never to do it again. There are people that cross two, three, or more times. Not me."

Lucía believed that the border was becoming more dangerous and that there is a greater chance of getting caught. By her calculations in 2004, "it is about five times more difficult to cross today. First, because of the wall and the other reason is that there is more surveillance. . . . Now they use motion sensors and helicopters. Before, the helicopters operated at a certain time. They had a routine, but now they patrol continuously."

Lucía was so focused on escaping domestic violence that she failed to consider the potential consequences of unauthorized migration. She left risk management to her father, who selected the coyote who would cross her. The separation of Lucía from her daughter was extremely stressful and traumatic and led her to never again attempt to cross the border unauthorized. Instead, she was fortunate enough to be granted permanent residency under the family reunion provision.

David: Migrating for a Better Life

It was June 2, 2004, and I was taking photos of the murals in Chicano Park, San Diego, when a man riding a bicycle stopped to see what I was doing. He did not approach me immediately but, instead, just lingered nearby. I turned toward him to say hello. He was Latino, medium height, in his forties, dark hair, and missing his two front teeth.

"Do you like these?" he asked, referring to the park's murals. "Yes, they're very beautiful and interesting," I replied, and then asked, "Do you know anything about them?" "Yes, these are my people," he said. We began to discuss how the murals tell the stories of Mexican Americans in San Diego's Barrio Logan, including those of unauthorized migrants.

To build some common ground, I told him I understood the problems associated with migration because I faced a similar situation: I could come and go from the United States but my Mexican fiancé could not. "Where's he from?" he asked, now speaking in Spanish. "He's from Mexico City, the D.F.," I replied. "I'm from there . . . look," and he unbuttoned the top three buttons of his shirt to reveal that he had "D.F." for "Distrito Federal" (Federal District) tattooed on his chest. He had survived there by fighting and stealing. He said that in Mexico City there are a lot of rich people, but you almost have to choke them in order to get any money. You have to rob to survive, and you always have to be on the defensive. He liked the United States because here he felt safe; he did not have to steal or watch his back.

Out of the blue, he said, "I can bring your husband over. I'll bring him through the hills. Because he is my *paisano* [countryman], I'll give you a discount . . . $1,500," he added, his voice fading out. "You can bring him over? It's definitely an option to consider but we're both living in Mexico now and he has to finish his studies. . . . Definitely something for us to consider in the future, though, because it is hard to get good work in Mexico," I said, respecting his offer but not encouraging false hopes.

"So what are you studying? Why are you taking the photos?" he asked. "I'm actually, if you can believe it, researching unauthorized migration and risks to the migrants." "Really? You must have a kind heart to open up and listen to our stories, to try to understand," he replied and then asked, "So how do you do the research?" "I do interviews with all sorts of people who have an experience of crossing the border without papers," I replied. "I have my recorder with me because I've come from another interview. Do you have time for a quick chat?" He checked his watch and said, "Yeah, I'm not in a hurry." I explained that the interview would be anonymous. "They won't find out about me?" he asked. I replied, "I only know your first name and I don't know anything else about you or where you live. I wouldn't even be able to find you again if I wanted to." He replied, "Yeah, that's true." We then sat on the grass, and I proceeded to record the interview.

God and the Coyote. David, who was now in his forties, migrated to the United States when he was 17 years old. He left Mexico to improve his quality of life and his prospects for the future because "wages are low in Mexico. Here the dollar buys you more, even if the cost of living is higher. That's why people risk it, that's why they come from Chiapas or even El Salvador. . . . You don't want your children to be born there, you want your child to have a better life, better opportunities."

He believed that most Mexicans were forced to be "illegal" because they could not get a working visa. This said, he believed that they should be entitled to legal entry into the United States because the land once belonged to Mexico, only ceded unfairly under the Treaty of Guadalupe Hidalgo: "They don't have the necessary documents to get a visa, but they want to return to the lands that were stolen from them."

David blamed the increasing risk of unauthorized migration on the United States and believed that it was part of a larger U.S. plan to deliberately oppress Mexicans and "keep the people ignorant. Those who are ignorant don't know, but those who see a little of the light realize that the white guys do this to keep the Mexicans underfoot."

To David, the choice of coyote was particularly important for reducing risk of physical injury during unauthorized migration. It was best to pick a coyote from your own village or indigenous group, but this was usually more expensive. The most reliable coyotes were "people who crossed years ago and are now dedicated to crossing people from your village. These coyotes cross their people and are honest, but they charge more."

The best strategy for dealing with unknown coyotes was to make sure that family members in the United States made all the arrangements and that payment would be on delivery: "If you pay beforehand, [coyotes] rob you. There is a song that says if you pay beforehand, you end up with nothing. It's like if you pay the mechanic up front, the mechanic is going to play with your car. He'll tell you it's been fixed but won't do anything."

Above all else, migrants needed to believe in God. When David was migrating, his group faced a dire situation. They had been ill prepared to cross the desert. When the water ran out, there were arguments, and people began to lose hope. To David, faith in God was an effective risk reduction strategy:

> Lalo and I were crossing. He didn't want to move, so I had to drag him, and I was also really tired. There was another couple as well. We didn't have water, and yet we kept walking and walking. Our coyote used psychology and told us that, just ahead, there was a prickly pear cactus with fruit that we'd be able to eat, even though it wasn't true. This psychology helped us to cross. It was a blessed lie; it was like words from God. I consider that, when a person speaks like that, it is because God put it in his heart because, if it weren't for God, you would kill people in the hills. Many people are dying because your mind is not your own. It becomes the mind of the natural elements that capture you, and you lose your mind with fear. Without faith in God, you are lost. If you cross with faith, God will get you out of there.

Migrants needed faith and a belief in God to get across the border safely. A good coyote believed in God and could even act on God's behalf in order to save the migrants from dangerous situations. David believed that it was dangerous for a coyote to cross nonbelievers because there was a greater risk of death or injury to the group. Faith may thus be seen as a risk reduction strategy from the perspective of some migrants.

Different Stories, Common Threads

Although, as these four narratives make clear, each migrant has a unique experience of unauthorized migration, there are also key commonalities that make it part of a larger shared experience for many migrants. Key common elements of the migration experience were fear and anxiety. All four participants believed they had been exposed to some level of risk. The women were most concerned about the risks faced by their children; the men, about the risks posed by the harsh physical environment and the criminality at the border and about the potential loss of freedom if they were discovered by the U.S. Border Patrol.

All four migrants traveled to the United States in search of a better life. Diana's family planned to spend enough time in the United States to buy a home in Mexico. Arturo wanted better pay and career advancement. Lucía and David were both escaping the violence they faced every day in Mexico.

All four migrants attempted to attain a legal status that would enable them to travel freely between the United States and Mexico. Diana was traveling on a tourist visa and had attempted to secure one for her son as well. Arturo traveled on a tourist visa but hoped to secure legal sponsorship to work in the United States. Lucía did not have documents at the time but subsequently attained a tourist visa and has now formally migrated to the United States under the family reunion provision. David now resides in the United States and has legal papers that authorize him to travel to Mexico and back.

The Hernández Cruz Family

With these commonalities in mind, and to shed greater light on the strategies Mexican migrants have used to facilitate unauthorized migration across the border into the United States, let us turn now to an in-depth case study of a particular migrant family.

Patricia's Story

Patricia Hernández Cruz, of all the migrants I interviewed, provides the richest account of post–Operation Gatekeeper risk at the border. Her migration experience will be treated at length on its own terms before placing it in the context of her family's over a 25-year period.

Patricia is from Irapuato (see fig. 1.1) and crossed the border in June 2001, after Operation Gatekeeper went into effect (but before the stricter measures introduced following the 9/11 terrorist attacks).

This is Patricia's story, as told by her in response to a single statement: "Tell me about your migration to the United States":

> My brothers and sisters were already in the United States and suggested that I come. I didn't want to, but, since my husband had already been here, we decided to. My husband said that my brother,

Figure 2.1 A solitary cairn in the desert near Mexicali marks the border between the United States and Mexico.

the first to migrate in our family, had a coyote who could cross us. First, my husband would cross, and then he'd arrange to get me over. My mother-in-law said, "Best you both go and leave the boys with me." And that's what happened. We came here and left my sons there. My brother said that the coyote would be in town on such and such a day. We traveled on a Tuesday to Tijuana and then went to San Luis [Río Colorado]. We traveled to where the coyote was waiting for us and he took us from there.

I crossed at San Luis Río Colorado. I remember it was a Friday when we tried the first time. My husband crossed on the sixth and on the seventh or eighth I tried to cross, but *la migra* [U.S. Border Patrol] caught me along with the guide. We were detained in Mexicali or Cuervos, somewhere close to the desert (see fig. 2.1). I was there all day before I was released with the coyote. We tried to cross for about a week, from the Friday of one week until the next week. I spent about 15 days with him altogether until I was actually able to cross.

The first time we crossed, it was about seven in the morning. It was June, so the sun was already high and it was fine. We waded through a large reservoir that separates Mexico from the United States. We climbed up a hill and there was a highway. From there, we ran a little until we were in a cornfield and then we just ran. We were running through an irrigation canal with lots of trees, so we didn't see la migra's vehicle. The guide said, "Run!" We turned back, but they got us.

They put us in the car for about an hour, but, since they didn't pick anyone else up, they took us to where they take migrants. They take down your details, ask your name, where you live, why you are going to the United States, your parents' names. . . . They treated us very well when we arrived at the jail, or whatever it is called; they took our fingerprints and a photo.

They treated me very well, but then lots of men began to arrive, and they treated them badly. They yelled many nasty things and started asking them why they came to this country, leaving their wives behind and alone. Many of the men came from Sinaloa, and [the U.S. Border Patrol officers] said that they would go to Sinaloa to sleep with their wives. Yelling, "You are the coyote, don't be an idiot. You are this, that, and the other," but they didn't treat me that way; they treated me well.

After la migra got us, the coyote said, "You know what, we'll try [again] another day." Next time, we were running and la migra came on horseback. We ran, but there were lots of branches, so I hid within them. Then the guide got me to run, and run, and run, and jump into the reservoir. At the moment he jumped, he broke his leg, so he couldn't take me again. . . . The coyote arranged for another guide, and that was the guy who got me across.

I crossed through part of a river, like a reservoir, but it was only up to my knees, it wasn't very deep, and we waded through it. After that, I climbed a mountain with lots of plants, lots of branches, trees with lots of limbs, very big trees, and I was alone. The coyote was going to take me with another two women, but they didn't show up, so the guide took me on my own. It was really bad because I was on my own, all alone. I mean, you see bottles of water, socks, and shoes from other people, and then it is just us going through there.

There is an area where they plant melons. It is like a marsh, and we ran through there for about half an hour. We arrived there, but so did the migra. There were two large trees, so my guide said, "Get down! Get down!" but there were also two beehives, so I hit my head. La migra went by, but, because it was almost their changeover time, we started back to the trees near the reservoir. We waited for about two hours until the [U.S. Border Patrol] changed shift and tried to cross again. We went past the mountain again and then had to run for half an hour until we were at another reservoir. It wasn't very deep, but it was still quite deep. We had to get through the reservoir and then run for an hour. We were running and running before we hid in a cotton field. We hid in the cotton's irrigation canals. It was very wet, and it took a long time to get through since we were always looking to see if la migra was coming. We reached some recently harvested wheat fields. We ran until we got to a small town. We crossed a highway into a sorghum field and just kept running. We had to run for another hour until we reached Yuma.

We arrived at a lady's house in Yuma, but she didn't want to invite us in. She was a friend of the guide, but she said no because her boyfriend was there, but then said yes, but only let us to wait in the garden. We were wet and arrived there at about ten at night. The coyote left, but then came back and picked me up about four in the morning and took me to a house, where I stayed until the next day. The next morning, I got up and showered, we had breakfast, and that's when they brought me here [to Santa Ana] by car.

We arrived in June and our sons arrived in August. [Our coyote] had crossed some people and dropped by to visit us at our house. I spoke to him about crossing my two sons. I asked him how much it would cost, and he said that he would charge what he had charged me for my crossing, $800 per child. So my brothers and sisters helped me to pay to cross my children. From what my children have said, they went through the same process that I went through but the first time la migra caught them, it was because . . . well . . . the guide likes doing drugs and he was high. The second time, he got them over. They didn't spend much time with him, only about a week. When they crossed, my eldest son was 16 and the [next eldest,] about 15 years old. It would have been more complicated if they had been younger because of the risk of child abduction. The first time you cross, you aren't afraid because you don't know what it's like. The second time we tried, la migra had us running scared. I was more frightened; I didn't want to go. I told my husband that I wasn't going to do it and that I was heading back because my nerves had got to me. The third time, you know the process and the places you will move through. La migra tells you not to cross because people can kill or rob you. They scare you. You get worried, I guess I started to think about it. . . . You endure a lot to reach this country.

Thank God, we knew a good coyote, who picked the guides for us and told them, "I am placing my faith in you, this is my family." I'm really grateful to my brothers and sisters [for arranging the coyote] because you are handing your life to them since they are the ones guiding you. "Now come this way, and now over there, and jump this, and swim over there," and through it all, they are guiding you, and it is sad because anything can happen at the border. You are surprised by everything you see, and you ask yourself, "Why am I going? You can lose your life on this journey." As a friend of mine said, "And all just for the American Dream?" It is sad because I didn't come to steal from this country but to work, to get ahead, and, so they say, without Mexicans this country wouldn't be so well off. Yes, you really endure a lot in order to cross.

I didn't suffer as much as others. When I was detained, another lady arrived at the jail without shoes. She had been walking in the desert for eight days, eight days! She was exhausted. The guide couldn't figure out where [they were] meant to go. There was a train line, and they followed it. They found a boxcar that they thought would be pulled, but it wasn't, so they stayed there sleeping another eight days until migration picked them up. The lady had blisters. Her 19-year-old and 10-year-old sons were with her. Her husband was [in the United States] and wanted the children to go alone, but they wanted her to go with them. . . . She was never going to try again. She told me that, on one afternoon, they found a tree, and all twenty migrants tried to sit in the shade. Later, the guide made them climb over sand dunes, and they were sliding back, but they had to try again and again to climb over them. They had eight days of this before they reached the boxcar.

More than anything else you have to pick the right people, you don't just travel with whomever. You find someone who you know or who other people in your family know or someone your friends know are a good person. The woman had said to her sons, "We must stay here by the tree so that la migra finds us." Her sons had said, "No, Mama, we must not stay here," but she didn't have shoes, she only had a sweater, and she'd cut off the sleeves to wrap around her blistered feet. Sometimes I think about how much people endure to come to this country. It's very cruel.

I didn't know that I was pregnant with my son until I arrived in the United States. I asked my sister to take me to the doctor for a checkup, and even the doctor did not realize I was pregnant! I told the doctor that I had only had a light period, but I thought it was because of stress [due to the migration]. So she gave me pills to take, but I took two and felt really, really, bad. I called my sister because I was really sick. The doctor said to take a pregnancy test—it would be a $40 fee if it were negative and free if it were positive. I didn't think

I was pregnant but I did it anyway. They did a blood test and the nurse told me I was four weeks pregnant—it shocked me. How could I be pregnant after everything I'd gone through? Later, I thought how amazing God is—after all that I had been through: the reservoirs and everything else—I was pregnant.

The good thing is that the guide was good and was always saying, "Watch yourself here, Señora, this can be slippery." When we were getting out of the water, he'd help me and say, "Run to the fence, and then there is a rock wall to climb when you get out." When the bees stung me, the guide asked me if I was allergic to bees, and I said that I had never had a problem before.

I didn't think that I'd be able to do all of this because I'm overweight. At times, the guide offered to carry me, but I said that I could do it. He said a skinnier women from El Salvador got to the middle of the journey, sat down, and wouldn't run. We ran a lot. When you want to get here and have made the decision and spent the money, you just have to get here. I just had to get here.

My son was born here, and they looked after me well. Once I knew I was pregnant, the doctor began taking care of me. She gave me some paperwork to fill out so that I didn't have to pay for the birth. You go to the doctor the whole nine months and you don't pay—that's what this country offers.

My husband got a job at my brother's [place of] work, where he'd worked last time. The original plan was that I'd get a job to pay to bring the children, but I was pregnant. I tried to get a Christmas job at my sister's church, but they turned me down because I was pregnant so we just had my husband's wage. Then my sister's mother-in-law left for [North] Carolina; she'd been working for a man who was on his own with a daughter. He rang my sister to ask if she knew of anyone who wanted work, so I called him. I explained that I was pregnant, but that didn't bother him. He just wanted someone because he travels a lot, and needs someone to stay with his daughter. I told my husband that I would clean when the man was home, and, when he was away, I would stay overnight with his daughter. My husband wasn't keen [on the idea] because I was pregnant, and he thought something might happen, but, thank God, there were no problems, and I still work for this man today. I didn't have to have any documents to work for him. He pays me $200 a week whether I am just cleaning or staying overnight.

As a migrant here, it is your job to work. Go to work, go home, go to work, go home—that's all that happens all week. The weekends are for washing and shopping—that's what you do when you're in this country. As a migrant, you do have some fun, but it's not the same as being in your own country. It's not too bad for me because my brothers and sisters are here, if I'm not with one group, I'm with the other.

With the raids, you don't go out because you worry that they might get you after all the effort and the sacrifice you've made to make it across—because it's horrible, really horrible, because you are alone, all alone, out on the tracks and it scared me. I said to God, "How many people have been killed? Will they kill or rape me here?"

We don't travel far and we take precautions. We are free to walk down the street like in our own country, but there is always a fear of the police stopping you. We keep the car insured, my son in a car seat, and we drive sensibly in the streets so we don't draw attention to ourselves.

Money isn't important to me since it comes and goes, but the return trip to and from Mexico is much more difficult since September 11 [2001]. According to my sister, things have changed a lot. If you were worried then, you are more frightened now since there is much more surveillance. There was always border surveillance, but now the government is smarter. My sister used false documents for ages and never had a problem, but now they investigate so you can't stay in any job without legal papers.

My eldest son has just returned to Mexico because he didn't like it here. My husband has become depressed and says he wants to leave, but I don't want to go. It's not that I like it here but my [U.S.] son will lose his opportunities, even just learning English. He will grow up in Mexico and want to be here. If I can stay so that he grows up here, learns English, and grows up like the other children, I will stay because [if we leave,] he will return here in the future, but he will start from scratch. I don't want that for him because my other sons came here older and went to school, and they found it difficult. On the other hand, I [also] want to leave because these are not my people. I want to go for a while and come back, but just thinking about the crossing . . . no. I think we will stay 15 or 16 years. I have to provide for my son and also my sick father. We were sending money every two weeks, but now we send monthly.

We had a house in Mexico before we came but it's not finished. My idea is to finish painting the house and buy another and if there is the opportunity to buy a house here or an apartment, why not? A

little while ago, my brother went back and said things were very difficult there. Here, he says, you have the opportunity to work each day,
and there are life's comforts. You live well, eat well, and you don't
have to worry about what to put on the table tomorrow. That's why
sometimes I think it is better to think about staying here. Yes, go and
visit the family, but remember that it is very difficult to live there.
Yes, it is worth everything that you endure to get here. It is worth it,
but it is a lot of suffering to be able to achieve something. Even still,
it is worth it.

Influences on Patricia's Decision Making. At home in Irapuato, Patricia
struggled with whether to travel to the United States. In her narrative, we
see the overt connection between her final decision to go to the United
States and the influence of family, but what was not so obvious were the
covert factors that influenced the decision, the societal factors surrounding Patricia in Irapuato.

Just being born and raised in Irapuato predisposed Patricia to migrate.
According to the municipal government, Irapuato had a population of
440,134 inhabitants in 2002, and the average age was 21. Some 150,340
of these residents were of working age and 98.8 percent had work, but,
of these, fewer than 15 percent (22,525) had a high school education, and
fewer than 5 percent (7,380) had a higher education.[1] Thus the Irapuato
of 2002 had a young and poorly educated population, which meant that
most of its workers would be poorly paid with considerable competition
for better-paying positions.

Although the 2002 census stated that 98.8 percent of the city's
working-age residents had work, this included those who were working
only part-time or in domestic jobs for low wages, such as Patricia's sister
Rosa, who now worked as a housekeeper after having recently returned
from the United States. Moreover, the employment statistic did not
include the unemployed who had to leave the community in order to find
work, many of whom were now unauthorized migrants in the United
States. Since Patricia was now almost 40 years old and had only completed
two years of high school, her job opportunities would be limited and low
paying in Irapuato. In contrast, in the United States there was a demand
for unskilled laborers and these workers were relatively better paid.[2]

The Irapuato that Patricia knew was undergoing a rapid process
of modernization driven by remittances sent by the migration of its
residents to the United States. Tradition and modernization were both

Figure 2.2 Tradition and the migrant world coexist in Irapuato.

aspects of everyday life now prominent in this colonial landscape. This is illustrated in figure 2.2, where Mexican musicians playing traditional *corridos* (ballads) walk through the local markets; Elektra, an appliance store, where locals can receive their remittances from the United States via Western Union money transfers, is prominent in the background.

The desire for a better way of life, often expressed in the purchase of U.S. goods, was plainly visible in Irapuato. What may have started as demand for household appliances to improve the customers' lifestyles had been transformed into a simulated American shopping experience, with an increasing number of malls and U.S. department stores such as Sears.

At home in Irapuato, Patricia was surrounded by new stores showcasing what the United States might be like. When she could not afford to buy some of the items from those stores, the temptation to migrate would have been even greater. Patricia's sister Rosa, who had moved back and forth between Irapuato and the United States, had built a house; her brother Miguel, who had left for the United States only a few years before, now had land and was also building a house. Patricia's other relatives living in the United States were also doing well. Patricia could compare this with the living conditions of those around her who have stayed in Mexico and were struggling, such as her older sister Ana, who was raising her children and looking after their father in a very modest house.

Patricia would also be aware that unauthorized migrants returning from the United States were stimulating the local economy by demanding a U.S. lifestyle on their return. Joshua Reichart's 1982 study found that "returned migrants raise consumption norms in their places of origin, leading other community members to emulate those consumption patterns by migrating themselves."[3]

Responding to this demand, U.S. stores in Irapuato now required bilingual workers. This provided an opportunity for unauthorized migrants in the United States to return home and get work with their newly acquired English skills. Just a few years living in the United States could provide Patricia's children with the skills to attain high-paying employment on return to Irapuato, unauthorized migration in this instance ironically creating long-term opportunities in Mexico.

Patricia could remember when her husband had gone to the United States and what they were able to do with the money he had sent back. Indeed, their simple home in Irapuato was partly the product of those years of work. At the same time, she could recall her separation from her husband, and this might encourage her to accompany him to the United States, especially since the children were now older. What would keep her in Irapuato if her immediate and extended family were in the United States? In the United States, she would be with her husband and children; she could find work there and contribute to fixing up the house in Irapuato for their old age.

Increasingly, if Patricia stayed in Mexico, she would feel left behind. There was a feeling in Irapuato that everyone was leaving and that unauthorized migration was a normal part of everyday life. Everyone knew someone who had just left or others who had just returned. Irapuato was filled with references to the United States, so it is not surprising that Patricia, in the context of a changing Irapuato and with the encouragement of family, would decide to migrate to the United States.

Patricia's Encounters with Risk. Once Patricia made the decision to migrate to the United States, her journey reflected her family's migration strategy. She relied on her family to select a safe coyote, who would choose a safe guide and route. She would then rely on family for a job on arrival to the United States. Patricia admits that she was too trusting and did not understand the potential risks until she undertook her first crossing, when she experienced some psychological trauma. Detained, she saw other would-be migrants who had suffered considerably and she began to rethink her decision to migrate. Overhearing the verbal abuse of Mexican males in the U.S. Border Patrol detention area, she did not want to keep trying to cross. But because she had not been personally threatened, and because she strongly wanted to work, finish building the family home, and get ahead for the future, in the end, she went ahead.

On her second attempt to cross, her guide suffered a physical injury, breaking his leg as he fell into a concrete irrigation canal. Patricia then had to change guides and travel alone with a stranger. She feared sexual assault and even death at his or other hands as they moved across desert, reservoirs, and irrigation canals. On that trip, she suffered minor injuries, bumping her head on a beehive and being stung by bees, when avoiding the Border Patrol. All this time, she did not realize that she was pregnant and could have miscarried her baby.

Although the original plan was to leave her sons with family in Irapuato, once safe in the United States, she and her husband made the decision to take a one-shot chance and bring the children to the United States to keep their family together. Once there and unable to control the situation, her children ended up traveling through the desert with a drug-addicted guide. Patricia became concerned when any of her family moved back and forth between the United States and Mexico; she perceived the border to be more dangerous to cross with the tightening of border policies since the terrorist attacks of September 11, 2001. Ironically, Patricia reunited the family only to find it fragmenting again: her eldest son, who failed to adjust to life in the United States, returned to Mexico. In her mind, her greatest achievement is that her young son is a U.S. citizen. Forced to choose between one son in Mexico and the rest of her family in the United States, Patricia is now determined to stay to provide him with the benefits of life in the United States.

Both Patricia's decision to migrate and the logistics of her travel and risk management were intertwined with family. Indeed, family residing in the United States determined her migration strategy. Chris Martin suggests that migration, particularly unauthorized migration, is rarely an individual endeavor but, instead, part of a family strategy. It is therefore

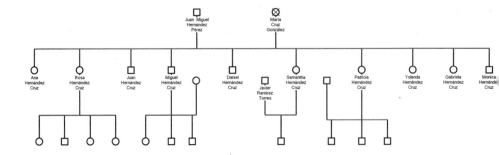

Figure 2.3 The Hernández Cruz family tree.

pertinent to consider how Patricia's journey is the result of family decisions, knowledge, and the practice of migration over time.[4]

The Migration of the Hernández Cruz Family

Since 1981, various members of the Hernández Cruz family participated
in unauthorized migration journeys to the United States. Before pro-
ceeding to the family members' narratives, let us take up the different
characters discussed in them (see fig. 2.3).

Of Juan Miguel Hernández Pérez and María Cruz González's ten
children, only Ana and Rosa currently reside in Mexico. Juan, Miguel,
Daniel, Samantha, Patricia, Yolanda, Gabriela, and Mónica are all living
in the United States, most residing in the vicinity of Santa Ana, California. In 1981, Juan Hernández Cruz set out from Irapuato in search of
work in California. He was following his father's footsteps but, unlike
his father, who had been a registered worker under the Bracero Program,
Juan would be crossing as an unauthorized migrant. This one successful
unauthorized crossing would change the destiny of the Hernández Cruz
family. Unauthorized migration would no longer be a dream but would
become, on the one hand, a feasible means of resolving a variety of challenges this family would face in the coming years and, on the other, the
source of problems for the family—in particular, risk to its individual
members and, more generally, fragmentation of the family itself.

Juan's brother Daniel was the next to follow. Abiding by the limited
instructions provided by his brother, he crossed into the United States
in the early 1980s. In the meantime, quite independent from the rest of
the family, in early 1988, Juan's sister Rosa Hernández Cruz decided to

cross. She did not find the crossing difficult; she just waited at the border in Tijuana, along with thousands of others, and made a run for it when the U.S. Border Patrol officers were distracted.

Also in 1988, Juan and Daniel's mother had become seriously ill. She had no private health insurance and Irapuato's public health services were quite limited. Juan decided to bring his mother to the United States, where she could receive free medical treatment. Because his mother was too sick to come alone, Juan's 21-year-old sister, Samantha, accompanied her on the journey.

Samantha, her mother, and their coyote (a friend from Irapuato) attempted to cross through the back hills of San Ysidro many times but without success. Her mother was so sick she could not run from the U.S. Border Patrol. The one time they did make it across, they were detained on Amtrak's San Diego–Los Angeles train service, picked out onboard by the U.S. Border Patrol (Samantha believes it was selection by racial stereotyping). All their belongings were taken out of bags and thrown onto the dusty ground. They were yelled at and taken to a detention center; when they arrived, officers severely interrogated a handcuffed Mexican man in their presence.

Because there was too great a chance of being caught and deported if they tried to cross over the hills, the coyote suggested they get false papers instead. Juan's mother was the first to cross because she needed treatment. Once across the border, Juan paid the coyote and took his mother straight to the hospital for treatment. Samantha crossed the next day. By using someone else's papers, altered to include their photos, they found it easy to cross via the San Ysidro U.S. Port of Entry.

When Samantha arrived in California, Juan was arranging his legal permanent residency in the United States. He recommended that Samantha also arrange her residency, taking advantage of the amnesty for long-term farmworkers. Through friends, they were connected with a farmer in the United States who signed all the documents they required for $800 each. They both received a letter that said they had worked on a farm for the required number of years and were both granted permanent residency.

Samantha was looking after her mother in the United States when she met her future husband, Javier Ramirez Torres. Javier had first traveled to the United States on March 17, 1986, when he was 16 years old. The idea of migrating would not have occurred to him except that a friend invited him to go, and Javier was looking for adventure. Although his parents felt he was too young to migrate, Javier was already independent. He had been living on his own since he was 14; they could not control his actions. Money to pay for this rebellious trip was lent by friends rather than by Javier's family.

Although migrating was his friend's idea, Javier's extended family was vital to the crossing. He traveled with his friend to his grandmother's house in Tijuana, where he stayed until Javier's uncle, a professional coyote, crossed the two boys. When they got to the United States, his friend's relatives found them jobs. The first crossing took a while, requiring them to advance slowly and to wait and retreat a little every time the migra came. After a week of attempts, they eventually made it across to a U.S. airfield (Brown Field Municipal Airport), where a private vehicle picked them up and dropped them off at a safe house. From there, hidden in a double-bottom truck, they drove through the San Clemente U.S. Border Patrol checkpoint to friends in Anaheim.

In August or September of 1986, Javier was deported to Tijuana after a raid on his workplace, a restaurant in Anaheim. He was given no chance to return and collect his belongings. Taken into custody at 4 p.m., he was dropped off in Tijuana by 9 p.m. When Javier returned to his coyote uncle, he was crossing other people. Eventually, a different uncle crossed Javier and a deported fellow worker to San Ysidro.

Confused and close to the border, Javier and his fellow worker asked a gringo to help them find their way north. The gringo, later suspected of being a drug addict, offered them a ride but only drove them around in circles. After taking a payment of $150 from them, he dropped them off back at the border where they had started. They then approached a Mexican American woman, who arranged for her boyfriend, also Mexican American, to take the two to Anaheim for $400 ($200 each). Javier, his friend, and their Mexican American coyotes were waved through the San Clemente checkpoint without any problems. About a year after this second crossing, Javier met Samantha (they would marry in November 1989).

Although Juan and Samantha's mother had responded to medical treatment, it became clear that her kidney disease would require a transplant. When tests showed that neither Juan nor Samantha was compatible for the operation, they sent for their brother Miguel, whom tests of the family in Mexico indicated was the most compatible of all the children. Issued a two-month visitor visa by the U.S. Consulate in Mexico City to help with his mother's health, Miguel traveled to the United

States in 1988. Interestingly, his mother's migratory status was never called into question. When, after all, he was found to be incompatible for organ donation, his family in the United States convinced him to stay there, even though he had planned to return to Mexico. Miguel then paid a coyote to cross his de facto wife and child.

Once Miguel's wife arrived, they worked together in a California sporting goods factory before moving, with the company, to Colorado. In 1991, Miguel's wife gave birth to their American son. Only a short time after, however, U.S. migration officials raided the factory where he was working; his de facto wife, four-year-old Mexican daughter, and one-month-old American son were deported to Mexico. Miguel stayed because, before the raid, an American woman who lived nearby had offered to marry him for $1,000 so that he could get legal status as a permanent resident. He decided to stay and plead his case with his nominal American wife because he would eventually divorce her and legally be able to immigrate his real family. The U.S. government, however, traced his information back to Mexico and found that he was living with another woman, his de facto wife, by whom he had two children. Miguel was deported to Mexico.

Rosa, who had now been in the United States for three years since her independent crossing in 1988, returned voluntarily to Mexico in 1992 because she had earned enough money to buy land in Irapuato. Her sick mother, María Cruz González, decided to visit her husband and youngest children in Mexico. Because she could not receive the treatment she needed there, however, she returned to the United States that same year. Although her daughter Samantha, who arranged the trip, believed that her mother would be crossed using false documents, María Cruz González was in fact crossed in the trunk of a car along with four other people. Samantha was shocked to realize this later, especially because her mother was critically ill.

Samantha, around this time, changed from being a migrant to a coyote and began using her papers to cross family members into the United States. She lent her papers to her sisters Yolanda, Gabriela, and Mónica so they could cross; this was her dying mother's wish. By the end of 1992, when her mother died, Samantha had crossed her younger siblings into the United States. In 1993, Samantha was granted U.S. citizenship and immediately stopped lending her papers for fear of losing her status. She then submitted paperwork to legalize her husband, Javier, whose employers had begun check the staff's legal status. By 1997, she had secured his permanent residency and by 2001, when their son was born, their immediate family members were all legal residents.

In 1993, after burying his mother back in Irapuato, Miguel crossed again to the United States, but, this time, as an unauthorized migrant. It was more traumatic: a girl in their group almost drowned in the river as they tried to cross. When he did get across, he sent again for his de facto wife. He always used the same reliable and trustworthy coyote for his wife because he did not want her to be at risk. This coyote was more expensive but usually smuggled Miguel's wife via official ports of entry rather than through the desert. This was particularly important this time because she was pregnant and, later that year, gave birth to their second, U.S.–born son.

Following Miguel's lead, Rosa decided to return to the United States also in 1993. This crossing was more difficult since it was through the desert near Mexicali rather than via Tijuana. Her group drove across the border in a pickup truck, all the time guided by an American on a motorbike. Even her coyote was nervous; he was drinking and ended up driving so erratically that Rosa convinced the other coyote to drive. On delivery to the United States, she was unable to contact her family. Eventually, one brother came to pick her up, but he had no money, so her coyotes held her until her sister Samantha arrived to make the payment.

Miguel and his family returned to Mexico in 1995; he left his family there and came straight back to the United States with Patricia's husband. They crossed via the Nogales U.S. Port of Entry by avoiding the security cameras. In 1996, Miguel returned home, and, that same year, Rosa crossed back to Mexico because her children, who were always smuggled to join her in the United States using borrowed documents, were becoming hard to manage. Rosa believed that they were being influenced by the unruly behavior of the American students at their school.

In 2000, Miguel crossed back into the United States via Mexicali, and his family followed. In 2001, his sister Rosa followed him. She crossed near Algodones, but, after running for several hours, she was caught by the U.S. Border Patrol. When she was released, the coyote was waiting for her. To increase her chances of a successful crossing, they decided to get hold of legal papers. They knew a woman who had a tourist visa. This woman was reluctant at first; she was pregnant and planned to give birth in the United States. She did not want to risk the opportunity of gaining U.S. citizenship for her child, but, in the end, she lent her papers in return for $200 so she could pay her rent.

Patricia's family was the most recent to cross. Her husband crossed on June 6, 2001, Patricia crossed on June 21, and her sons in August of that year. The extended family's trips across the border have been return trips to Mexico. Rosa returned to Irapuato with her children in mid-2004; they plan to stay permanently. Unable to adjust to life in the United States, Patricia's eldest son returned to Mexico later that same year.

The Family's Migration and Risk Management Strategies

Although each individual member of the Hernández Cruz family had a different migration experience, all were shaped by the family's collective migration strategy. This is a result of decisions made by the family's coyote in light of changing circumstances at the U.S.–Mexico border. Thus the coyote is a key element in risk management. Coyotes believe that it is safest to cross with legal tourist documents, followed by documents borrowed from family members, followed by altered fake documents, and, finally, by crossing in isolated areas where likelihood of detection by the U.S. Border Patrol is minimal, although the risk of physical and psychological trauma is greater.

Finally, the narratives demonstrate that, over time, by changing the location of their physical crossing, the Hernández Cruz family has been able to continue to successfully enter the United States, but the number of their attempts has increased, and there has been a greater exposure to, and experience of, risk. Nevertheless, overall, it can be seen that the outcomes have been good for the Hernández Cruz family. Its members are on track to reaching, or have already achieved, their personal and economic goals.

The Hernández Cruz family's migration strategy is based on using social networks to select and manage coyotes. Juan is the family's leader and continues, even today, to be a key player in the organization of his family's unauthorized migration strategy. He was what Peter Stalker would call a "pioneer," the vital connection who would establish a chain of migration by helping other family members link into unauthorized migration networks and establish themselves once in the United States.[5]

Juan's father, a bracero worker, also played a role in setting up the family for unauthorized migration. The Bracero Program broke down many of the psychological barriers to unauthorized migration: family members were now familiar with the American way of life; when they migrated back as unauthorized workers, they could reintegrate into their well-established social networks.[6] As Graciela Orozco, Esther González, and Roger Díaz de Cossio explain, "It is a structural phenomenon of our [Mexico and the United States'] complex bilateral relationship, which, in essence, responds to the different levels of economic development of the economies of each country but, also, has its origins in the many interactions between Mexican social networks on both sides of the border that motivate the continual migratory flow."[7]

Social networks are pivotal to providing information that may reduce risk, or at least perceptions of it. Once established in the United States, Juan could quickly arrange the necessary contacts as the need arose. He would vary strategies as circumstances changed and better options became available. For example, in the early crossings, according to Samantha in 1988, Juan "had a friend from Irapuato . . . a coyote as they say. . . . My brother told us that a man would come by the house, he was a friend and he was going to cross us."

Once Samantha met Javier, however, Juan was then made aware of Javier's uncle, who was a professional coyote based in Tijuana and, by marriage, was now family. Juan then started to use Javier's uncle as the contact because this was a better risk management strategy: the coyote was family and should have their interest at heart.

In part, migrants shape their risk reduction strategies around whom they blame, or hold responsible, for the risks associated with unauthorized migration. In this case, the Hernández Cruz family was unanimous in blaming coyotes as the primary source of risk to unauthorized migrants. According to Patricia, "More than anything else you have to pick the right people, you don't just travel with whoever. You find someone who you know or who other people in your family know or someone your friends know are a good person."

Miguel explained that choosing a coyote was risky because there were good and bad coyotes: "Many people who would cross you are trustworthy, good people, but there are some who are not. There are some who are very bad." According to Samantha, when the coyote was bad, people suffer as her mother did:

After five years in the United States, my mom decided to go back [to Mexico]. We let her go because supposedly they were going to treat her illness there, but there weren't the facilities, so she was getting sicker and sicker. So she decided to come back [to the United States] again.

This time, we saved up money because the crossing is very expensive and it's a risk. It's risky because the coyote said to my brother that he was going to bring her across in a car at the line [U.S. port of entry]. She was going to drive across as a passenger. Do you know where they put her? In the trunk! My mom says she was with a pregnant woman, a child, and a man. That's how they crossed. It was a miracle that Mom could cross back again without any documents but when Mom told us how she'd crossed . . . well, it was very dangerous.

Javier blamed a negligent relative, a less experienced coyote, for exposing him to a greater risk of deportation and leaving him vulnerable to being tricked out of money by an American: "You could say that we were tricked because the guy dropped us right on the other side of the U.S. side entry point and no further. Nothing more than 'You stay and I go,' so we didn't give him a cent. Why would I give him money when he just dropped us there? It didn't matter that I was family; he just dropped me and rushed off."

A migrant's social network is crucial to selecting a coyote because the fundamental prerequisite of a safe coyote is that you know him and you know people he has safely crossed to the United States. The more vulnerable the potential migrant, the more you need to trust the coyote and the more you are willing to pay to ensure safe delivery of loved ones. "I always bring my wife," Miguel explained,

I get them to cross my wife. It is a bit more difficult for her, but I don't want to take any risks. The boys were born here [in the United States], so it's no problem for them since this is their home, but it's difficult for us. I arrange for a different, more trustworthy guide, who crosses women safely. You don't want to put the women at risk. I can run and defend myself, but women can't, so I arrange for an easier crossing for her. When we cross my wife, we look for trustworthy people because, although they charge me a little more, they either walk or drive across at the line [U.S. port of entry]. It is more expensive but less risky.

Miguel's strategy, and that of his extended family, coincides with Katherine Donato and Evelyn Patterson's findings that "when women migrate, Mexican families attempt to safeguard traditional gender roles by controlling their trips and seeking extra protection in the process of border crossing."[8]

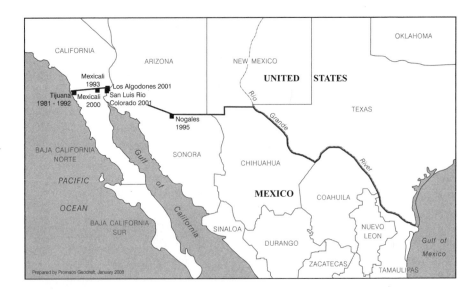

Figure 2.4 The U.S.–Mexico border, outlining the unauthorized border crossing patterns of the Hernández Cruz family. (Map by Promaco Geodraft)

Another thing the family could do to reduce risk was to always ensure that payment took place in the United States. As Miguel told me: "You cross before you pay, that's the deal. Once in the United States, they asked me where I lived, and they took me there before we paid the money. In any case, they hold you [in a safe house] until they get their money."

The most important factor in unauthorized migration risk reduction is an integrated and informed family network on both sides of the border. The migrant is more likely to be referred to a coyote who has a good record for successful crossings with minimal psychological or physical trauma. This coyote then develops a migration strategy and manages migrant risk at the border.

Responses to Border Policy Change

In the case of the Hernández Cruz family, there is an obvious shift in undocumented unauthorized crossings over time from Tijuana in the early 1980s, when U.S. border security was relatively lax, to farther east via San Luis Río Colorado into Arizona by 2001, when strategies such as Operation Gatekeeper had come into play (see fig. 2.4).

From 1981 until 1988, family members were involved in overt undocumented crossings at Tijuana. Rosa and presumably Juan and Daniel, who went before her, crossed near Playa Tijuana and were part of a mass crossing, a spontaneous surge of Mexicans onto U.S. soil in numbers that were uncontrollable, even at official ports of entry. This style of migration, Joseph Nevins explains, was quite common up until the early 1990s,

> when the sector would sometimes apprehend 2,000 people on busy nights—the vast majority in Imperial Beach, by far the busiest station in the United States. (Migrants liked crossing in the Imperial Beach area because it was the closest point to an urbanized area—San Ysidro.) Most afternoons, large numbers of migrants would gather along the boundary and cross once night fell. According to [Gustavo] De La Viña[, whom Nevins interviewed in 1997], the first time he toured the boundary in the San Diego Sector he saw groups of three to four hundred unauthorized migrants at different hills—on the U.S. side of the boundary—in the Imperial Beach area, all waiting to travel northward. Given such numbers, it was impossible for the Border Patrol to control them. And, in certain areas along the boundary, only the remnants of a chain-link fence existed. In many ways, the boundary as a physical, visible line barely existed. This led De La Vina to conclude that what he had to do was "delineate the border . . . to show the migrants and us where the U.S. began and where Mexico ended." Building the new steel wall (or "fence," in INS parlance) was the way to do so.[9]

To prevent the gathering of migrants and the rush across the border described by migrant participant Rosa (and also by Nevins), in September 1989, floodlights were installed at San Ysidro on the U.S. side of the border. U.S. Border Patrol Officer numbers were increased by one hundred. By 1990, the metal border wall was under construction, and there was already limited evidence that migrant traffic was shifting eastward to the outskirts of urban Tijuana.[10] The general trend was "when crossing was made more difficult in one sector, the migrant flow was diverted to other sectors where enforcement was less intense."[11]

In 1993, the family had shifted undocumented crossings eastward to Mexicali, with Rosa and her brother Miguel crossing there that year. By this time, undocumented migration had gone underground; the swell in antimigrant public sentiment that led to Operation Hold the Line in El Paso, and then to Operation Gatekeeper, had made itself felt.[12] The exception to the Mexicali rule for the Hernández Cruz family was Rosa's mother's crossing at Tijuana in 1992, but this was a covert crossing in the trunk of a car rather than an overt one using false documents.

In October 1994, Operation Gatekeeper was implemented in California.[13] In 1995, Miguel and Patricia's husband crossed at Nogales by outsmarting security cameras at the official U.S. port of entry. In 2000, Miguel returned to Mexicali, but, from then onward, the Hernández Cruz family used Arizona as their region of unauthorized undocumented entry into the United States, with Rosa crossing at Algodones, followed by Patricia and her husband crossing in the same vicinity, but from San Luis Río Colorado en route to Yuma.

Coyotes as Risk Managers

Although it attracted little media attention, in 2004, some 3.6 million of the 9 million unauthorized migrants in the United States simply overstayed their visas.[14] David Salazar, head of Customs and Border Protection, explained that, in that year, the number one crossing strategy was by passing as a U.S. citizen or with authentic permanent resident documents that were either borrowed or stolen. Number two was by using a false document. Number three was by altering an original document to add the photo of the person who wished to cross. And number four was by crossing at night hidden in a vehicle (at night because of the better climatic conditions and shorter lines). Since the trunk was very commonly searched, to avoid detection many migrants ended up being smuggled in more dangerous parts of the vehicle, including under the hood around the motor.[15]

Indeed, we see that Miguel, given the opportunity, overstayed his U.S. tourist visa. For the other, most vulnerable undocumented members of the family, we can see that the coyote obtained borrowed or stolen original documents. "They also crossed my little two-and-a-half-year-old daughter," Miguel told me, "but they brought her over at the line [U.S. port of entry] with somebody else's documents."

After Rosa had made several risky and unsuccessful attempts at Algodones, the coyote said, "We'll try again. We'll see if my wife's friend will lend us her passport [U.S. tourist visa]." But the friend told Rosa, "No, I'm about to give birth and I want to give birth in the United States, that's why I have my passport and what if they get you." Rosa said to her,

"If they get me I will tell them that I found it in such and such a place. You can tell them you lost your document there." "She didn't really want to," Rosa explained, "but the next day she knocked at the door and said, 'Okay, I'll lend it to you. I'll lend it to you but you have to give me the 200 dollars you promised. I have to pay the rent.' We agreed. It's like I say, we all do this for necessity. We don't do it for fun."

These options were not available to Samantha on her first crossing because she still had not met Javier and was not crossing with his highly experienced coyote uncle. The best that their coyote from Irapuato could do, even at greater expense, was to get them modified original documents, where the photo had been replaced with their own. "Eight times we'd attempted to cross the hills near San Ysidro," Samantha told me.

Really early in the morning, about four or five, we'd cross but then they'd get us. The next day we'd be up early again, they'd get us and so on. They got us seven or eight times, because my mother was sick and couldn't run, before the coyote spoke with my brother and suggested it would be better to get us false papers; to get documents for people about our age who looked like us—so that's what my brother did. He bought us false papers and we walked across at the line [U.S. port of entry]. At last, after all the hassle, the guy arrived and said we were going to cross via the line [U.S. port of entry]. "Don't worry and act like nothing's wrong." Thank God, we crossed.

Unlike Javier's uncle, who had a strong sense of duty and who automatically sought out safer options for vulnerable migrants (such as children and the sick), Samantha and her mother's coyote suggested this safer option only after they had tried to cross again and again. Samantha was upset with the coyote, but, at the time, there was a crackdown on the use of fake documents, so the coyote might have left this as a last resort.[16] Or he might simply have been better prepared to deal with healthy young males from Irapuato than a sick, middle-aged woman.

The next best strategy, according to David Salazar, was to be crossed via an official port of entry. Indeed, Miguel also had one of his safest and most successful crossings this way:

It was 1993 and, this time, I returned as an illegal. I crossed with my brother-in-law, Patricia's husband. We crossed at a border entry point where there was just a wire fence. We crossed beside the entry point where they check your papers. There is a camera that goes around in circles and just a wire fence. There was no wall, just wire and a dry riverbed. We were following behind the camera so they wouldn't see us. . . . We got to Tucson. When we arrived, a young guy took us to his house for three days before my brother-in-law and I caught the bus to Los Angeles.

By crossing unauthorized at a U.S. port of entry, there is a greater chance of being detected, but there is also less risk of exposure to the elements or of being attacked by bandits. Crossing in isolated desert areas is a migrant's very last resort, but, by 2001, several members of the Hernández Cruz family were exposed to these risks due to the tightening of U.S. border controls.

Changing Migration Strategies

Woven into the patterns established by the coyote in response to changes in U.S. border policy were the ebbs and flows of migration activity in response to changing circumstances within the Hernández Cruz family itself. As the most obvious instance, the mother's illness led to a peak of activity in 1988, with the mother, Samantha, Miguel, and Rosa all crossing within the one year.

The principal motivation for that first peak was to secure publicly funded medical treatment for the mother. "I crossed with my mom," explained Samantha. "We didn't come to make money, like most people do; we crossed because my mother was sick. She couldn't have the operation she needed in Mexico because we didn't have the money for it. My brother was [in the United States] and said, 'I'm going to send money so that you can cross and Mom can get taken care of.' I'm not sure if you know but the [U.S.] government helps you if you have money or not, so that's why we came."

Although Samantha believed that the reasons her family had migrated differed from those of most Mexican migrants, the rationale was still financial. Her mother could have received appropriate treatment in Mexico if they had been able to pay for it. Mexicans' "notion of the migrant as an economic mercenary has no relation whatsoever to the way migrants regard themselves," writes Rubén Martínez. "Ask Mexicans why they cross the Rio Grande and they will invariably say, 'to seek a better way of life.' They do not mean only material gain." [17]

Samantha, and perhaps some other members of the family, may have considered getting health care for their mother to be an honorable reason for their unauthorized migration to the United States. In the eyes of the general U.S. population, however, seeking publicly funded health care feeds the stereotype of Mexican migrants as excessive users of social services.[18] Some studies show that unauthorized migrants can, indeed, put a strain on welfare, health, and education services; others show that migrants account for greater tax revenue than government expense.[19] Thus, even though the use of health services by the Hernández Cruz family for the mother and later for the various children's births does suggest that family members have been a burden on California's health system, the taxes they have paid since then may well have offset this expenditure of public funds.

In 1992, there was a second peak in the Hernández Cruz family's unauthorized migration. When the mother returned to the United States, just before her death, she asked Samantha to lend her permanent residency papers to Samantha's younger sisters, Yolanda, Gabriela, and Mónica, so that they could make documented unauthorized crossings. After Samantha was granted U.S. citizenship in 1993, however, she decided to stop risking her legal status to help family members cross unauthorized into the United States. From then on, she helped them only by accompanying their U.S. citizen children across the border or by arranging to borrow documents from others—she no longer lent them her own documents.

In time, Miguel was motivated to migrate, unauthorized, to the United States to take advantage of jus soli. Under this legal precept (as recognized in the Fourteenth Amendment of the U.S. Constitution), any child born in the United States is automatically a U.S. citizen.[20] In 1991, Miguel's first American child was born, but, that same year, he and his family were deported back to Mexico. Although they crossed back into the United States in late 1993, by early 1995, they had all returned to Mexico by choice. This year-long stay in the United States appears to have been motivated by jus soli, to ensure that their third child, born early 1994, would be a U.S. citizen, as is their second child.

It can also be seen how certain family members might have influenced others. For example, Rosa who seemed to have had a close relationship with her brother Miguel, tended to follow him back and forth between the United States and Mexico.

In contrast to the attitudes of the Hernández Cruz family, Javier (who married into the family) had very different motives for migration; he crossed as a young man looking for adventure or, as he put it, "freedom, the opportunity to explore other things and I wanted to see new places."

Cynthia Lightfoot, a specialist in the culture of adolescent risk taking, explains that this type of risk-seeking behavior is common among young males. Adolescents are often classified either as troublemakers, associated with rebellion, or as heroes, taking advantage of opportunities. Young males set out to prove they are heroes by taking risks that are viewed positively by society.[21] Although Javier's parents did not approve, classifying him as a rebel, other societal influences, including popular culture, might have suggested to Javier that, in the eyes of the broader Mexican society, he could become a hero or, even if he were unsuccessful and suffered the severe consequences of risk, at least a martyr-hero. Soon after Javier was deported to Mexico, however, and after his job was threatened by a revision of his migration status at the workplace, his unauthorized status became more of a threat than a thrill.

In contrast to Javier, who considered unauthorized migration an adventure, the Hernández Cruz family considered it to be a necessary evil. "One [U.S. Border Patrol] agent asked me why I was crossing," Rosa told me. "'Necessity,' I said. 'Do you think I'd be here if I didn't need to be? I know it's dangerous.'"

Rosa believed that she had no legal options and would therefore have to take the risk of unauthorized migration to reach and work in the United States. This suggests that she would have taken a documented alternative, if it had been available; indeed, when Miguel had the opportunity to obtain a legal tourist visa, he took it. The Hernández Cruz family saw attaining legal status as one important way of reducing future potential risk. As the first real example of this, Samantha, a recent arrival to the United States, sought to achieve legalized status under the 1986 Immigration and Reform Act, which granted amnesty to long-term farmworkers. In contrast to its goal of legalizing an existing unauthorized migrant population, "the 1986 Immigration Reform and Control Act (IRCA) . . . led to the legalization of large numbers of unauthorized immigrants as a way of ultimately reducing unsanctioned immigration. The IRCA's main effect, however, was 'to reinforce and expand already well-established cross border migration networks' and to create a booming business in fraudulent documents."[22]

Likewise, Miguel tried very hard to attain some sort of legal status to provide stability and a secure income for his family, even by participating in a false marriage: "An American had asked me if I wanted to marry her so I could get papers; I accepted. I paid $1,000 for us to marry." He was detained, however, and had to undergo legal proceedings, which ended up denying him the chance to become a legal resident in the United States.

Aspirations of family members also appeared to change according to the migration status attained. For example, after he became a permanent resident of the United States, Javier came to realize that this was not enough for him, that he also wanted the right to vote: "Yes, I'd become a citizen. I'd do it for the right to vote. I've never voted in my life, not even in Mexico. When I came [to the United States], I was too young to vote, and I don't even have a voting card or military service papers, none of that. When I came here, I was young, so I didn't have the chance to get any of these documents."

The Hernández Cruz family thus associated legal authorization and U.S. citizenship with freedom of movement across borders, the right to earn a living, and entitlement to other rights, such as the right to vote.

Determined to Migrate

Despite being deported or failing again and again to cross the border, members of the Hernández Cruz family kept trying until they were finally able to make it into the United States. This is partly because most migrants assume that, over time, their family will achieve legal status. "Once a [migrant] network was established and family members were in place to provide communications and assistance," David Lorey tells us, "the migrant flow could not simply be shut off whenever the U.S. economy cooled down. The fact that migrant populations from Mexico had historically been recognized and accepted as U.S. citizens after a period of work and acculturation, regardless of reforms in U.S. immigration laws, reinforced migration networks and migrant lore." [23]

Operation Gatekeeper did appear to shift the undocumented crossings of the Hernández Cruz family eastward, but not to actually reduce their unauthorized migration. The Hernández Cruz family continued to cross, despite the risks, but the journey became more difficult and they had to undertake several attempts before they successfully crossed into the United States. In 1993, Miguel had to make several attempts in Mexicali before making it across. In 2001, Rosa made several attempts to cross at Algodones, but eventually ended up paying to borrow papers when it became too difficult to cross undocumented. Patricia, in the same year, spent 15 days trying to cross before finally making it to the United States, surviving treacherous conditions in remote desert areas.

Indeed, Wayne Cornelius's 1998 study found that the overall average number of attempts before successful crossing was increasing: "Those who arrived in 1995 averaged 1.18 attempts, and migrants arriving between January and June 1996 required 1.63 attempts on average. In terms of successfully crossing on the first attempt, [on the other hand,] 78 percent did so before January 1995, 87 percent during 1995, and 81 percent in the first half of 1996." "Prospective illegal immigrants," concluded Cornelius, "have learned quickly to avoid the most heavily fortified segments of the border altogether and cross elsewhere."[24]

U.S. border officials expected that implementation of Operation Gatekeeper would lead to the migrants undertaking pretrip risk assessment and deciding not to cross.[25] In general, however, the Hernández Cruz family tended to focus on the task of crossing and only reflect on risk after their journey. Speaking generally, Rosa told me that "people come back to visit but then risk [crossing to the United States] again. People cross no matter what. They find a way to cross. I'd love to have a visa!"

Ironically, despite the risks, each migrant ends up deliberately or inadvertently encouraging others to migrate. "They see me and say, 'Rosa did it, so why can't I.' When I showed my bathroom to my brother he said, 'Wow, what a bathroom!' and that's where his curiosity [to migrate to the United States] began."

It is clear from Patricia's narrative that at least some migrants presume migration to be of greater risk to children than adults and therefore parents seek out safer strategies for their children: "First my husband would cross and then he'd arrange to get me over. My mother-in-law said, 'Best you both go and leave the boys with me.' And that's what happened. We came here and left my sons there."

Adolescents were one group, in particular, that did not undertake pretrip risk assessment. Or, to put it in Javier's words: "No, to be honest, it didn't occur to me to think about that, although crossing the border is an odyssey. [After a friend suggested he and Javier cross,] I went home and told my parents that a friend had invited me to the United States. They said, 'No, you can't go. You're too young. You can't go!' So then I said, 'I'm not asking for your permission, I'm going.'"

Indeed, Lightfoot tells us, adolescents have impaired risk assessment capabilities. Peers heavily influence their decision making, such as Javier's friend convincing him that it would be an adventure to cross to the United States. Moreover, "Just don't do it" demands, such as those made by Javier's parents, do not work because the young will always overlook the potential for negative consequences when most people achieve good outcomes, in this case, when many other migrants successfully cross into the United States each day.[26]

It may be surmised that pretrip risk assessment for adults was minimal because "everyone" was migrating and so it was assumed to be a viable, and relatively safe, option. Moreover, in the majority of cases, family in the United States ("successful migrants") undertook planning for the migrant's journey, so there was little consideration of the risks by the individual. In other circumstances, the situation was so desperate that the benefit relative to even a perceived high level of risk was considered to be worth it. Finally, and less commonly, migrants who sought out adventure, in particular young males, perceived risk to be minimal through a positive attitude toward potential mishaps.

In contrast, for vulnerable groups, serious risk reduction strategies were adopted. For children, the sick and, in some cases, women, families undertook serious and considered pretrip assessment to determine the least risky strategy. Women and children in the Hernández Cruz family sometimes borrowed Samantha's documents or used modified or false documents to cross via a U.S. port of entry. This strategy coincides with what Katherine Donato and Evelyn Patterson found: "A common strategy is for women to obtain and carry valid documents but to use them inappropriately. A woman may 'borrow' a green card or other visa from a look-alike sister and cross with it, counting on the inspecting officer (who is processing dozens of entries an hour) not to notice or care that the person in the picture looks slightly different."[27]

Thus, in response to Operation Gatekeeper, family members did not decide to stay in Mexico, but, instead, moved their undocumented unauthorized crossings farther eastward into more and more remote, and dangerous, terrain. The easy Tijuana crossings of the 1980s were replaced by complicated journeys where migrants were subject to more difficult terrain. By the time Patricia crossed at San Luis Río Colorado in 2001, the journey was arduous and quite traumatic: "I guess I started to think about it. . . . You endure a lot to reach this country. . . . Thank God, we knew a good coyote, who picked the guides for us and told them, 'I am placing my faith in you, this is my family.'"

At the time of their interviews in 2004, the Hernández Cruz family members believed that the border had become more dangerous. Patricia believed the crossing to be more dangerous to unauthorized migrants because of the higher levels of U.S. border security: "The return trip to and from Mexico is much more difficult since September 11 [2001]. According to my sister, things have changed a lot. If you were worried then, you are more frightened now because there is much more surveillance. There was always border surveillance but now the government is smarter."

Javier attributed the dangerous nature of the border to the fact that migrants were being forced into ever more difficult terrain: "Today, it is very difficult [to cross]. In the past, you didn't have to go far or through the desert, we crossed through some desert but it was nothing."

Javier tended to discourage people from crossing because it was so expensive that it was almost worthwhile for him to just send the money to help them out, rather than pay to cross them to the United States. "Nowadays I tell people to think twice about the crossing because it's quite difficult. It costs 2,000 to 3,000 dollars to cross, so I say it's better that I send them the money to use rather than spend on the crossing."

As a result of the dangerous nature of the border crossing, Miguel had decided to remain in the United States for the long term: "We can't leave now, not in the near future. Our family has told us that it is very difficult to cross because there is a lot more surveillance because of the [war on] terrorism. That's the problem so, for now, there's no returning to Mexico . . . because it's more difficult, it's more expensive. When I crossed I paid $1,000. . . . We don't want to lose time coming and going. If I am going to spend $4,000 to get back [after a visit to Mexico], it is better to just save it for the children's university."

What Operation Gatekeeper, in particular, appeared to have done was to increase the Hernández Cruz family's length of stay in the United States. The family was beginning to stay longer within the United States to avoid the repercussions of more unauthorized crossings. By reducing the frequency of trips across the increasingly dangerous U.S.–Mexico border, they were managing risk. From 2000 to 2001, when crossing conditions were more difficult, family members decided either to reside in the United States or to return and stay in Mexico. This was because "in general, the experts believed U.S. policies based in efforts to drive up the cost of migrating actually lowered the odds of repatriation and increased the numbers of permanent undocumented residents, converting a circular movement into a unidirectional flow."[28]

Whereas, before, Miguel and Rosa used to cross the border on a semi-regular basis, now Rosa decided to return to Mexico permanently and

Miguel to stay in the United States until his house was finished and his children were old enough to make their own decisions about the future. Aspirations for the future motivated Patricia to remain in the United States even though she did not feel culturally adapted. She wanted to ensure that her son had access to all his legal entitlements as a U.S. citizen and that she would be economically stable when she returned to Mexico. Because it has become increasingly difficult to cross back and forth between Mexico and the United States, Patricia preferred to stay for the long term and achieve all her goals before returning to Mexico.

These observations and changes in strategy are consistent with David Spener's findings immediately after the implementation of Operation Hold the Line in El Paso: "In addition to resorting to more extreme efforts to cross, [migrants] also reduced their number of crossings by staying over for longer periods of time on the Texas side. Thus instead of crossing daily, they would cross and spend an entire week or even a month in El Paso, staying with friends or relatives, or even camped out in the desert. Others actually decided to set up residence in El Paso for the first time because crossing, while still far from impossible, had become much more of a chore as a consequence of Operation [Hold the Line]."[29] Increased border security had led to migrants' increasing dependence on coyotes, who then raised their fees and made it even more undesirable economically to move back and forth between the two countries.[30]

The Hernández Cruz Family: A Success Story?

Overall, despite the risks, the outcomes were good for the Hernández Cruz family. At my study's end, they were on track to reaching, or had already achieved, their personal and economic goals. Rosa had returned to Mexico after working in the United States for several periods of time. She was both pleased and proud of her achievements: "What I wanted was a house. You can be proud of building a house. My friends know that I was over there [United States] and they say 'You built this house!' Yes, I built this house and not everybody could do it."

Even at home, there were benefits from the unauthorized migration, with better employment opportunities for Rosa's children, who were educated on and off in the United States. Her daughter applied for a front desk position at the new Holiday Inn hotel opening in Irapuato in 2005, but there were other employment opportunities: "Anyone who speaks English and has done preparatory school has no problems getting work. It's more difficult for the accountants and lawyers. We're up to here with lawyers and accountants. Work is available for people with computer skills, English, and Preparatory School."

Back in Irapuato, Rosa also enjoyed a new social status: "Things from [the United States] are a novelty here. Like your car, they'll see the Baja California plates. 'Who has come from the United States to visit Rosa?' They admire it. Just like if I take things from here to there they say, 'How pretty!' We are here and we want to be there; we are there and we want to be here."

Rosa took me on a tour of her "American" kitchen and upstairs to two bedrooms and a full bathroom. We then went next door to see Miguel's house. With the money he had earned in the United States, Miguel renovated his original home into a two-story building; a month before I interviewed him, he remitted $18,000 to Mexico to purchase another property.

Miguel believed, despite the problems he faced, that unauthorized migration to the United States was worthwhile: "When I arrived from Mexico, I didn't have anything, nothing more than a very small house. I arrived with a dream to build a bigger house and, thank God, I have achieved this. I now have two houses to my name."

He had the benefit of his nominal marriage, which provided him with a valid social security card that has meant that he has the opportunity to appear to be legal and thus reap the economic benefits: "I've been working as a painter for ten years with the same company. I started earning $4.25, and now I earn $13 an hour. I couldn't earn that in my country."

Javier recognized the benefit of having crossed into the United States. As a legalized permanent resident, he could return to Mexico and compare his current circumstances with those back in Mexico: "Yes, I think that I would do it again. Do you know why? Unfortunately in my country, and it will always be my home, I don't like the political system. There I'd never have a new car or even a car in the first place. I'd never make this amount of money, and I earn good money. In Mexico, I just couldn't do it because I don't have the education to be able to do it. . . . I would never have made it in Mexico. I would do this all over again."

Javier thus achieved a much-improved economic status in the United States despite his low level of education, but his overall satisfaction was linked to his personal development and opportunities for advancement in the workplace: "I was a cook, now I am head cook. I'm a leader at work and, if I put in more effort, I could become a supervisor or a manager."

Unlike Rosa, Miguel, and Javier, Patricia was still far from reaching her goals but believed that the United States, rather than Mexico, was her best opportunity for economic security. She had a balanced perspective on the outcome of her risky journey; on the one hand, the journey frightened her but, on the other, she felt that, as a mother-to-be, she was compensated with the full, publicly funded medical treatment she received in the United States.

Unfortunately, unauthorized migration had negative outcomes for some family members. Both Patricia and Rosa experienced family fragmentation, with Patricia's son returning to Mexico, unable to adjust to life in the United States, and with Rosa unable to legally visit her eldest daughter, who had cancer and resided in the United States.

On reflection, Samantha thought it ironic that her father, having lived and worked in the United States under the Bracero Program, could have gotten legal residency for all his family but decided not to. How much easier life would have been if he had filled out that simple paperwork all those years ago.

Except for María Cruz González, family members suffered no serious physical or psychological trauma during their unauthorized migration journeys. The outcomes of undertaking the journeys were positive, with the different members achieving both personal and economic aspirations.

The family's migrant "pioneer," Juan, left Mexico poor and uneducated. By 2004, his youngest sister Mónica had graduated from a high school in the United States and planned to go on to college. Most of Juan's siblings who followed his trail to the United States now own property in Mexico and have increased their asset base substantially. Four of the family's children became U.S. citizens—this new generation was more American than Mexican. Unauthorized travel across the border will soon be part of family heritage rather than everyday reality.

Over time, the Hernández Cruz family developed a sophisticated detection and risk reduction strategy based on their solid social network. It enabled them to appropriately select coyotes, who then managed the crossing and safety issues according to the vulnerability of the migrant family member; healthy adults usually undertook cheaper undocumented unauthorized crossings in isolated areas, whereas vulnerable members, the sick and children, were crossed at greater expense via official ports of entry to the United States using borrowed, stolen, or fake documents. In the worst-case scenario, when documents were unavail-able or there was a crackdown on fraudulent documents, migrant mem-bers were smuggled across concealed in vehicles. Once successfully in the United States, most family members reduced the frequency of visits to Mexico and planned longer stays in the United States to avoid the increasing dangers and expense of border crossings. As the opportu-nity arose, family members also sought to legalize their status through amnesty or marriage, and that of their children through jus soli, U.S. citizenship by birth within the United States.

Insights into Unauthorized Migration and Risk

All the participants in this study migrated to the United States in search of a better life. Most wanted to improve their economic status; others wanted to receive medical treatment (María Cruz González) or to escape domestic violence (Lucía). They undertook unauthorized migration because there was no legal alternative available to them at the time.

Among the migrant participants, healthy adults did not really think about risk, perhaps because "everyone" was migrating, therefore unau-thorized migration was assumed to be a viable, relatively safe option. Individual migrants entrusted risk assessment to family members in the United States, who were presumed to have greater knowledge about the border. The exception was the migrant Arturo, who had received a higher education and was quite aware of the risks he faced at the border. In contrast, a less-educated young male in the study (Javier) had a reduced perception of risk, deliberately seeking out risk and adventure. In gen-eral, the risks of unauthorized migration were seriously considered only when more vulnerable family members were planning to cross, such as the sick (María Cruz González) or children (Diana, Miguel, Rosa, and Patricia's children). This pattern matches what Pia Orrenius found to be the case: "In general, younger, less educated migrants are more willing to bear risks, whereas educated older individuals are less willing—either because they have access to better information or because they have 'more to lose.' Being married and having children also lowers the tol-erance for risk, as an unfortunate accident or death could leave family destitute."[31]

Migrant participants considered the coyotes to be the greatest source of risk at the border. The family would pick the best coyote they knew and pay for the best crossing strategy they could afford (because the greater the cost, usually the safer the migration journey). They determined that the safest way to migrate into the United States was by overstaying a tourist visa (Diana, Arturo, and Miguel), followed by crossing via a U.S. port of entry using someone else's documents (Rosa, Yolanda, Gabriela, and Mónica), followed by crossing at a U.S. port of entry using false papers (María Cruz González [first time], Samantha) and crossing without papers at or near to a U.S. port of entry (María Cruz González [second time], Lucía, Javier, Miguel with Patricia's husband). They determined that the most dangerous was crossing in areas least monitored by the U.S. Border Patrol because they would be most vulnerable to the elements and criminals and least likely to get rescued by either U.S. or Mexican officials (David, Rosa, and Patricia). The family paid more to secure false papers for vulnerable members so they could cross via official ports of entry rather than through the more physically demanding remote areas of the border.

There was an overwhelming belief among all the migrant participants that the U.S.–Mexico border was more dangerous today than in the past and they associated this with increasing border security measures in the wake of 9/11, which made crossing the border more expensive and difficult. The migrants responded by choosing their coyotes carefully, who then managed their migration; by staying longer once they reached the United States (Diana, Miguel, and Patricia); and, finally, by using any means available to become legalized (Juan and Samantha) or, at the very least, to ensure that their children were U.S. born (Miguel and Patricia).

Despite any difficulties, most migrant participants were pleased to have migrated to the United States and, at the conclusion of the study, were achieving their goals, such as building houses in Mexico (Diana, Rosa, Miguel, Daniel, Javier, and Patricia). Only two of the migrants decided that unauthorized migration was not "worth it": Lucía, who could attain legal migration to the United States, and well-educated Arturo who had better work opportunities than most in Mexico.

Having examined migrant experiences of the unauthorized migration process and the risks involved in this chapter, let us next consider the responses of the Mexican government, civil society, and the news media to the unauthorized migration of its citizens to the United States to determine the role that formal, institutional responses play in migration risk management.

3
Government, Civil Society, and Print Media Responses

In chapter 2, migrant encounters with unauthorized migration revealed the vital role that family networks play in protecting migrants from harm. This chapter examines the role Mexican society plays, through its institutions, in managing the unauthorized migration of its citizens to the United States. It begins by reviewing the Mexican government programs apparently designed to mitigate the risks of unauthorized migration. It then briefly reviews the role of civil society efforts (both binational Mexican and Mexican American) to lobby for political change and a decrease in the actual levels of risk experienced by unauthorized migrants. Finally, it analyzes the Mexican news media responses to the risks of unauthorized migration, as evidenced in how media institutions attempt to shape the Mexican public's perceptions of those risks. And, finally, it considers the interplay between the Mexican government, civil society, the news media, and the unauthorized migrant participants in this study.

Official Responses of the Mexican Government

For many years, it suited both U.S. and Mexican governments to avoid official discussion of, or response to, unauthorized migration.[1] This would change, however, with the integration of Mexican and U.S. economies since the 1994 North American Free Trade Agreement (NAFTA), which has had consequences for labor markets in both countries, most notably, the tightening of border security by the United States, accompanied by increasing levels of risk for unauthorized migrants. The risks to migrants have led to growing public pressure, which in turn has made it impossible for the Mexican government to avoid this issue.

According to the 1997 *Binational Study: Migration between Mexico and the United States*, by the mid-1990s, the Mexican government undertook three major policy initiatives: (1) "the protection of migrant rights"; (2) "avoiding abrupt changes in U.S. immigration policy"; and (3) "in light of the reaction to the recent negative U.S. climate towards immigrants, seeking recognition for their contributions to the host society."[2]

The election of Mexican President Vicente Fox in 2000 led to a reevaluation of the rationales, benefits, and risks of Mexican unauthorized migration to the United States. With a new agenda and a relatively favorable diplomatic climate (U.S. President George Bush being acquainted and friendly with President Fox), the Mexican government recognized that there was an opportunity to seek a legal means for Mexicans to continue working in the United States. At the same time, this strategy could win the favor of Mexican citizens residing in the United States who would soon secure voting rights in Mexican elections.[3]

Within Mexico's political structure, two Mexican government entities were assigned responsibility for managing the issues associated with Mexican unauthorized migration to the United States: the Secretaría de Relaciones Exteriores (Ministry of Foreign Affairs) for migration issues at an international policy level, including the protection of Mexican migrants in foreign territories; and the Instituto Nacional de Migración (National Migration Institute) for specific migrant-related programs on Mexican territory. Responsibility for Mexico's five official migration-related strategies has been divided between these two entities:

1. Establishing a diplomatic dialogue between Mexico and the United States on unauthorized migration (Secretaría de Relaciones Exteriores);

2. Expanding consular responsibilities to include the protection of any Mexican residing in a foreign territory, the legal defense of migrants' human rights, and the creation of unauthorized migration risk awareness strategies (Secretaría de Relaciones Exteriores);

3. Implementing an awareness campaign for potential migrants and a rescue plan facilitated by the Instituto Nacional de Migración's rescue team Grupo Beta (Beta Group; Instituto Nacional de Migración: Programa Nacional de Protección a Migrantes [Migrant Protection Program];

4. Protecting and helping migrants returning from the United States to safely reach their Mexican communities (Instituto Nacional de Migración: Programa Paisano [Countrymen Program]);

5. Detaining and deporting foreigners entering, unauthorized, into Mexico en route to the United States (Instituto Nacional de Migración: Plan Sur [Southern Plan]).

Although not associated with any specific programs, the Comisión Nacional de Derechos Humanos (Mexican National Commission for Human Rights) collaborates with the Instituto Nacional de Migración to prevent and respond to human rights violations on Mexican territory.[4]

Having identified the strategies the Mexican government uses to respond to the increasing risk to Mexican unauthorized migrants, let us examine each strategy to determine its goals and to evaluate, where possible, the extent to which it has reduced the risks associated with unauthorized migration to the United States.

The Diplomatic Response

Of all the diplomatic issues between the United States and Mexico, unauthorized migration is one of the most difficult and sensitive.[5] For this reason, until recently, both Mexico and the United States have attempted to overlook it or to avoid dealing with it. "During the first 75 years of the twentieth century," David Heer tells us, "the Mexican government held an ambivalent attitude concerning Mexican emigration to the United States. During the last decade, it has come to believe that such migration represents a safety valve and has expressed its opposition to U.S. legislation intended to restrict its flow."[6]

The Secretaría de Relaciones Exteriores has shifted from disengagement to proactively seeking an official dialogue with the United States on unauthorized migration.[7] In an interview for this study, a former Mexican consul to the United States interpreted the situation differently: "U.S. authorities did not want to recognize this problem. Until the mid-1990s, it was practically impossible to sit at the table and talk about migration. . . . Mexico took the initiative to gain recognition of this problem between our two countries and suggested that we should sit down and talk."

In any case, with regular meetings between Mexican and U.S. officials since the 1990s, considerable progress had been made toward establishing an accord on migration until the September 11, 2001, terrorist attacks on the United States, which effectively stalled further progress and resulted in a tightening of U.S. borders.[8] Despite setbacks and a constantly changing dynamic, both countries continue to discuss unauthorized migration. Overall, this dialogue should be considered to be positive because, in the words of Peter Stalker, "much of the abuse directed at immigrants results from a failure of government leadership. Few politicians are prepared to acknowledge the contribution of immigrants.

Faced with a contradiction of real demand for workers on the one hand, and the political unpopularity of admitting more people on the other, they prefer to stand back and let the market decide, leaving immigrants to pay the price, if necessary with their lives."[9]

Efforts by the Mexican government to recognize, and react to, the risks of unauthorized migration—and to have these risks acknowledged by the U.S. government—should be considered a positive step even if, at this point in time, the benefits for migrants are limited.

The Protection of Mexican Expatriates

In addition to its role in international diplomacy, the Secretaría de Relaciones Exteriores is responsible for protecting, or at least for acting as advocate for, Mexican citizens in foreign territories. To that end, the ministry has a network of embassies and consulates throughout the world, including 45 across the United States. Its capacity to assist Mexican migrants is, however, limited both by a lack of resources on the ground and by a lack of local knowledge. "The Mexican consulates can do many things," a representative of the Instituto Nacional de Migración told me, "but they are not all powerful. After all, they are diplomats and can't be everywhere. They see how they [ranchers] capture and treat migrants. They have a lawyer and if there was violence . . . they make an energetic prosecution."

Increasingly, civil society, migration lawyers, and other migrant advocates are of enormous assistance in gathering the information necessary to act on infringements of migrant rights. In one such instance, a U.S. couple had shot a young migrant, leaving him paraplegic. Evidence and documentation provided by a human rights nongovernmental organization was vital to the Secretaría de Relaciones Exteriores undertaking the court case and winning compensation for the Mexican victim's family.

The ministry is also involved in measures to reduce risk to migrants: "On a national level," a representative explained, "Mexico undertakes preventive protection of migrants. We cannot impede the free movement of Mexicans on national territory but we do attempt to warn them of the risks of undocumented migration to the United States."

The "Guía del migrante mexicano" (Mexican Migrant Guide) is a booklet designed both to inform potential migrants about the risks of unauthorized migration to the United State and to "provide some practical advice [about U.S. society] which may be of use if [they] have made the difficult decision to search for work outside [their] country."[10]

As can be seen from this brief quotation, the tone of the guide is clearly sympathetic toward would-be migrants.

The Mexican government's apparent complacency, or acceptance of, the status quo of Mexican unauthorized migration was not well received in the United States. Instead of effectively discouraging unauthorized migration, the Mexican government was seen to be helping migrants reach the United States by unauthorized means.[11]

It would seem, however, that the guide has had little actual impact on the decision making of migrants. When *New York Times* journalists Charlie LeDuff and Emilio Flores presented it to recently arrived unauthorized migrants residing in the United States, the migrants were not aware of the guide and scoffed at its recommendations. Indeed, they believed that the Mexican government should replace it with more practical tips. Hire coyotes based on recommendations, one suggested, and never at border towns, where the risk of robbery, rape or being held for ransom is higher. Pick a local coyote so that family members will know if something bad happens. Find out the cost of your crossing in advance by asking those who have been before. Have a code word so that, once you are locked in a safe house waiting for the coyote's money to be delivered, you can let your family members know if something is wrong and they need to contact the coyote's relatives or the authorities. Never tell on the coyotes, another migrant offered, otherwise, you will end up dead or in jail. "Try never to cross the river," said a migrant named Travolia. "Never do it. If you have to, write your name in your underpants in case you drown. Then they can find your family and you can be buried by a priest."[12]

These comments demonstrate that the migrants have created a hierarchy that helps them reduce risk. Thus, even though the guide emphasizes that migrants should avoid human traffickers and crossings in remote regions, the migrants themselves recognize that successful crossings are more likely to occur using a human trafficker in less-monitored, remote areas. Those interviewed suggested that, to be truly helpful, the guide should offer tips on how to make the migration journey actually safer, such as how to use family networks to secure an experienced human trafficker.[13]

Some media commentators claim that the risk awareness campaigns by the Secretaría de Relaciones Exteriores are a token effort, a charade designed to impress certain sectors of Mexican and Mexican American society for political purposes.[14] According to the Secretaría de Relaciones

Exteriores representative, however, the ministry's efforts are genuine, although somewhat futile. So as long as migration to the United States is a viable means for Mexicans to support their families, the Mexican government will talk about the risks of unauthorized migration rather than moving to reduce it, much less stop it. With limited input into U.S. policies, all the ministry can do is "inform potential migrants about the laws of the United States and important differences in culture . . . we have to give them the opportunity to benefit from this chance." The appropriateness of the risk reduction programs of the Secretaría de Relaciones Exteriores should be considered, however, because the Mexican government continues to pursue them despite binational political criticism and their seemingly limited benefit to migrants.

The Programa Nacional de Protección a Migrantes

The Migrant Protection Program comprises two facets. The first is awareness campaigns to discourage unauthorized migration, through signage both in communities with large numbers of outbound migrants and at the border. The second is rescue efforts through intervention by Grupo Beta when migrants are at risk from physical and psychological threats at the border on Mexican territory.

Risk Awareness through Signage. The Instituto Nacional de Migración has strategically located risk awareness posters in central and southern Mexico. "Look after your life!" they warn. "The search for a dream could be your worst nightmare. The paths that migrants take to cross the border could take them to their death." In contrast, the signs at the border encourage the migrants to be cognizant of specific risks as they undertake their crossing because, practically speaking, once migrants have traveled to the border, they are unlikely to be dissuaded from crossing.

The effectiveness of these poster and signage campaigns is unknown: as of this writing, there have been no formal studies to investigate how these strategies actually influence migrant decision making. It is yet to be determined whether migrants gathered at strategic locations (see fig. 3.1) have open minds and can be influenced by signage, or whether they have already made up their minds and have no room for second thoughts.

There are indications from the field, most notably defacement, that the signs and warnings are disregarded. Thus, on the Mexican side of the Tijuana–San Ysidro border wall, one of the Programa nacional de

Figure 3.1 Prospective migrants gather to cross into the United States at Playa Tijuana.

protección a migrantes signs has been defaced (see fig. 3.2). On the sign's desert scene, the word "KIDS" has been sprayed using Mexico's national colors of red and green. The word itself may imply that the sign is childish, depicting risks of the desert not present in Tijuana. English may have been used to refute the government's assumption that only illiterate *campesinos* (peasants) are attempting to cross the border. In any case, this graffito plainly seems to convey some level of contempt for this government program.

Migrant Rescue and Grupo Beta. In contrast to passive signage, a much more hands-on approach to migrant protection is the rescue of migrants at risk of physical or psychological injury as a result of climatic conditions or human rights violations.[15] The human face of this Mexican government response is Grupo Beta, an elite rescue group founded in 1991 to "protect migrants from attacks or abuse by traffickers or criminals along Mexico's border regions, regardless of their nationality or migration status on Mexican territory" and coordinated by the Instituto Nacional de

Figure 3.2 "KIDS" graffitied onto a Mexican government migration warning sign.

Migración.[16] The Comisión Nacional de Derechos Humanos then assists Grupo Beta with follow-up on violations by documenting and, where possible, prosecuting human rights abuses reported by Beta.[17]

In 2003, Grupo Beta rescued 2,800 migrants in Mexico from adverse climatic conditions.[18] In addition to their reconnaissance trips, Grupo Beta has established a network of desert shelters on the Mexican side of the border with beacons designed to attract the attention of distressed migrants in need of shade, potable water, and rescue. These structures are required in Mexico because unauthorized migrants, in crossing long distances over inhospitable terrain to avoid detection and reach less secure parts of the border, may become distressed and suffer from exposure to the elements before they even reach the United States.

Although the effect of the Programa nacional de protección a migrantes poster campaign is unknown, it does appear that the efforts of Grupo Beta have reduced the incidence of violent attacks against potential unauthorized migrants on Mexican territory. An indirect benefit of Grupo Beta's activities has been a better relationship on the ground between Mexican authorities and the U.S. Border Patrol, with the two groups often training together and working to curtail the activities of smugglers, including human trafficking networks. Indeed, this symbolic and practical alliance may have helped further diplomatic negotiations between the two countries on migration.[19]

The Programa Paisano

Although aimed at protecting Mexican unauthorized migrants at the border, Programa Paisano is focused on those returning to Mexico from the United States. It is important to include this program, despite this study's focus on risks to outbound migrants, because the Mexican government considers it to be an integral part of their "migrant protection" strategies. As a representative of the Instituto Nacional de Migración interviewed for this study explained:

> The Paisano Program is responsible for protecting Mexican migrants returning to Mexico. It aims to protect them from extortion, so that no one robs or abuses them. When a Mexican comes from the United States they come with dollars, with presents for the family and, without fail, there is always someone who wants to extort them. . . . We are responsible for those who enter [Mexico] . . . we see them returning at airports, ports and through customs, we are trying to see that they get just treatment.

Each year, the institute is responsible for updating a guide that provides contact details for a myriad of Mexican government departments and that advises migrants on how to avoid physically, psychologically, or economically threatening situations on the return journey to their communities. "We recognize that you are returning after a long absence," the 2003 guide begins, "so we have prepared the COUNTRYMAN'S GUIDE 2003 to provide you with information so you will return safely."[20]

It informs returning migrants about the different documents they will need to resettle in Mexico as well as how to transport their goods from the United States so they can avoid any problems with federal, state, and municipal authorities. Indeed, it gives the impression that government institutions are much more of a threat than any roadside bandits, and even tells returning migrants exactly how to lodge official complaints should they be harassed, threatened, or robbed by any government employee. This was a reality in the past, an institute representative told me, with "many migrants saying that upon arrival [to Mexico] they were mistreated; migration officials, government officials, and the state police, municipal police, federal police and the tax authorities took things. This is mistreatment, and we want to provide them with a better service from the time they arrive until they have reached all parts [of Mexico]."

Scattered throughout the guide are commonsense recommendations such as "Countrymen, do not risk traveling with a large amount of cash."[21] Since the inception of Programa Paisano, the risks for unauthorized migrants returning to Mexico appear to have diminished in one significant respect. "The current administration did a survey [in 2004]," an institute representative explained, "and 97 percent of returning migrants said they didn't experience extortion. And that is an important advance. Ten years ago or even four years ago, 97 percent would have said they had been extorted." Whether this occurred as a result of the program's efforts is uncertain, but the advance seems unmistakable.

The well-coordinated efforts of the Mexican government in Programa Paisano do, however, bring into question the disparity between programs designed to protect outward-bound, poor, and vulnerable Mexican migrants, and those designed to protect more affluent migrants returning home. To a certain extent, migrants are encouraged by Mexican society to leave, despite the risks—they are the "heroes"—and are then welcomed back and protected, to a degree, when they return.

The Southern Plan

Like Programa Paisano, the Southern Plan (Plan Sur) does not directly address risks experienced by Mexican migrants bound for the United States. As part of a Mexican strategy to placate the United States in order to negotiate better conditions for Mexican migrants, however, it plays an important role in the Mexican government's efforts to reduce the risks facing Mexican migrants.

Implemented in 2001, the Southern Plan was designed to tighten security at Mexico's southern border with Guatemala by increasing both the number of migration checkpoints and the presence of police and military. "In exchange for better conditions for Mexicans working in the U.S.," Mexican government spokesman Santiago Creel explained in April 2001, "our government is prepared to increase measures aiming to arrest foreigners crossing the country heading for the U.S."[22] Although its purpose was clearly positive, however, the Southern Plan has had a troublesome unintended consequence. Mexico's management of its border with Guatemala has come more and more to resemble the United States' management of its border with Mexico, creating many of the same problems for Guatemala that Mexico itself has experienced.

On a visit to the southern Mexican border, *Time* magazine journalist Peter Katel found that, despite the increasing difficulties and risks for migrants, unauthorized migration into Mexico was continuing: "Central Americans are dodging the crackdown, using remote routes to cross the border into Mexico. Two thousand miles to the north, Mexican immigrants to the U.S. are doing precisely the same thing."[23] In effect, U.S. border policies at the U.S.–Mexico border have set the tone for border management practices not only in southern Mexico but also down into Central America, with Central American migrants responding in much the same way that Mexican migrants have. More recently, however, the Mexican government has endeavored to replace the Southern Plan's border policy with a more humane one, which would set an example for the United States.[24]

Implications of the Government's Responses

Although the diplomatic dialogue between Mexico and the United States may hold potential for the future, Mexico's implementation of the Southern Plan is an extreme compromise early in negotiations, and indicates the power imbalance in the U.S.–Mexico relationship. In any case, this long-term diplomatic approach is of little immediate benefit to migrants facing the risks of unauthorized migration today.

The Mexican government's programs to defend migrants' human rights and to rescue migrants at risk using Grupo Beta are largely Band-Aid solutions whose contribution to risk reduction is suspect. The sole exception may be Programa Paisano, which appears to have significantly reduced economic threats to returning migrants. If so, this may be because the Mexican government can exert greater control over Mexican territory or because it sees greater political advantage in protecting better-off migrants on their return home than poor migrants on their way to the United States.

Overall, the actions of the Mexican government may have helped quell public discontent in Mexico and among Mexican Americans over the increasing number of border deaths and the government's lack of a clear stance on border issues. Although some on both sides of the border perceived that the Mexican government was reducing the risk of unauthorized migration through its various strategies, as of 2006, the actual situation on the ground had not improved and, if anything, had worsened.

It would seem that the Mexican government is more concerned about the opinion and potential reaction of the United States than about the protection of its citizens, as illustrated by its implementation of the Southern Plan. What, then, is the true purpose of the government's migrant protection programs? Are they designed to help migrants or to help the Mexican government avoid serious criticism by the Mexican public while posing no threat to the United States? With that question in mind, let us see how Mexico's civil society interprets the activities of its government and how it responds to current migration policies on both sides of the border.

Mexican Civil Society: Coalitions and Collaborative Responses

According to the Centre for Civil Society at the London School of Economics and Political Science, *civil society* "refers to the arena of uncoerced collective action around shared interests, purposes and values. . . . Civil society commonly embraces a diversity of spaces, actors and institutional forms, varying in their degree of formality, autonomy and power. Civil societies are often populated by organizations such as registered charities, developmental non-government organizations, community groups, women's organizations, faith-based organizations, professional organizations, trade unions, self-help groups, social movements, business associations, coalitions and advocacy groups."[25]

Although there are many U.S. civil society groups to lobby against unauthorized migration, such as the Minutemen, this study will focus on Mexican civil society responses to the increasing risks of Mexican unauthorized migration. Among these groups are human rights organizations, Christian faith groups, and migrant advocacy groups. In pursuing their common goals, these groups have developed close interrelationships as they raise awareness of the risks associated with unauthorized migration, lobby against policies that increase risk, provide human rights documentation and education, or coordinate migrant rescue programs.

Migrant Risk Awareness: Into Sight, into Mind, into Action

Mexican civil society organizations have used all the means at their disposal to raise awareness of the risks of unauthorized migration and to lobby for change, predominantly in U.S. border management policies. As Benjamin Prado of the Raza Rights Coalition explained during an interview:

> It's about public awareness. That is the fundamental tool that we have . . . to bring public awareness to the realities of these policies. . . . If you go to San Ysidro, Tijuana, right now, you see what could be considered "order," people coming in and out, trade happening in an orderly way, but that's [just] an appearance that hides the fact that people in the mountains and deserts are dying. . . . Our organization feels it's important to unmask the reality, the objective reality of this is that too many people are dying. Too many people are dying trying to survive. . . . It's our obligation as Mexicans, as Latin Americans, as human beings, to bring this to the attention of the entire population. We must be concerned if we are truly a civil society, a truly democratic society. If we are truly about justice, then we must expose the injustices that happen systematically.

Awareness of an issue is limited so long as the general public is not exposed to it. Indeed, one of the goals of Operation Gatekeeper was to prevent encounters between urban populations and unauthorized migrants, to create an appearance of "order" at the border.[26] Mexican civil society groups at the border thus strive to create awareness of unauthorized migration, particularly the risks. Because their resources are limited, however, they must seek out inexpensive but effective ways to get their message across. Increasingly, the Internet is a mechanism by which these organizations can directly communicate with the public, for example, the California Rural Legal Assistance Foundation's Web site (http://www.stopgatekeeper.org). To get people interested in searching for information about organizations associated with unauthorized migration, these civil society groups often use the radio, television, and print media for free publicity.

In Tijuana, Victor Clark Alfaro, director of the Centro Binacional de Derechos Humanos (Binational Center for Human Rights), has come to understand that the print media are an important tool for the diffusion of information on human rights abuses. At the same time, his center and the media have a mutually beneficial relationship: "The press is always looking for our opinion . . . after 20 years, I have observed that we have become a vital source of information for the press on three issues: migration, violence at the border, and drug trafficking."

One of the most effective strategies that Mexican civil society groups have used to create awareness and attract media attention is to hold a public event. Different groups have taken the initiative for different events at different times of the year, thus providing a calendar of outdoor activities that has attracted attention and, through media coverage, reached homes throughout the United States and Latin America.

One event, for example, was the celebration of a Mass on October 3, 2004, on both sides of the border at Playa Tijuana / Border Field State Park. Organized by the Casa del Migrante en Tijuana (Tijuana Migrant Hostel), the Mass was celebrated by Hostel Director Father Luis Kendzierski and by Father Henry Rodriguez of Saint Jude's, San Diego.

In full view of a crowd that had gathered at the border wall and the news media, including the Telemundo news camera broadcasting by cable to all of Latin America (see fig. 3.3), the Catholic priests took the opportunity to espouse their cause and to lobby for change. "Lord," Father Henry prayed, "bless the men, the women, the young people who have died seeking a better way of life crossing our borders, and we ask forgiveness and healing for a lack of response to the needs of those who are seeking a better way of life—seeking justice and seeking peace." He concluded the Mass by saying, "Thank you for joining us today for our liturgy. Jesús is telling us that if we have just enough faith to believe we can make a change—to be a voice for people who have no voice . . . by our gathering here at this wall this morning it shows that, as men and women of faith, we want to be those instruments of change."

Father Henry's message is clear. Mexican (and other) unauthorized migrants who die trying to cross into the United States where they aim to work hard to improve their lives are society's poor, vulnerable, and "voiceless" people. The situation must change, and for that to happen, people must support his cause and be seen at the different border events.

The Casa del Migrante en Tijuana has been actively participating with other civil society organizations in organizing outdoor events, such as this Mass, since the year 2000. The hostel's core work, however, is providing accommodation, food, and human rights education to Mexican

Figure 3.3 The cable network Telemundo broadcasts the Mass commemorating the deaths of unauthorized migrants at Playa Tijuana / Borderfield State Park.

unauthorized migrants. Its hope is that, thanks in part to their awareness programs, more migrant-friendly border policies will be adopted, and the need for their other services will diminish over time.

Linda Arreola is assistant director of the Catholic Diocese of San Diego's Office for Social Ministry. "We work with different coalitions," Linda told me, "like the Interfaith Coalition for Immigrant Rights and the American Friends Service Committee to . . . do vigils, so we have the 'Posada without Borders,' that's along the border during Holy Week. There are the visits to the Hope Cemetery where about 200 unidentified migrants are buried. We have the Migrant 'Way of the Cross,' one year it's in Tijuana and the other it's in San Diego. So there are religious . . . events, advocacy efforts. We do vigils through to advocacy just to educate the public."

New York Times journalist James Sterngold reported on one such event: "One group, the California Rural Legal Assistance Foundation, held a march today at the Southern California cemetery where some of the hundreds of immigrants who die every year after illegally entering into the United States are buried in unmarked graves."[27] Appearing, as it did, in a prestigious and well-syndicated publication, Sterngold's article would have had exposure to a wide audience promoting national, and even international, awareness of the issue. In the local media, such civil society events are also frequently reported. In 2004, for example, Jeff McDonald of the *San Diego Union-Tribune* wrote that the "10-year anniversary of Operation Gatekeeper was observed in different ways at different places yesterday. But at both venues, those who died were prayed for and remembered, as activists and others worked to find a way to end the dying. . . . South of the U.S.–Mexico border on Friday, a small group of demonstrators marked the anniversary by walking eight miles from the beaches of Tijuana to the airport. They hung an empty casket on the border fence to symbolize those who have died trying to find work in the United States."[28]

Just as civil society groups strategically use the print media to promote their message, so, too, does the antimigration lobby. "The Minuteman Civil Defense Corps volunteers," reported Chris Moran, also of the *San Diego Union-Tribune*, "gathered by a brown metal post-and-rail border fence south of Jacumba to watch for illegal border crossers and report them to the [United States] Border Patrol. The group invited the media so it could transmit its message to Washington: that the federal government has failed in its responsibilities to secure America's borders."[29]

Nevertheless, with regular media coverage of the risks and consequences of unauthorized migration, and with events to stimulate public awareness, the civil society organizations can rally public support and, with this support, begin to lobby the government to create change. Because public support is not always enough, however, Mexican civil society groups have also turned to documenting violations of universal human rights as a tool for political change.

Human Rights as a Legal and Political Tool

Human rights are a universally recognized code of conduct for the ethical and appropriate treatment of all human beings. They can be used to protect unauthorized migrants by providing both a legal mechanism for appropriate treatment and a deterrent to violations through prosecution; through documentation of systemic infringements, human rights also serve as a tool to press for political change.

By constructing walls and increasing levels of security in urban areas, U.S. border management strategies such as Operation Gatekeeper were designed to shift migration into remote areas with difficult terrain. This, it was hoped, would discourage migrants and much reduce, if not stop, unauthorized crossings. Unfortunately, the actual outcome has been that Mexican migrants continue to migrate, and in growing numbers, but experience greater risks. Indeed, according to Americas Watch, "changes in U.S. law and policy have led to a climate along the border that is even more likely to contribute to serious abuses of human rights."[30] Migrants have increasingly come to rely on human traffickers, a varied but often dangerous group, and because crossings now take place in remote areas, migrants are at greater risk not only from the harsh environment but also from criminal attacks.[31] As the number of human rights abuses rises, so has the number of civil organizations dedicated to human rights protection at the border.

In Tijuana, the Centro Binacional de Derechos Humanos (Binational Center for Human Rights) is dedicated to recording human rights abuses, taking statements from victims, and working to achieve positive legal outcomes. It also has programs dedicated to educating vulnerable groups about their human rights so that they can avoid or at least officially complain about abuses. Recently, the center gathered with other nongovernmental human rights organizations to start a new program with the U.S. Border Patrol. "Nine months ago," Clark Alfaro told me in August 2004, "we changed our approach with the Border Patrol. Historically, Border Patrol has been an enemy of human rights defenders; we saw how they would pick on the migrants. We decided to stop fighting with Border Patrol but, instead, sit down and meet on a monthly basis. We are trying to get them to put a human rights awareness program into Border Patrol officer training."

The center works closely with the American Friends Service Committee in San Diego to raise human rights awareness in the border region. According to Christian Ramirez, U.S.–Mexico Border Program director, the American Friends Service Committee is focused on two principal themes: "promoting awareness of human rights, especially among communities that are subject to human rights violations, and . . . the documentation of human rights violations along the border."

"Victims can come to our office and lodge a complaint," Ramirez explained. "We collect statistics and publish these complaints. . . . Through documentation, we try to influence the policies of U.S. legislators, in particular border policies. We use the documents as a source of evidence demonstrating human rights violations. We lobby, we speak with congressmen, sometimes it is a waste of time, but at least our goal is to convince the public and civil society that these human rights violations exist and there must be a change."

At the same time, the information of the Centro Binacional de Derechos Humanos and the American Friends Service Committee is increasingly used by Mexican government entities, such as the Secretaría de Relaciones Exteriores, to legally defend Mexican nationals whose human rights have been violated. This is a symbiotic relationship: the human rights organizations have the capacity to record and document human rights violations, as they occur, across the United States, whereas the Mexican government has the capacity, once armed with these documentary records, to prosecute human rights cases.

Migrant Rescue: Dealing with the Reality of Today's Border Policies

In contrast to creating greater public awareness or documenting human rights violations to lobby government, humanitarian groups have formed along the length of the border to address a more immediate problem: unauthorized migrants at risk of death or serious injury in desert or mountainous regions.[32] One of the largest and best-known groups is the Border Angels, whose more than 800 volunteers have set up over 400 water stations in desert areas of California and Arizona and in Baja California.[33] As Border Angels Coordinator Enrique Morones told me: "In the summer, we do not have to worry about the mountains that much, and in the winter we don't have to worry about the desert that much. We concentrate our efforts in these particular areas because the people come when the jobs are there. Why don't they just wait until the winter? Well, there are more jobs now, that's why they're crossing in the summer, and in the winter lots of times they're heading home, although now [with changing border policies] they're heading home less [often]."

Although groups like the Border Angels receive some level of support from the U.S. Border Patrol, the patrol is always suspicious, believing they harbor unauthorized migrants rather than merely rescue them from precarious situations.[34] Enrique Morones counters: "A point that comes up regularly is that we are encouraging people. No one comes here for the water. All I said to them was the time to cross is not the daytime. We don't give them instructions or anything but I know it's a lot safer to cross at night because of the heat factor." Although only a humanitarian response and not a tool for change, rescue will be required as long as U.S. border policies that exacerbate risk remain in place. Nevertheless, Morones says, he will continue the work because

> there's a parable that made an impact on me. There's a father and a son walking by the beach, and, as they're walking along, his son picks up starfish and throws them back into the ocean. It's really hot and all the starfish are dying. The father says to the son, "What are you doing?" "I'm saving these starfish." "Whatever you do, you're not making a difference because there's thousands." And the little boy[, who] had a starfish in his hand[,] says, "It will make a difference to this one," and throws it into the ocean.

Morones is satisfied if he has managed to save one life with his hundreds of water stations.

Implications of Civil Society Responses

Most civil society organizations dedicated to issues at the U.S.–Mexico border focus on raising awareness of the risks of unauthorized migration. That said, their programs are mostly targeted at the general public (particularly in the United States). They do this to press politicians to change border and migration policies and thus reduce the risks experienced by unauthorized migrants. The materials they direct at migrants are designed for those who have already taken up residence in the United States, to help this vulnerable group avoid human rights abuses and to support them when things go wrong. Their documentation of human rights abuses has served both to assess the risks of unauthorized migration and to lobby for policy change. There are some efforts to rescue migrants, or at least to prevent death from dehydration by providing water supplies in strategic locations, but the extent to which these efforts actually save lives is unknown. The success of civil society's efforts to raise awareness of the risks of unauthorized migration in the voting population might best be measured by their frequent appearance in the print media, on both sides of the border.

Mexican Print Media: A Constructed Dialogue of Risk and Migration

To understand how the risks of unauthorized migration are represented in the Mexican print media, I chose to examine Tijuana's and Ensenada's newspapers, whose journalists are particularly aware of border issues. Between March 2003 and October 2004, I collected articles from Tijuana's daily *El Mexicano*, from Sunday editions of its *Frontera*, and from pertinent editions of Ensenada's *El Vigia*. A preliminary analysis revealed three types of migrant risk-related articles: migrant death statistics with limited discussion of the causes of death, overviews of the risks to unauthorized migrants, and daily news reports of specific incidents involving migrants.

Following the recommendations of anthropologist Mary Douglas, I read the articles to determine how journalists assigned responsibility and blame.[35] I then categorized the journalists' rationales and tabulated these (see table 3.1).

According to the articles, migrants were exposed to a wide variety of risks: abduction and extortion, assault, or coercion into the sex trade, exposure to a criminal environment, robbery, drugging, reckless driving, concealment in confined spaces, exposure to the elements, accidental shooting, abandonment, detention, family fragmentation, and criminalization. The consequences were physical injury, psychological trauma, or death. Migrants suffered physical injury or death from hyperthermia, dehydration, exhaustion, asphyxiation, gunshot, automobile accidents, drugs, physical, sexual, or verbal violence, or sexually transmitted disease. They suffered psychological trauma when they lost contact with their children, lost their money or freedom, or when the safety of their families was threatened.

Risk Scenario 1: The Naive Migrant

In articles and editorials on migration, Mexican journalists clearly held human traffickers accountable for most of the suffering endured by unauthorized Mexican migrants. In this scenario, journalists tended to exonerate migrants of personal responsibility for the consequences of risks they took by labeling the migrants "naive": "The migrant doesn't know the area and trusts whoever offers to help him to reach the 'American Dream.'"[36]

Journalists reported that, by their unquestioning trust in human traffickers, naive migrants increased their risk because the traffickers could be associated with organized crime, feel no sense of duty toward the migrants, or downplay the dangers of the migration journey. If the human trafficker was associated with organized crime, the migrant might

Table 3.1 Mexican Print Media Representations of Risk to Unauthorized Migrants Crossing U.S.–Mexico Border

	Risk Scenario 1: Naive Migrant	
(A) Human trafficker is associated with organized crime	(A1) Abduction and extortion	Psychological trauma from loss of freedom
		Death, physical injury, or psychological trauma from physical, sexual, or verbal violence
		Psychological trauma from threats to safety of family
		Psychological trauma from financial loss
	(A2) Abduction and coercion into sex trade	Psychological trauma from loss of freedom
		Death, physical injury, or psychological trauma from physical, sexual, or verbal violence
		Psychological trauma from threats to safety of family
		Death, physical injury, or psychological trauma from sexually transmitted disease
	(A3) Exposure to criminal environment	Death, physical injury, or psychological trauma from physical, sexual, or verbal violence
	(A4) Robbery	Psychological trauma from financial loss
		Death, physical injury, or psychological trauma from physical, sexual, or verbal violence
(B) Human trafficker feels no sense of duty	(B1) Reckless driving	Death, physical injury, or psychological trauma from traffic accidents

	(B2) Concealment in confined space	Death, physical injury, or psychological trauma from asphyxiation
	(B3) Drugging	Death, physical injury, or psychological trauma from detrimental effect of drugs
	(B4) Abandonment	Death, physical injury, or psychological trauma from hyperthermia, dehydration, or exhaustion
(C) Human trafficker downplays risks of migration journey	(C1) Family fragmentation	Psychological trauma from family losing contact with children
	(C2) Exposure to elements	Death, physical injury, or psychological trauma from hyper- or hypothermia, dehydration, or exhaustion.
Risk Scenario 2: Migrant Encounters with People near Border		
(A) Migrant encounter with people having racist or antimigrant attitudes	(A1) Abduction and assault	Psychological trauma from loss of freedom
		Death, physical injury, or psychological trauma from physical, sexual, or verbal violence
(B) Migrant encounter with bandits	(B1) Abduction and extortion	Psychological trauma from loss of freedom
		Death, physical injury, or psychological trauma from physical, sexual, or verbal violence
		Psychological trauma from threats to safety of family
		Psychological trauma from financial loss

(Continued)

Table 3.1 (*Continued*)

	(B2) Robbery	Death, physical injury, or psychological trauma from physical, sexual, or verbal violence
		Psychological trauma from financial loss
(C) Migrant encounter with hunters	(C1) Accidental shooting	Death, physical injury, or psychological trauma from being shot
(D) Migrant encounter with law enforcement officers having racist, antiterrorist, or antimigrant attitudes	(D1) Assault	Death, physical injury, or psychological trauma from physical, sexual, or verbal violence
	(D2) Detention and criminalization	Psychological trauma from loss of freedom

be subject to abduction and extortion, abducted and coerced into the sex trade, exposed to a criminal environment or robbed. For example, Barry Joseph Vanbrocklin and Hector Jesús Soria abducted three unauthorized migrants and then attempted to extort $1,500 from each migrant's family.[37] A Mexican woman contacted police in a desperate effort to see her baby, who had been taken as a guarantee by traffickers. Originally, the traffickers had agreed on $400 to cross the woman's mother but now were demanding an extra $700 in return for her child.[38] Mexican girls abducted to become sex slaves were forced to cross the desert in high heels and tight dresses into the United States, where they would be subjected to constant sexual assault, while their families believed they were working as maids or nannies.[39] Some migrants unwittingly became involved in drug smuggling and were subjected to outbreaks of violence between different gangs.[40] One migrant was robbed in a coordinated effort between human traffickers and Tijuana's municipal police.[41] As is clear from just this sample of articles, Mexican journalists portrayed unauthorized migrants as victims subject to the ruthlessness of traffickers often connected with organized crime networks.

Human traffickers who felt no sense of duty toward their migrants subjected them to reckless driving, concealment in confined spaces, drugging, or abandonment in the desert. Thus a truck with 17 migrants hidden in the back was stopped for excessive speeding; its driver had already had his license suspended for reckless driving.[42] Four migrants died and 18 were injured when another trafficker's van overturned.[43] Reporting on the same incident, Samuel Murillo noted that the van had sped up when pursued by a U.S. Border Patrol vehicle.[44] In some cases, journalists exonerated traffickers, at least in part, finding their behavior to some extent justified: "The traffickers sped up when they realized they were being followed by the American authorities and that's when [the U.S. Border Patrol] shot at one of the tires of the panel wagon and it fell into a gully."[45]

On the other hand, the print media had little sympathy for human traffickers who subjected migrants to death by asphyxiation. On May 14, 2003, there was a report that 19 migrants had asphyxiated in the back of a refrigeration truck.[46] The tragic nature of this incident attracted considerable media attention and inspired graphic reporting on both sides of the border. Thus Daryl Strickland and Scott Gold of the *Los Angeles Times* reported that "the victims apparently tried to get fresh air by scraping away insulation that clogged small holes in the trailer's back door."[47]

On May 16, 2003, 28 migrants were discovered by the U.S. Border Patrol trapped in a railroad boxcar; that same day, 10 migrants were discovered, thirsty and hungry from days without food or water, hidden in a vehicle in Texas. The implication from the print media was that concealment was becoming an increasingly popular means of smuggling migrants, but this generalization failed to consider that the spate of "discoveries" in Texas might have been due to a crackdown by U.S. Border Patrol rather than any change in trafficking patterns.[48]

Mexican journalists were particularly critical of human traffickers who ignored their duty to take care of migrant children. Reporting in February 2004 that U.S. officials in Arizona had discovered two cases of migrant children drugged into a state of unconsciousness, Virginia Viana and her colleagues strongly emphasized the immorality of this mistreatment of children.[49]

More commonly reported was the deliberate abandonment of migrants in desert areas. Thus, in June 2003, 10 men and 8 women were abandoned in a desert valley near Mexicali, although fortunately an anonymous phone call to Mexican authorities facilitated their rescue.[50] Then there were cases where individual migrants would become exhausted and were left behind by their group. Five such cases were reported in Arizona in the week ending May 29, 2003.[51] The journalists implied that the lack of a sense of duty toward migrants was primarily associated with novices, who had just entered the lucrative business of human trafficking.[52]

When human traffickers downplayed the potential dangers of migration, perhaps to boost the spirits of migrants but often merely to secure a commission, migrants were more likely to experience family fragmentation or exposure to the elements. In this first risk scenario, naive migrant parents believed it was safer to have a stranger cross their children via official ports of entry than to have the children travel with them through the desert, but this was not always the case.[53] Parents failed to have a contingency plan with the trafficker should either parents or children be detained by the U.S. Border Patrol. In 2003, this resulted in 4,426 children (70 percent of all children detained) being returned to Mexico unaccompanied.[54] Almost all of these children were collected by Mexican child protection services, thus reducing the possibility of physical or sexual abuse, but they were still subjected to the psychological trauma of being separated from their families, sometimes for a protracted time.

In the case of Karen Tepaz Tepaz, a six-year-old detained on September 7, 2004, a group of migrants who claimed to be her relatives later turned out to be merely traffickers. Unable to provide accurate details about her family, Karen remained a government ward until her family could find her.[55] In most cases, the parents would remain in the United States and send another relative on the Mexican side to arrange another attempt to cross the child.[56] In August 2004, a mother detained by the U.S. Border Patrol and unable to reach her child, who had been successfully crossed, suffered a nervous breakdown.[57]

When traffickers downplayed the dangers of the migration journey, migrants often failed to carry sufficient supplies or to adequately "train" for the journey. Thus, reported Mercedes Ortiz, deserts, mountains, and rivers could pose serious dangers to migrants unprepared for them.[58] *El Mexicano* elaborated by explaining that the heat of the desert could kill in summer, whereas the cold of the mountains and rivers could kill in winter.[59] In one article, Andy Adams, spokesman for the U.S. Border Patrol, pinpointed human traffickers as a principal source of risk: "Many [migrants] are tricked by the coyotes, who assure them that they only have to walk a few hours through the desert."[60]

Because it is a struggle to climb over sand hills, migrants with poor physical fitness were easily subject to exhaustion in the desert. Even strong swimmers were at risk of drowning in the rivers and canals. In California's Imperial Canal, for example, there are surface currents of 10 miles (16 kilometers) an hour and undercurrents of 20 miles (32 kilometers) an hour.[61] On February 25, 2004, the U.S. Border Patrol rescued 46 Mexican migrants from the mountains near Nogales, Arizona, some suffering from hypothermia and on the brink of death.[62] Mexico's Grupo Beta rescued 35 migrants on August 1, 2004; the migrants had been misinformed about the distances they would have to travel across the desert and did not have enough water for the trip.[63]

In summary, the Mexican print media have established a strong connection between the selection of a human trafficker and exposure to risk. Although, on the one hand, they have identified human trafficking as a source of risk, on the other, they have also presented it as a necessary evil to reduce risk. Mexican journalists have tended to assign blame to subgroups within human trafficking networks, such as novice or get-rich-quick traffickers. This implies that there are safe traffickers, hence the emphasis on finding those with a strong sense of duty toward their migrants. The emphasis thus has been on selecting a "safe" human trafficker rather than avoiding all risk by not migrating. Migrating is understood to be inevitable.

The journalists were constantly reinforcing the stereotype of the "naive migrant," a trusting Mexican who can be easily fooled and is extremely vulnerable to risk at the border, a construct that served to convey their sympathy for unauthorized migrants without forcing them to take a stand on the morality or legality of unauthorized migration. This approach allowed the media to raise awareness of the risks of unauthorized migration in Mexican society without being controversial. They presented child migrants as the most innocent of all victims, being exposed to risk because of a lack of risk assessment by their "naive migrant" parents. All articles referring to children suggested that only "selfish" parents would subject their children to the risks of unauthorized migration. Taken together, the articles implied that an effective migrant risk reduction strategy would be to select human traffickers who are not associated with organized crime, who feel a sense of duty toward the migrants, and who help them prepare for the migration journey, rather than underplay its dangers.

Risk Scenario 2: Migrant Encounters with People near the Border

In articles where human traffickers were not identified as the source of risk, journalists attributed the threat to encounters with dangerous people from either side of the border. Migrants could be at risk of serious physical or psychological harm if the person they encountered held racist or antimigrant attitudes, was a bandit, or was a hunter who mistook them for wildlife. If the migrants encountered law enforcement officers, such as the U.S. Border Patrol, they might be subject to assault, detention, and criminalization.

Quoting defenders of human rights, some articles identified racist groups as a particularly grave physical and psychological threat to migrants. For example, American Border Patrol, a private membership vigilante organization (not to be confused with the U.S. government's Border Patrol), undertakes military-style surveillance on private land at the border and makes unsupervised citizen arrests neither endorsed nor opposed by the U.S. government. Human rights defenders claim that, in recent years, there have been at least nine clear-cut cases of race-incited murder of Mexican migrants.[64]

Another threat to migrants were the *bajaderos* (badlanders), a new type of border criminal who abducted migrants from their human traffickers upon their arrival in the United States. Some articles suggested that this type of criminality has emerged because of increasing security measures at the border. There is less risk involved for those who abduct migrants once they are in the United States because they can receive the payment from the family without incurring any of the risks associated with the unauthorized border crossing. In November 2003, four migrants died when they were caught up in a shootout between smuggling gangs.[65] Migrants who survive extortion or robbery can remain in the United States to recover economically. Should they be returned to Mexico, however, whether by the U.S. Border Patrol or the traffickers (if they default on payment), they can remain trapped at the border, unable either to return home or cross into the United States.[66]

Journalists also presented "no-fault" incidents when migrants encountered farmworkers who accidentally shot them while out hunting wildlife. On July 3, 2003, Juan García Mendoza shot Jesús Barrera Vasquez in rural Texas after mistaking him for a wild boar.[67] On February 6, 2004, Jaime González shot Mexican migrant Celestino Lopez Espino when he was out hunting porcupines.[68]

When a migrant encountered a law enforcement officer, it was most likely to be a U.S. Border Patrol officer, whose duty it was to protect the United States' borders. Although not all law enforcement officers were considered a threat, individuals holding deep-seated racist, antiterrorist, or antimigrant attitudes were seen to pose a serious threat to Mexican migrants. Claudia Smith, a human rights activist, noted that, in 2003, three migrants had been killed by U.S. Border Patrol agents. All had been shot; one migrant multiple times. The evidence that these shootings were in self-defense was not conclusive, and Smith pointed out that they represented only the reported crimes.[69] Since September 11, 2001, U.S. law enforcement officers have been encouraged to consider all unauthorized migrants as potential terrorists.[70] This gives rise to aggressive, potentially violent interactions between officers and migrants.

Detention and criminalization can themselves be both physically and psychologically damaging. According to Alejandro Gutiérrez, the trauma of contact with law enforcement may be even greater for children than adults: "Many times, a child's first contact with Border Patrol is when they are being chased by them, with a policeman 1.90 meters [6 feet, 3 inches] tall, who speaks a foreign language and is an expert at frightening people. The children go through interviews, paperwork, fingerprinting, and so they must be very frightened."[71]

In November 2003, a group of 30 frightened migrants was detained after being chased through the desert by the U.S. Border Patrol for three hours.[72] Journalists suggested that, although U.S. border management strategies were often tokenistic and ineffective in stopping unauthorized migration, for Mexicans, encounters with U.S. migration officials could lead to serious repercussions such as motor vehicle accidents.

In conclusion, the Mexican newspaper articles implied that any encounter by migrants with people near the border during the migration journey could pose a threat. By their very nature, such encounters were hard for migrants to manage, but journalists implied that the U.S. government should act to curtail extremist behavior. Articles emphasized the need for both the Mexican and the U.S. government to abide by international human rights conventions, the need for Mexico to defend its migrants against human rights abuses, and the need for the United States to enact legal mechanisms that make individuals accountable for their mistreatment of migrants.

Mexican Institutions and Organizations: Different Agendas, Common Desire

Though their agendas may be quite different, in an everyday context, the responses of the Mexican government, civil society, and the print media to escalating risk are intertwined. For example, when Border Angels undertakes its visits to the desert on Mexican territory, policy requires that Grupo Beta accompany them. However, on these visits, it is not uncommon for a representative from the Comisión Nacional de Derechos Humanos to also participate or for a journalist to come along to cover the story (see fig. 3.4).

Such everyday cooperation between the different Mexican institutions is both natural and desirable. The Mexican government, for example, needs the rigorous documentation undertaken by the human rights organizations both in Mexico and the United States, in order to defend Mexican nationals from human rights abuses. In turn, these civil society organizations have limited capacity to undertake legal human rights defense cases, and are keen to support the Secretaría de Relaciones Exteriores when it decides to prosecute human rights violations in the U.S. legal system. There is also a mutually beneficial relationship between civil society organizations and media organizations because civil society groups need to raise public awareness to secure support, funds, and

Figure 3.4 Representatives of Border Angels, the *San Diego Union-Tribune*, and Grupo Beta at a migrant rescue shelter prepare to place water in the Mexican desert for migrants.

political clout, while media organizations want interesting or different perspectives on important issues affecting society. The anti-Gatekeeper events and festivals held by the faith-based organizations are beneficial to both groups. In Tijuana, however, there is a spirit of goodwill and cooperation between the local representatives of all these entities that goes beyond any logistical necessity to pool resources. It has emerged from their common desire to protect the well-being of Mexican unauthorized migrants.

But even with cooperation on the ground and their common desire, the civil society groups could not in good conscience support the approach of the Mexican government toward management of unauthorized migration, particularly the decisions made by the ruling hierarchy in Mexico City. In turn, the government could not support the shocking, attention-seeking tactics of the civil society organizations that, in many cases, misrepresent government. Nor could it be said that the unauthorized migrant is always the primary concern of the Mexican government, civil society, or the print media. Indeed, political priorities and agendas are too often the underlying focus of one or all of these different Mexican institutions.

One thing is plain from this analysis: awareness of the issues surrounding the risks of unauthorized migration is a battleground. Whereas the U.S. government is attempting to reduce visible unauthorized migration with the implementation of Operation Gatekeeper, the Mexican government is trying to sustain the status quo without drawing too much attention to any of its negative impacts. For their part, civil society organizations are working against both processes by trying to raise wide-scale awareness of the issues in dramatic ways. The print media, for their own journalistic purposes, feed off these different opinions to create an overall point of view, which they then present to the general public. In the end, the original experiences of the migrants themselves have been shaped into something quite different.

Returning briefly to consider the migrant experiences outlined in chapter 2, it is worth noting that none of the migrants was assisted by, or even mentioned, any of the government programs. Most were aware of the increasing risks of migration due to the tightening of border controls after September 11, 2001, however, and this implies that civil society awareness strategies, facilitated by the print media, were successful. It appears that information provided by civil society, and their social networks, informed the migrants' decisions to stay in the United States rather than travel to and from Mexico. Because U.S.–based family members tend to organize the migration strategies for the next generation of migrants, it was also interesting to note some migrants were now providing money for their relatives to live in Mexico rather than to cross into the United States (see Javier in chapter 2).

Having considered the responses of the Mexican government, civil society, and the print media to unauthorized migration, let us now examine sociocultural responses to the risks of unauthorized migration as expressed in border art.

4
Mexican Border Art as Activism

At the U.S.–Mexico border, there is a convergence and hybridization of culture, particularly in the popular arts, where Mexican and Chicano arts collide and combine.[1] Because border communities are on the geographical demarcation of national sovereignties, and at the interface of migrant sending and receiving communities, unauthorized migration has logically become an important focus of the border arts.[2]

Up until implementation of California's Operation Gatekeeper in October 1994, Tijuana was the site of the greatest number of unauthorized crossings into the United States.[3] For this reason, the people of Tijuana have long been closely connected with unauthorized migration and its negative consequences. As U.S. border security has intensified, the artists of the Tijuana community have sought to depict the increasing tension between the United States and Mexico and, in particular, the escalating risks faced by Mexican unauthorized migrants. But, Maria Eraña tells us,

> it was not until 1990 that artists and activists from Tijuana took to the streets to call attention to the increased dangers to those who enter the United States without documents. . . . Wooden crosses were erected, following the Latin America tradition of marking the place where someone dies with crosses, flowers, and candles. The crosses at El Bordo were dedicated to the thousands of anonymous people who throughout the years, and all along the border, have paid with their lives . . . in order to be accepted into the "land of opportunity."[4]

It was in 1990 that the U.S. military erected a border wall outside Tijuana, a wall immediately perceived by locals as a symbol of violence between two supposedly peaceful neighbors.[5] And, with the wall, the United States adopted ever stricter border security measures.

To the people of Tijuana today, however, the border wall has become a fixture of everyday life. They have claimed the Mexican side as their own and made it their projection screen. Here Tijuana's artists can present their ideas, particularly about migration and the debate surrounding it, not only to locals but also to a broader audience through reproductions and imitations of their art.

The artistic expression on Tijuana's border wall is part of a rich Mexican tradition. "Art associated with social movements helped to constitute—not simply reflect—Mexico's dramatic social and political change over the last century," explains Edward McCaughan. "National identity, notions of citizenship, democracy, and justice . . . have been shaped, in part, by the content, form and institutional context of activist art."[6]

Diego Rivera (1886–1957), José Clemente Orozco (1883–1949), and David Alfaro Siqueiros (1896–1974) are synonymous with the Mexican mural movement and have defined many of the themes that continue to be used to express the ideas of Mexican and Chicano artists today.[7] For example, in his mural *Tierra y Libertad* (Land and Liberty) at the Palacio Nacional in Mexico City, Diego Rivera has painted still-popular iconic images of Mexico's political forefathers, campesinos, indigenous peoples, Catholic clergy, the eagle, and corn, to refer to just a few.

Across the border, during the 1960s and 1970s in the United States, the Chicano rights movement sparked an impressive number of mural projects. Those in Chicano Park in Barrio Logan, San Diego (see fig. 4.1), are fine examples of mural art's privileged position both in promoting Mexican political activism and in reaffirming Mexican identity outside of Mexico.[8] Being such a rich source of expression and information on the experiences of Mexicans and Chicanos, mural art has been readily adopted to express artists' views of unauthorized migration right at the border wall.

Because they have been isolated, not only geographically but also politically, from decision-making capital cities,[9] border communities have felt neglected; border art is therefore deliberate in its attention seeking. Susan Herbst explains that "artistic media are particularly useful to groups who find themselves on the fringes of the public sphere, because these media are so malleable. One can express an infinite number of concepts and emotions through painting, drawings, performance, art, cartoons, and the like."[10]

Within this context, the border wall at Tijuana has taken on its own identity and become a community bulletin board to discuss different facets of migration. Juan Villoro suggests that the wall is as ineffective in stopping unauthorized migration as it is effective in promoting awareness

Figure 4.1 The Mexican American mural of the Virgin of Guadalupe at Chicano Park, San Diego.

of the risks of migration: "The worthless scrap iron functions merely as advertising. It foretells the horrors that the adventurous may suffer. It's no coincidence that the landscape is ugly. Since October 1994, when Operation Gatekeeper was implemented, approximately 400 Mexicans have died trying to reach that temporary heaven we call 'el otro lado' (the other side)."[11]

The wall has become part of an "alternative" medium. The artworks on it provide uncensored information: there is no authority to determine what can or cannot be placed on the wall. This, according to Joseph Nevins, is in contrast to traditional news, where, particularly in the United States, reporting on border issues has often been closely aligned with government policies and has strived to shape rather than accurately reflect public opinion.[12] Moreover, graffiti-style popular art exhibitions allow for anonymity, if desired, and debate of taboo issues, particularly those that appear to be unpopular with government.[13]

Although most of the images on the wall address the border and migration, I have chosen only the most informative migration-related, risk-centered examples, produced by independent artists, by a civil society coalition, and by the Tijuana arts community, funded by both private and public institutions, for consideration here. My analysis is ethnographic, and my discussion of the images inspired by in-depth interviews with artists who created the images and by writings on these works. In most cases, my understanding and interpretation have been informed by the artists themselves, presenting the objectives and symbolic meanings of their art. Along with my analysis, I have provided photographs of the artworks for the readers' scrutiny.[14]

My documentation of artworks began at Playa Tijuana (32° 32′ 03.5″ N, 117° 07′ 21.9″ W) and concluded at (32° 32′ 50.4″ N; 116° 58′ 05.0″ W) on Cuauhtemoc Boulevard, the eastern end of the road adjacent to Tijuana's international airport. There are two independent artworks, *Paradise Ahead?* in Playa Tijuana and *Bienvenido paisano al sueño americano* (Welcome, Countryman, to the American Dream) in downtown Tijuana. And there are two border wall art exhibitions at Tijuana International Airport, La frontera la llaga abierta, produced by a civil society coalition, and La tercera nación, produced by Tijuana's local arts movement with support from the Mexican government and sponsorship by private organizations.

This chapter analyzes the cultural production of border art by different groups as a response to escalating risks for Mexican unauthorized migrants crossing the border. It considers the significance of this popular art genre both at the border wall in Tijuana and in the broader Mexican national debate on unauthorized migration. Through reproduction and imitation of these symbolic images of border life in a variety of media, different sectors of Mexican society are creating an awareness of the risks of unauthorized migration.

Independent Artists: A Critique of Risk and Migration

Along the border wall are a variety of independent artworks, ranging from product advertising to graffiti. There are two independent artworks, however, that directly address the topic of risk and unauthorized migration: one is *Paradise Ahead?* situated in Playa Tijuana, a popular beachside suburb, and the other is *Bienvenido paisano al sueño americano*, located in downtown Tijuana.

Paradise Ahead?

One meter high by three meters long (three feet by ten feet) and painted in Mexico's national colors, red, green, and white (see fig. 4.2), this mural is situated in Playa Tijuana, Tijuana's beachside suburb. Being so close to the ocean, the steel wall that underlies it has become severely rusted; the mural's white is now tinged with orange.

Vertical strips mimic the bars that act as a barrier to the United States at the nearby beach, Playa Tijuana (see fig. 3.1). Observed more closely, the vertical lines actually depict skulls mounted one on top of the other. Red paint is used to depict blood running down the wall. People passing through the barrier are shown as dismembered bodies; only arms and legs can be seen. On the left side of the mural, although its clarity has been corroded, is an indigenous woman with a bullet belt between her naked breasts. At her feet, a dog feeds on a human leg trapped on the Mexican side of the wall. On the right side are workers about to enter the United States.

Shente, as he is known, is a local Tijuana graffiti artist who worked on this mural. He explained that a Mexican friend, known as "Copras," returned from San Francisco, where he had seen anti-globalization murals, and he wanted to express some of these concepts in the context of Tijuana, and therefore chose to represent the risks facing Mexican

Figure 4.2 The mural *Paradise Ahead?* in Playa Tijuana.

unauthorized migrants. Shente remembers that it was one of the first murals on the border wall, undertaken in late 1999 or early 2000. Producing the artwork was a collaborative effort: "We bought the paint and went to the wall and there were more friends there and we all painted together. One did the letters, another drew the worker with his overalls. . . . We put many skulls like a painting by Orozco or Diego Rivera, somebody like that. So a friend drew the skulls, and he drew the countrywoman without a shirt with the belt of bullets around her and a black dog."

Shente suggested that, to those unfamiliar with Mexican culture, some aspects of the mural might seem odd. For instance, Mexicans consider death to be a part of life. He explained that "the skulls represent the Mexican culture. [But] the Day of the Dead for us isn't scary, it's not like 'Oh, I'm going to die!' or in other cultures where you can't talk about that. It's like you're going to die and that's cool. Well, it's not cool, but it's something that you accept."

Risk of death might not be as culturally significant to Mexican migration decision making as U.S. border management strategists might have expected when they devised Operation Gatekeeper. Shente implied that, on some level, Mexicans might reach paradise either by arriving at the United States or by dying. That said, Shente suggested that *Paradise Ahead?* was also a question for Americans, not just for Mexicans, and thus its title was written in English. The mural is for Mexicans looking forward but also for Americans looking back into Mexico. In other words,

> Just like the dog was looking toward the United States, the idea is that you are standing here and looking toward them but it is also in reverse, they are looking at Mexico. Here is paradise, there is everything from petroleum to all types of fruits, jungle, we have everything. It is saying to Mexicans that here we have what their paradise does not . . . better still, why are you going to the United States looking for an American dream when you have a Mexican dream. You can do it here, you can do it in Mexico but it is a question of you wanting the country to go forward. If we say that we don't have anything good and that the good things are only always in other places, you won't realize what you have. If you want to go to the United States because it is better there, you will later realize that it is the same or worse.

In *Paradise Ahead?* dismembered bodies crawl through the border wall as blood oozes. Skulls commemorate those Mexicans who have died in their efforts to reach the United States, the "paradise" they seek. The mural questions, however, whether "paradise" is really ahead, through the border wall and in the United States, or whether Mexicans could achieve a better life by striving, perhaps even through revolution, to economically develop Mexico.

Bienvenido paisano al sueño americano

In contrast to *Paradise Ahead?* no direct contact was possible with the artist of *Bienvenido paisano al sueño americano* (Welcome, Countryman, to the American Dream; see fig. 4.3). Although the mural is totally anonymous, with no reference to the artist by signature, initials, or code, we can safely assume by its use of Spanish that the artist was a Mexican painting for Mexicans.

The words "Bienvenido paisano al sueño americano" stand out in red, white, and blue against the gray border wall, the reference to the United States reiterated with the icon of the American flag painted on the right side of the mural. The use of green with white and red is most likely a

Figure 4.3 The mural *Bienvenido paisano al sueño americano* in downtown Tijuana.

reference to Mexico. On a concrete barrier just at the bottom of the mural, someone has written in black "Mensaje desde la gran Tenochtitlán" (Message from the great Tenochtitlán), Tenochtitlán being the original name of the Aztec settlement that would become Mexico City.[15]

Images, Symbols, and Meanings

In both of these independent artworks, the wall is metaphorically the space between paradise and its opposite, misery, and, to judge from strong depictions of blood, skulls, and crosses in both, also the threshold, not simply between Mexico and the United States, but also between life and death.

From precolonial, through colonial, to modern art, death is perhaps the most consistent archetypal theme of Mexican artists, expressed, in particular, with images of skulls.[16] According to Shifra Goldman, who has catalogued iconography from Chicano and border art, the black west Mexican funerary dog, which appears in *Paradise Ahead?* is a guide accompanying humans on their journey after death.[17] This religious belief, Linda Schele and Mary Miller tell us, dates back to the ancient Maya.[18]

Bienvenido paisano al sueño americano contains a cross, a symbol of Christianity, sacrifice, and death,[19] frequently used both by border artists and pro-migrant demonstrators to represent the death of Mexican migrants at the border. Consider, for example, the green cross clutched by a man in the crowd at a Mass celebrated on both sides of the border at Border Field Park / Playa Tijuana on October 3, 2004, to commemorate the loss of life attributed to Operation Gatekeeper (see fig. 3.3).

The association between the murals and death implies that in *Paradise Ahead?* the concept of paradise can be considered as a place not only of pleasure on Earth but also of death, as Shente implied. Mexico's dominant faith is Catholicism, which holds that paradise (heaven) awaits the faithful upon death.[20] Indeed, in Luke 23:42–43, Jesus refers to heaven as paradise: "Amen I say to thee, this day thou shalt be with me in paradise."[21]

Bienvenido paisano al sueño americano, in contrast, is based on a more worldly ideology, that of the "American dream," whereby Americans can achieve wealth and happiness by working hard. It defines the values and actions appropriate to U.S. society.[22] Migrant Americans, including unauthorized migrants, may aspire to achieve the American dream by reaching the associated standard of living.[23]

A green cross appears again, in *Bienvenido paisano al sueño americano*, where the artist uses it to present the American dream, not as a promise, but as death. Merely seeking the American dream can lead to a migrant's death. But even if the migrant succeeds in reaching the United States and achieving the American dream, migration can lead to a different kind of death: fragmentation of the migrant's family or culture.[24] The U.S. flag flying above the pile of Mexican skulls would seem to symbolize U.S. political dominance over Mexico and the unauthorized migrant.[25]

Whereas *Bienvenido paisano al sueño americano* implies a passive acceptance of death as a potential consequence of unauthorized migration, *Paradise Ahead?* contains two icons associated with revolution. First is the widely recognized icon of the worker, a representative of political and social ideals, holding a hammer and sickle, revolutionary workers' symbols from Soviet Russia (see fig. 4.2).[26] This stands well within the tradition of revolutionary Mexican muralists such as Diego Rivera.[27]

The second revolutionary icon in this work is that of the indigenous woman.[28] The mural's indigenous Mexican woman, with a belt of bullets between her breasts, seems a likely symbol of the women who served as soldiers and officers in the Mexican Revolution.[29]

Independent artists thus have used iconic images such as skulls and blood to express to their Mexican audience the risks of unauthorized migration. *Paradise Ahead?* questions whether the United States is really better for Mexicans than their homeland, and *Bienvenido paisano al sueño americano* suggests that the consequence of trying to achieve the American dream may be death. The murals' images are fundamental responses to the wall that has come to symbolize the increasing militarization of the U.S.–Mexico border.

Activist Art for Protest and Political Change

On November 2, 1998, a group of volunteers gathered at the border wall to commemorate Mexico's Día de los muertos (Day of the Dead). They attached commemorative crosses to the wall, one for each of the unauthorized migrants reported dead since the start of California's Operation Gatekeeper. The crosses remained in place for the month of November and were then taken down.

In the year 2000, the volunteers decided to leave the crosses up and create a permanent exhibition. The annual event was changed from Mexico's Day of the Dead in November to the anniversary of the implementation of Operation Gatekeeper in October. With time, the volunteer initiative developed into a well-coordinated effort involving the Casa del Migrante en Tijuana (Tijuana Migrant Hostel), the Border Arts Workshop, and a variety of migrant rights groups, including the California Rural Legal Assistance Foundation represented by Claudia Smith, a prominent spokeswoman for migrant rights in the United States.

The exhibition, as established in 2000, begins with a simple shrine to the migrants that depicts a migrant, dead, up against the wall (see fig. 4.4). Wearing work clothes, the migrant is placed within a cross, and artificial flowers decorate the shrine. According to Eraña, objects such as crosses and flowers are popularly used by Mexicans to commemorate the site where someone has died.[30]

Next to this shrine, the total number of migrants who have died crossing the border (since the start of Operation Gatekeeper) is displayed up on the wall, as though it is clicking over like an electronic counter. And

Figure 4.4 A Border Arts Workshop shrine to deceased unauthorized migrants in Tijuana.

Figure 4.5 Coffins commemorate the annual unauthorized-migrant death toll since the implementation of Operation Gatekeeper.

next to the number is painted the question "¿Cuántas más?" (How many more?).

Adjacent to Tijuana International Airport, a row of crosses commemorates the migrants who have died attempting to cross into California since the start of Operation Gatekeeper. Each cross contains the name of a migrant, if known, or "No identificado" (Not identified), if the U.S. Coroner was unable to identify the remains.

After a kilometer (half mile) or so of crosses, colorfully painted coffins represent the annual death toll among migrants attempting to cross, unauthorized, into California since the beginning of Operation Gatekeeper (see fig. 4.5). The coffins are decorated with images reminiscent of Mexico's Day of the Dead celebrations; their skulls and flaming hearts are signature icons of Chicano art.[31] This mix of imagery illustrates the fusion of artistic ideas, and the interaction between Mexican and Chicano artists, at the border. It is also a reminder of their collaborative participation in this civil society activist art exhibition on the border wall at Tijuana–San Diego.

Figure 4.6 La frontera la llaga abierta (The border, an open wound) art exhibition in Tijuana, marking ten years of Operation Gatekeeper.

October 2004 marked the tenth anniversary of the implementation of Operation Gatekeeper. This was commemorated by a number of community events (as discussed in chapter 3), including the renovation of the civil society anti–Operation Gatekeeper border art exhibition. Although the four key features of the exhibition remained in place, the original slogan "No puedo pasar indiferente ante el dolor de tanta gente" (I cannot pass by indifferent to the pain of so many people) was replaced by "La frontera la llaga abierta" (The border, an open wound) and artists repainted sections of the wall with much bloodier imagery (see fig. 4.6).

This revised slogan, "La frontera la llaga abierta," may be a reference to Gloria Anzaldúa's well-known work *Borderlands = La Frontera*, where she writes: "The U.S.–Mexico border es una herida abierta (is an open wound) where the Third World grates against the First and bleeds. And before a scab forms it hemorrhages again, the lifeblood of two worlds merging to form a third country—a border culture."[32]

The change in slogan in October 2004 may also be a response to a nearby, new border wall art exhibition called "La tercera nación," which is discussed in greater detail in the following section. Put in place in April 2004—six months before the renovation of the civil society exhibition, La tercera nación presents Tijuana as a positive example of cultural integration between the United States and Mexico. The La frontera la llaga abierta exhibition, in contrast, is a gruesome reminder of the pain, suffering, and risk experienced in this very same border space. Gloria Anzaldúa's concept of a "third nation" as a bloody wound, contrasts with the imagery of that same "third nation" by Tijuana's arts movement. Changing the title and slogan of the civil society border art exhibition in October 2004 may have been one way of attempting to undermine the positive imagery of La tercera nación.

Overall, the civil society alliance considers that their border wall art exhibition has been successful in boosting community awareness of the risks of unauthorized Mexican migration to the United States. As a representative from the Casa del Migrante en Tijuana explained, "You see the crosses, and all that area is respected, even by the graffiti artists." These groups believe that the respect their artwork is shown is a positive sign of its acceptance and influence in the community.

The Politics behind the Representation of Migrant Deaths

As shown in chapter 3, civil society organizations have strived to promote awareness surrounding the risks of unauthorized migration; art has been an essential component of their risk awareness strategy. The border wall artworks are designed to promote community sensitivity but also to attract the news media, which in turn disseminate these images and stimulate broader awareness of the cause, preventing the deaths of unauthorized migrants at the border.

The relaunch of the civil society art project as a permanent exhibition in the year 2000 was highly strategic. Nevins observed that, by 1999, there was a distinct lack of news media interest in Operation Gatekeeper; it was "old news."[33] Creating a permanent art exhibition and combining it with an annual commemoration of migrant deaths, on the anniversary of the implementation of Operation Gatekeeper, have captured media attention and exposed the general public to the human face of unauthorized migration, risk, and migration-related deaths.

The tenth anniversary of Operation Gatekeeper, marked by a series of civil society events, led to the San Diego Union-Tribune running five in-depth front-page stories on the risks of unauthorized migration. The articles focused on U.S. border management strategies and the human consequences.[34] The border wall artworks, with their stylized images of death, attracted the attention of both the newspaper's readers and the syndicated U.S. media. In a *Union-Tribune* editorial, journalist Logan Jenkins wrote:

> Looking south, the heart can take a beating. You may have seen the arresting photograph in Friday's *Union-Tribune*, the one of artists placing on the Tijuana border fence a large painting of a stylized human skeleton. He's striding across a desert landscape, carrying a plastic water jug in each bony hand. According to the caption, the painting recognizes the 10th anniversary of Operation Gatekeeper, the famous crackdown that drove illegal border crossers to the east, exposing them to harsh, often fatal, conditions. I ask you: What should those of us living comfortably in San Diego feel as we regard the skeleton? Anger? Pity? Detachment?[35]

The civil society organizations have used their border artworks and events to gain attention and create an opportunity to speak out about the risks facing unauthorized migrants. For example, journalist Edward Sifuentes reported in the *North County Times* (based in Escondido, some 30 miles north of San Diego) that the tenth anniversary of the implementation of Operation Gatekeeper had sparked numerous protest events aimed at creating public pressure to reject this style of border management.[36] And migrant rights spokeswoman Claudia Smith took advantage of the presence of a *San Diego Union-Tribune* reporter at the renovation of the border wall art exhibition in October 2004 to state that "giving the appearance that the border is under control, especially in the San Diego sector, has come at an enormous price."[37]

Because Operation Gatekeeper had pushed unauthorized migration into remote desert areas, the populations of Tijuana and San Diego were no longer experiencing its realities. Realizing this, civil society organizations decided a permanent border wall exhibition would be an effective way to attract attention and promote awareness of the life-threatening consequences of Operation Gatekeeper. Even as the U.S. government strived to make unauthorized migration "invisible" to the urban voter, civil society organizations would try to maintain awareness and make the deaths of unauthorized Mexicans unacceptable, in the eyes of the U.S. and Mexican people.[38] Thus the civil society art exhibition on the border wall is both a protest against the risks to unauthorized migrants associated with U.S. policy initiatives and a tool to stimulate political change.

Tijuana's Arts Movement: Defining Self

La tercera nación (The Third Nation) encompassed a visual display along two and a half kilometers (one and a half miles) of the border wall in Tijuana, as well as artworks on the Tijuana River canal, exhibitions at the Tijuana Cultural Center and a variety of music, literature and poetry events. Together, these events were known as the "Grito creativo" (Creative Cry), a presentation of Tijuana's creativity before the world.[39]

La tercera nación was an initiative of the Spaniard Antonio Navalón Sáchez, a well-known Mexico City–based businessman and friend of Mexican President Fox (who, with his wife, Marta Sahagún, presided over the official opening on April 20, 2004).[40] Navalón secured the required private-sector funding (90 percent of the project's cost) for the exhibition to go ahead.[41] The official sponsors were prominent private organizations such as Telefónica Movistar, Mexicana, Milenio, Coca-Cola, Forum Barcelona 2004, Santillana, and Tecate Cerveza. These were joined by Mexican public entities such as the Consejo de Promoción Turística (Mexico Tourism Promotion Board), Instituto Municipal de Arte y Cultura (Municipal Institute for Art and Culture), Municipio de Tijuana (Municipality of Tijuana), Instituto Cultural de Baja California (Cultural Institute of Baja California), Gobierno de Baja California (Government of Baja California), Consejo Nacional para la Cultura y las Artes (National Culture Council) and the Secretaría de Educación Pública (Ministry for Public Education).

Speaking at the launch, Navalón explained his motivation for La tercera nación: "Tijuana is . . . the city that embraces everyone and is an example of life which, through its culture, rises above borders of origin, race, language and converts itself into a symbol of understanding, this third nation that is only possible with equality, vitality and creative capacity."[42] He chose to mount the exhibition in Tijuana because it is one of the most visited and creative cities in the world. La tercera nación is a celebration of those people who, 3,000 kilometers (1,850 miles) from the Mexican capital, welcome people in and out of the Mexican nation.[43] Though Tijuana flexibly adjusts to changing global circumstances, Navalón went on to say, the city's identity is sometimes overwhelmed by the images created by foreigners and transients. By using plastic sheeting to cover different parts of the city, La tercera nación would wrap Tijuana in its own identity.[44]

He chose the border wall because he felt that, there especially, the new exhibition could show how creativity could overcome the barriers between the United States and Mexico: "Before, when you arrived in Tijuana and left the airport, you could only see the wall until you reached the crosses, testimony to the tragedy and to that we pay respect. But that overlooks the other part of the truth."[45]

Although the crosses in the civil society art exhibition (La frontera la llaga abierta) were one aspect of life in Tijuana, in his opinion they were not the only truth. Now people arriving at Tijuana by air could look down on La tercera nación before driving beside the wall and seeing images flicker by as though it were an old movie.[46]

In early 2004, Tijuana graphic artist Jhoana Mora and fellow artist Maximiliano Lizárraga were invited to coordinate the exhibition's two graphic design installations: one on the border wall and the other on the edges of the canal in downtown Tijuana. Local artists were invited to submit images for these installations or to provide permission for prese-lected images from their work to be integrated into the project.

For the border wall installation, to design a series of images that would appear like a film being screened on the wall, Lizárraga used vibrant color to frame upbeat images of Tijuana. Color, according to Lizárraga, "is one of the most penetrating visual experiences that we humans share. Color encloses symbolic meanings and offers us an enormous vocabulary of great use in visual literacy."[47]

The images were reproduced on plastic sheeting that could then be attached to the three-meter (ten-foot) border wall for the length of the road adjacent to Tijuana International Airport, two and a half kilometers (one and a half miles). The border wall was selected as one of the two sites for La tercera nación because it had become part of the visual identity of Tijuana. "The city's boundaries motivate the mural writers to be like the community muralists, Lizárraga explained, "where self-assertion, pride and expression are the essential basis for an ephemeral art. . . . When growing up with walls of all kinds, we can ignore them and become indifferent; become violent and try to bring the walls down, or as a last resort carry on a magical ritual that neutralizes the power of walls, by decorating them with signs, symbols and art, which have been selected by these mural writers as a way of saying, 'Here I am.'"[48]

However, not everyone or every artist was impressed with the concept of "decorating" the border wall. Heriberto Yepez was both a participant and an outspoken critic of the border wall installation. He felt that it was inappropriate to beautify a wall that is essentially a symbol of violence. He saw La tercera nación as part of the "NAFTA arts movement," a feel-good presentation about Tijuana that coincided with a visit by Mexico's President Fox. In his published open letter to the organizers of La tercera nación, Yepez wrote:

> Border art is being manipulated to create a favorable image of cultural integration with the United States, a supposed colorful Fusion. This is clearly an intellectually irresponsible use of visual and verbal language in a public space for pro-globalization propaganda. What significance has "The Third Nation"? I'm not referring just to the concept according to the organization currently using it (with events from April to July 2004) but this point in time where this concept is generally being used to define border art as though there were a happy synthesis between Mexico and the United States.

Yepez speaks to the contradiction that, even as there is greater economic integration of the United States and Mexico under NAFTA, physical and social divisions between the two countries are growing deeper. These divisions have manifested themselves as a border wall and stricter migration controls in traditionally integrated border communities such as Tijuana. Yepez finds it highly incongruous that Tijuana's artists are "decorating" the border wall that divides the two countries and then claiming that Tijuana and San Diego are united, as part of a "Third Nation."

Another participant was more enthusiastic: "It really, really, helped me to be part of the show. There are some people who will regret not being part of that show; it's definitely going to be part of history in TJ [Tijuana]." Such artistic displays are important to participate in because they mark important points in Tijuana's history, even if the overall outcome is not perfect: "It's kinda odd because I don't really think that we, you know, the arts community would have done something there [at the wall] because it's too much of a cliché at the border. I mean, the border by itself tells you a lot of things. For me, it's very obvious to do a show there because it's something that's already been done."

That said, the artist believed that the images of La tercera nación would provide a contrast to the traditionally negative ones of Tijuana

Figure 4.7 La tercera nación art exhibition on the Tijuana–San Diego border wall.

presented in the U.S. media, including movies. The exhibition could provide a local sense of identity by expressing the unique feeling that is Tijuana, by being "more about living in TJ than illegal crossings. . . . It's the United States' influence on your life just by living on the other side [of the border]. In a way, the whole thing about the border is not the border itself, but the way it makes you feel."

The border wall installation of La tercera nación (see fig. 4.7) blends stereotypical images of Tijuana, such as its share taxis, with those of America, such as the American flag. Tijuana's self-identity is also juxtaposed with its image as a stopping point for migrants. By reproducing and displaying the border wall on the wall itself, the installation plays on the symbolic nature of its space.

La tercera nación is very much a border arts project created by the people of Tijuana to define their city and to combat images produced by outside groups, including images contrived within the United States or even in central Mexico. As Maximiliano Lizárraga explained, "We feel like we are an island. . . . We're not gringos because we don't have that nationality and we're not from Mexico City where everything is centralized and when they talk about the great cities they only talk about Mexico [City], Guadalajara, and Monterrey."

La tercera nación allows the artists of Tijuana to define, on their own terms, the character of Tijuana.[49] In stark contrast to the other risk-centered art exhibitions, however, what is noticeably absent from this exhibition are representations of the risks of unauthorized migration. This absence speaks to Tijuana's struggle both to define itself as independent from the commerce of unauthorized migration and to emphasize its role in the new, integrated commerce of NAFTA. That President Fox supported this regional art exhibition and even attended its opening suggests that this "integration art" was politically endorsed, or at the very least politically correct. Use of art on the border wall by private interests and the Mexican government, potential beneficiaries of the greater integration of the U.S. and Mexican economies, could be seen as a strategic co-opting of a space traditionally used by the local community to criticize both countries' governments and their unauthorized migration policies.

The Reproduction and Imitation of Border Art throughout Mexico

Clearly, the border wall on the Mexican side has become a community art space, with exhibitions that provoke contemplation, reflection, and dialogue on unauthorized migration. Indeed, the wall itself has become an icon continually referred to in songs, paintings, the news media, and policy documents. Strategic placement of artworks on the wall, near Tijuana International Airport, for example, ensures that locals, migrants, and visitors who come to one of the world's most visited cities see these images. As one art critic points out, "Choosing the right site is crucial to activist art."[50]

That said, perhaps most interesting of all is the fact that the identity of the wall now stretches beyond Tijuana. The messages of these local art exhibitions and the wall itself have taken on a symbolic nature, reproduced and disseminated by a variety of media. Many of these images, however, are then used and controlled by organizations that are not based at the border. These images come to "represent" the border rather than depict the actual realities of life there.

So iconic had the border wall become that a larger-than-life replica was put on display from August to the end of September 2005 at the

Museo Nacional de Cultura Popular in Coyoacán (a suburb of Mexico City). The exhibition Culturas en fronteras (Culture at Borders) reviewed the culture of migration from prehistoric times (the human race leaving Africa) to the present-day unauthorized Mexican migration to the United States. The entryway to the exhibition was a replica of the border wall, with migrant manikins and with the visitors themselves appearing to be unauthorized migrants crossing into the United States (see fig. 4.8).

What was most interesting about this replica of a border wall were the messages in the art and graffiti on it. These messages, contrived in Mexico City, sometimes mimicked and sometimes contrasted with those ideas actually expressed at the border region and, more specifically, on the border wall at Tijuana. For example, the drawing of the human body against the wall on the replica in Coyoacán resembles the tracing of a migrant body for the shrine on the actual border wall in Tijuana (see fig. 4.4). On the other hand, the message "Todos somos ilegales" (We are all illegals; see fig. 4.9) stands in stark contrast to the one displayed at Chicano Park, San Diego, "Ningún ser humano es ilegal" (No human being is illegal; see fig. 4.10).

Among the images depicting the risks of unauthorized migration on the replica wall in Coyoacán is one of an aggressive U.S. Border Patrol officer threatening migrants (see fig. 4.11). On the back of the migrant's T-shirt is a picture of the Virgin of Guadalupe, reflecting his faith in her protection of Mexicans, and implying that religious beliefs must be considered a logical risk reduction strategy. That said, the Virgin of Guadalupe is both a religious and nationalist symbol. The symbol was adopted by Mexicans during their battle for independence from Spain. Revolutionary Father Hidalgo used it to call the people to arms.[51] Indeed, as a revolutionary symbol, the Virgin of Guadalupe remains popular in both Mexican and Chicano art (fig. 4.1).[52]

Most of the images on the replica wall imply that blame for the risks of unauthorized migration should be assigned to the United States. In contrast, those on the actual border wall at Tijuana seem either to condemn the situation in general (civil society exhibition; fig. 4.6) or to put more of an emphasis on the migrants' decision to leave Mexico for the United States (independent artworks; figs. 4.2 and 4.3).

The replica wall also depicts some of the suffering caused by unauthorized migration, including family fragmentation. A woman with a young child is depicted as being left behind as two men, one of whom

Figure 4.8 A manikin of an unauthorized migrant hiding behind a tree, Coyoacán.

Figure 4.9 The mural *Todos somos ilegales* (We are all illegals) in Coyoacán.

is presumably her husband, are climbing the wall into the United States (see fig. 4.12).

A graffito on this same section of the replica wall states, "Si el de Berlin kayo . . . este tambien kaerá" (If the Berlin Wall fell, so, too, will this wall). This statement perhaps speaks to the irony of the Tijuana–San Diego wall being built in 1990, just after the Berlin wall, which had divided Germany, fell in 1989.[53] A graffito below this says, "¿Tierra y Libertad?" (Land and Liberty?), a likely reference to the values of the Mexican Revolution, as depicted in Diego Rivera's mural *Tierra y Libertad* at the Palacio Nacional in Mexico City. This comment would seem to be more closely aligned with political values in central Mexico than at the border, where the artworks tend to assert that Mexicans have an inherent entitlement to land in the United States, an idea that reflects Chicano attitudes toward the Treaty of Guadalupe Hidalgo.

Although there are differences behind the politics of the images on the replica wall in Coyoacán and those on the border wall at Tijuana, both walls testify to the role of the wall as an iconic symbol of the militarization

Figure 4.10 The Mural *Ningún ser humano es ilegal* (No human being is illegal) at Chicano Park in San Diego.

Figure 4.11 A migrant encounters a U.S. Border Patrol officer in Coyoacán, Mexico.

of the U.S.–Mexico border and as a space to represent the risks facing unauthorized Mexican migrants. The artists working on both walls have the common goal to

> inform public opinion and foment sentiments similar to their own, is it any wonder that they would marshal an arsenal of pictures and words wedded together? . . . What better means through which to undermine the discursive foundation of immigration policy than a visual culture at once discursive and penchant? These rhetorical questions find an answer in the premise that the duel of words and images that rages across borders involves the audacious and creative co-optation of the dominant culture's systemic codes.[54]

Besides being a physical structure, the border wall has become part of the United States' and Mexico's collective imagination. It is a place to discuss points of contention between the United States and Mexico in a post–NAFTA political arena, where openly discussing conflicts has become increasingly difficult.[55] Art on the wall has become part of the Mexican national symbolic response to the escalating risks of

Figure 4.12 A woman and child look away as two men cross what is supposedly the U.S.–Mexico border, Coyoacán.

unauthorized migration. Artists who make use of the wall are rewarded by the reproduction and imitation of their art and messages across the United States and Mexico.

Migration Risk and Border Art

To the people of Tijuana, the border is a physical reality but, at the same time, it is a fascinating international symbol. To others, Tijuana is a place of curiosity, where the imagined becomes physical reality. The border divide between the United States and Mexico at Tijuana inspires a creative response.

Independent artists responded to the wall almost immediately after it was built, largely with temporary exhibitions during the early 1990s.[56] In 1999 or 2000, Shente began to participate in the production of *Paradise Ahead?*, a response to NAFTA (implemented in 1994) and the stricter border controls of Operation Gatekeeper. By 2000, media interest and attention on the human consequences of Operation Gatekeeper were dropping off.[57] Strategically, the civil society coalition mounted their permanent anti–Operation Gatekeeper art exhibition (La frontera la llaga abierta) in the highly transited Tijuana International Airport thoroughfare and began to mark the anniversary of the implementation of Operation Gatekeeper. By 2004, Tijuana's artists were responding to a decade of negative media coverage of their city, due both to the deaths and injuries associated with Operation Gatekeeper and to Tijuana's traditional image as a city of vice.[58]

The independent artworks on the border wall at Tijuana, such as *Paradise Ahead?* and *Bienvenido paisano al sueño americano*, depict unauthorized migration as a risky, indeed deadly, endeavor through commonly recognized symbols of death, including blood, crosses, and skulls. That said, their artists do not usually go beyond informing the public. They see their role, not as actively lobbying for change, but as provoking thought and discussion.

The collaborative civil society organizations, in contrast, seek to inspire community and voter responses to the risks of unauthorized migration both in the United States and in Mexico. For its part, the Tijuana arts movement has responded to an increasing number of negative portrayals of the risks of undocumented migration in Tijuana by creating positive images that are designed to represent the "other" Tijuana, a city that is culturally integrated with the United States.

The artworks on the border wall demonstrate deliberate responses to the increasing level of risk to unauthorized Mexican migrants at the border. The independent artists critique, the civil society organizations lobby to bring about the demise of Operation Gatekeeper, and members of the Tijuana arts movement try to assert the city's own identity while struggling with the fact that it is intrinsically linked to unauthorized migration. The success of all these artistic endeavors may be seen in the frequent reproduction and dissemination of their images throughout Mexican and U.S. society.

5
The Migrant's Voice in Popular Song

Successful Mexican musicians are adept at reading community sentiment; when they incorporate shared beliefs, experiences, and meaning into a song, they usually boost its popularity.[1] By understanding such songs, we can understand how Mexicans respond to an issue. With that in mind, this chapter analyzes Mexican popular songs that deal with unauthorized migration, performed by two leading bands, to gain useful insights into Mexican experiences of its risks.

Although music is an integral part of many different cultures, for Latin Americans, it is central to communication and cultural expression.[2] This is indeed the case in Mexico, where music is deeply rooted in everyday life and is part of a dynamic dialogue and debate between musicians and the larger community on the critical issues affecting Mexican society.

The pivotal role of music is due, in part, to Mexico's struggle with illiteracy, particularly among its rural citizens, for whom song is an especially important source of information and a well-accepted form of communication.[3] Moreover, because radio is the nation's most effective public communication medium, popular music is widely distributed in Mexico.[4] Song is thus highly pertinent to socially centered studies that investigate Mexican community opinion.[5] And just as unauthorized migration is central to the lives of many Mexicans, so song is central to the Mexican cultural expression of its risks. In 2003–2004, the songs of Los Tigres del Norte and Molotov permeated Mexican society by radio and television. Los Tigres' album *Pacto de sangre* (Blood Pact) is a clear example of the prominent role that traditional Mexican ballads (corridos) have come to play in Mexican popular culture.[6] Historically, the corrido has been a vital source of information for the less literate members of rural communities. During the battle for Mexican independence and the Mexican Revolution, it was also a song of criticism and protest.[7] Corridos can cover all aspects of everyday life but, for over thirty years, Los Tigres del Norte have built their success on narratives from the border, on poignant portrayals of the risks and consequences of unauthorized migration.

Molotov's "Frijolero" (Beaner), in contrast, was a one-shot critique of unauthorized migration by a band that debates a wide variety of political issues facing Mexican society. An overwhelming commercial success, reflected in industry awards and music sales rankings, "Frijolero" clearly portrays the frustrations that Mexicans face in light of the U.S. political stance on border management and unauthorized migration.

Although the songs of Los Tigres del Norte and Molotov are quite different, both are popular; analyzed together, they represent the sentiments of a broad cross section of Mexican society. "Different groups possess different sorts of cultural capital, share different cultural expectations and so make music differently," Simon Frith explains, "pop tastes are shown to correlate with class cultures and subcultures; music styles are linked to specific age groups."[8] Thus analysis of two different types of music contributes to a broader understanding of Mexican responses, in song, to the escalating risks for unauthorized migrants crossing into the United States.

This chapter first explores how Los Tigres del Norte use the corrido to portray the risks of unauthorized migration on their album *Pacto de sangre*. It then undertakes an in-depth analysis of the tune, lyrics, and music video of Molotov's "Frijolero," a more spontaneous popular cultural response to the escalating risks of unauthorized migration, to identify the contextual and covert meanings of the song. It concludes by reviewing the key migration issues raised by these musicians and by discussing the different strategies they use to reflect community sentiments and inform societal perspectives on unauthorized migration to the United States.

Los Tigres del Norte: Voice of the People

The Hernández brothers (Jorge, Hernán, Eduardo, Luis, and Raúl, who would later leave the band) and their cousin Oscar Lara were teenage musicians who migrated to the United States in 1968. When the U.S. Immigration officer who checked their papers called them "little tigers" (a nickname for kids), because they had come north in search of success, they decided to call their band "Los Tigres del Norte" (The Northern Tigers). Despite being authorized migrants to the United States, Los Tigres have always felt an empathy for their unauthorized migrant countrymen. On the one hand, all Mexican migrants in the United States share the common experience of cultural adaptation to life there, but, on the other, Los Tigres respect the sacrifices that unauthorized Mexican migrants must make to reach the United States.[9]

Over their thirty-year career, Los Tigres del Norte have recorded 30 records and sold 32 million albums. Their musical signature is the corrido interpreted in the style of *música norteña* (northern music).[10] Indeed, their corridos about unauthorized migration have been so popular they have inspired fourteen feature films.[11]

The corrido genre, George Lewis tells us, includes "songs about smuggling, immigration, racism, bilingualism, and even living in a culturally alien land[; these] co-exist with the more traditional themes of romance and nationalism."[12] José Manuel Arce Valenzuela suggests that the corrido is the voice of the Mexican masses making itself heard ever since the Spanish Conquest. Corridos let Mexicans rediscover and reidentify with their pain, heroes, virtues, and misery.[13]

In this vein, Los Tigres have been acclaimed as being the voice of marginalized sectors of Mexican society. To which Hernán Hernández has responded that he and his fellow band members "never imagined people would look at us as spokespersons; as the people who would say what no one dared to say . . . suddenly we were going to interviews, and people were writing that we were the voice of the silent people."[14]

Los Tigres have, however, come to embrace their role as spokespersons for Mexico's marginalized peoples. They feel both honored and obliged to speak out about injustice and tragedy in the lives of Mexicans.[15] That said, they recognize that, if indeed they are the voice of the unauthorized migrant, this has only come about because of public demand. When their audience asks to hear corridos on particular themes, Los Tigres have commissioned songs that feature those themes; in doing so, they sustain a market for their music.[16] Selection of material is crucial to the success of Los Tigres. When they get it right, the band appears to "read" the migrants' mind and receives informal endorsement to speak on the migrants' behalf.

At the same time, Los Tigres also play to people's romantic notion of themselves. Their audience connects with the music because their corridos usually depict the common person as a hero.

Ramón Pérez writes of how a novice coyote, having successfully led his first migration journey to the United States, could relate to and assume the identity of the coyote depicted in the songs of Los Tigres del Norte:

The drivers arrive, those who days earlier had carried the first load of us. They seem haughty and high-spirited, especially the one who had made his maiden trip. . . . The novice asks Chuco to lend him his cassette player, then takes a cassette still wrapped in cellophane from his pants pocket. The cassette is of Los Tigres del Norte singing corridos, or ballads, about smugglers. The novice puts the tape player to his ears, then pulls a ten-dollar bill from his pocket and orders one of his companions to go buy a six-pack of beer.[17]

The corridos of Los Tigres del Norte appeal mainly to working-class Mexicans, most likely because their songs depict the daily struggles of this group. They are usually based on an ordinary person, someone who encounters a particular situation and is then transformed into a hero, whether a survivor or a martyr. The songs introduce listeners to situations in someone else's life that are similar to their own. They can identify and empathize with the central character and relate to the moral of the story.[18]

A corrido with a migrant protagonist, for example, will speak both to unauthorized migrants residing in the United States and to potential migrants listening in Mexico as they consider crossing unauthorized into the United States. The migrants established in the United States may have suffered like the corrido's protagonist or at least will come to understand that they were fortunate not to have. For potential migrants, the corridos provide clues as to how to avoid dangers; ideally, they make migrants more aware of the risks. Thus the migrant David in chapter 2 mentions a song that taught him never to pay his coyote before crossing.

These messages of risk and danger in music often contrast with the constructed stories of success created by migrants who return to impress family and friends back in their hometown. Los Tigres are relaying an important alternative message: things do not always work out as planned, migrants should be careful because unauthorized migration to the United States is not as easy as it may appear from a distance, and any one of them could become the next border death.

Pacto de sangre: Mingling Life and Fiction

Los Tigres del Norte's emotive portrayal of risk, danger, and the personal experience of unauthorized migration is nowhere better exemplified than on their album *Pacto de sangre*, released on May 30, 2004, which debuted at number one on the Billboard Top Latin Albums chart.[19] It is a compilation of 14 songs, three of which are dedicated to unauthorized migration: "José Pérez León," "El niño de la calle" (Street Kid), and "El santo de los mojados" (Patron Saint of Wetbacks).

This album continues Los Tigres' tradition of revealing and openly discussing the most secret aspects of Mexican society: the drugs, corruption, violence and, in particular, the risks associated with unauthorized migration. They bring these issues out of the shadows. As Los Tigres' Hernán Hernández says, "Maybe a song can't resolve a problem, but you can at least let people know about what's not being done. More people can hear a song than will read a newspaper."[20]

The title *Pacto de sangre* itself has multiple layers of meaning. Los Tigres' Luis Hernández says it reflects the strong and emotional connection between the band and its fans both in Mexico and in the United States—it is a blood tie to the homeland.[21] It is also a pact, a two-way agreement, where Los Tigres del Norte, as activists, promise to address the tough issues if the audience will lobby for change. The "blood" relates back to the principal theme of the album: border violence and death. On another level, it reflects the band members, who are all blood related: four brothers and a cousin.[22]

On *Pacto de sangre*, Los Tigres del Norte introduce listeners to the death of a migrant in "José Pérez León," to the life of a street kid in a border city in "El niño de la calle," and to the prayers of a migrant in "El santo de los mojados." Through these emotive personal stories, the band provides both insight into the lives of the "voiceless" unauthorized migrants and accounts of the little-discussed and often unforeseen risks and consequences of unauthorized migration. They bring life back to the often-dehumanized, constructed identity of the "migrant." The corridos of Los Tigres provoke an emotional response in their listeners, raising awareness of the risks of unauthorized migration. With that in mind, let us see how the three migration-related corridos in *Pacto de sangre* inform societal dialogue on the escalating risks to Mexican unauthorized migrants crossing the U.S.–Mexico border.

Humanizing the "Migrant" Identity. Crossing a border is more than a physical journey; it is part of a psychological transformation of self. A migrant's understanding of self is challenged when, suddenly, the migrant is subject to a whole new categorization system that automatically defines and establishes the migrant's identity within the context of life in the new country.[23]

This new identity is troubling because unauthorized migrants are either invisible to mainstream U.S. citizens or classified by them as a menace. The moment they leave home, they become "migrants." When they successfully cross the border, the United States deems them to be "illegal aliens." If caught by the U.S. Border Patrol, they are "detainees" and become deportation statistics, or if they die on their journey, they become part of the migrant death toll. Dead or alive, the individual migrants are lost in policy and statistics.[24]

One of the most important and powerful features of the corridos of Los Tigres del Norte is that they strive to reestablish the personal identity of migrants, to tell their stories. This is achieved by creating composite stories, narratives that draw on a number of experiences to create one fictitious identity. On the album *Pacto de sangre*, the three migration-related corridos ("José Pérez León," "El niño de la calle" and "El santo de los mojados") use this technique to establish a narrative that the listener can both relate to and learn from.

The protagonist of *Pacto de sangre*'s feature single is José Pérez León, a nineteen-year-old country boy from the state of Nuevo León. When his distant cousin, an unauthorized migrant already working in the United States, tells him he knows of work picking cotton there, José bids his wife farewell and leaves for the United States. At the border, he seeks out the "most renowned" coyote and strikes a deal: he will be smuggled across the border by train. The next day, he unquestioningly gets into a boxcar with other migrants. They cross the border, but, because the boxcar is sealed shut, after several hours, they run out of air and all of them suffocate. José leaves behind his wife, who, unbeknownst to him, is pregnant with his child. The narrative ends by reflecting that José is just another Mexican with hopes and dreams who has died trying to get to the United States.

Los Tigres based their song on a real person. Sifting through interviews with Los Tigres del Norte and news articles revealed that real person to be José Antonio Villaseñor León, one of eighteen unauthorized migrants who died of asphyxiation inside a refrigerated semitruck in Texas in May of 2003.[25] The song is certainly a moving tribute to this young man, but his story is both more tragic and more gruesome than the corrido suggests.

According to his mother, Cristina León Soto, José Antonio Villaseñor León was a 31-year-old taxi driver who, up until the week of his death, lived in a small apartment in Netzahualcóyotl City, which borders on Mexico City. His wife had left him four months before, and he was struggling to raise their five-year-old son, Marco.[26]

The Tuesday before his death, José Antonio visited his mother and sister to announce that he and Marco were leaving for the United States. He had sold all his possessions, including his taxi, in order to pay a coyote to cross them. He wanted his son to have a better education and hoped his luck would improve in the United States. The next Monday, he called his mother to let her know that he and Marco had safely made it across the border and were about to get into a semitruck that would take them to Houston. Later, when survivors of the tragic incident described how one migrant tried to lift his young son up to an air hole, his mother realized that her son and grandson were dead.[27] According to his affidavit, the truck driver had heard a woman screaming "¡El niño!" (The boy!) over and over, almost certainly referring to the suffering and death of the youngest victim, Marco Antonio Villaseñor Acuña.[28]

There are several differences between the life of José Antonio Villaseñor León and that of the fictitious José Pérez León. In contrast to the popular image of the young and naive country boy from northern Mexico, Villaseñor León was from a populous suburb just beyond the outskirts of Mexico City and had already fathered a five-year-old son, who would die in the incident. Far from having the close and loving relationship portrayed in the corrido, Villaseñor León was estranged from his wife. What is more, father and son died in a truck after safely arriving in the United States, not in a railroad boxcar during the border crossing.

The character and the tale of José Pérez León were developed from the interplay between real, imagined, and musical elements. To set the rhythmic tone of the corrido, the songwriter chose a train rather than a truck. The accordion, a traditional instrument in música norteña, mimics a train whistle blowing, while the drums and bass tap the beat of a train moving along the rails. Together, this builds the slow and steady rhythmic basis of the song. Los Tigres' Raúl Hernández explains that the beat was carefully selected to convey the song's feeling: "It tells a story about someone who comes to the U.S. but in a different way. The subject doesn't show anger, he's more nostalgic. It made us sad when we first listened to it. So we came up with the idea of using a less aggressive beat. We tried to make the song be that way with accordion, bajo sexto and flutes."[29]

Even the decision to replace "Villaseñor" with "Pérez" appears to have been strategic. The most comprehensive article on this incident appeared in the *Washington Post* on May 16, 2003. Journalists Mary Jordan and Kevin Sullivan interviewed the family of Villaseñor León and a local by the name of Ricardo Pérez, who, despite the news of the recent deaths, was saving money to pay a coyote to take him to Texas.[30] Los Tigres and their songwriter may well have seen this same article and selected Pérez to represent the thousands of prospective migrants who would continue to risk their lives.

Alternatively, because Pérez is the Spanish equivalent of "Smith," they may have chosen this name to protect the name of the actual victim while representing a "common man." An unauthorized migrant informant in Grace Halsell's migration study, for example, uses "Pérez" as an alias when captured by the U.S. Border Patrol.[31] As for the content of the lyrics, changes have been made to the actual life story of José Antonio Villaseñor León, most likely for dramatic effect. Thus José was made considerably younger than José Antonio to tap into the sympathy commonly felt when the deceased is young and beginning life. José Pérez León had only just become an adult and started to make a family; he did not even know that his wife was pregnant. With these changes, the songwriter captures the suffering caused by family fragmentation: José's life was lost and his wife was left with a child to raise alone. Why did this happen? He was trying to grow up and take on his responsibilities by going to the United States to work, earn money, and create a better life for his family. This is indeed tragic.

What is remarkable, however, is that the death of José Pérez León is not as tragic as the death of José Antonio Villaseñor León. For one thing, both José Antonio and his son died of suffocation. More tragically still, José Antonio had tried to save his son by holding him up to an air hole but had been unsuccessful. The truth may have been too much for the corrido's audience to bear, and it would also be offensive to the surviving family, who would be forced to continually relive the gruesome deaths whenever they heard the song being broadcast, as it would be almost everywhere in Mexico.

José Pérez León, from Nuevo León, is a country boy. Although traditionally migrants tended to come from rural areas and worked in agriculture in the United States, today's migrants, like Villaseñor León, are often from urban areas and work in the service industries of U.S. cities rather than in the fields.[32] But, knowing that nostalgia plays an important role in keeping their fans happy, Los Tigres del Norte chose to make their corrido hero José a country boy.

Corridos and Composite Characters. José Cantoral, songwriter for Los Tigres, carefully selected fragments of real life to create "José Pérez

León." This interplay between real events and fictitious characters in corridos raises the question, why would songwriters construct these often complex composite characters?

Essentially, the creation of a composite migrant character allows the songwriter to focus on risk and its consequences in a way that is both highly believable and highly sympathetic. For prospective migrants, it provides information on situations whose high potential risk, however unlikely, may not justify the migration journey.

Again, in "Niño de la calle," songwriter Luis Torres tells the tale of the many children of the border by introducing the listener to a ten-year-old boy brought to a border town by his parents. His father, just like Villaseñor León, wanted to migrate the impoverished family to the United States so the children would have a better start in life, and the opportunity to get an education. On the journey, the boy's sister dies, and his mother also dies a little later, at the border. His father leaves for the United States, never to be seen again. The child suspects that his father has died because this is easier to face than that his father has abandoned him. The child now earns his keep working as a fire-eating circus clown in the streets of the border city.

Based in Tijuana, Luis Torres could create this corrido by extracting one clear and logical story from thousands of stories and media articles on border life.[35] His eloquent and moving account of one migrant presents Los Tigres' listeners with a character to which they can relate and emotionally respond.

The Subtext in Los Tigres del Norte's Corridos

Portrayals of the negative consequences of migration in corridos provide messages, sometimes subtle, on the risks of unauthorized migration. In "José Pérez León," for example, Pérez León dies because he does not question the decision of the coyote to lock him into the boxcar and because he chose the "most renowned" coyote at the border. In "Niño de la calle," there is the general warning about the potential consequences of risk to children with the underlying message that migrant parents should leave their children at home while the parents are working in the United States. By crossing their children, they subject them to greater danger and their families to greater risk of fragmentation.

In contrast to "José Pérez León" and "Niño de la calle," the third corrido, "El santo de los mojados," is a generalized presentation of the threats facing unauthorized migrants. In this corrido, the central character is a migrant sharing his prayer for protection before embarking on his migration journey. He asks the patron saint of migration to "let your shadow blind those who chase us, / those who try unsuccessfully to stop us. / Protect us, Lord, in . . . the deserts, / so that there will be no more deaths from heat or cold. We are in danger of losing our lives / but we can't stay here, there is no other choice. / Saint Peter, Patron Saint of All Wetbacks, / please grant us the legalization / of undocumented migrants."[33]

This corrido presents the risks of unauthorized migration so that they may be considered before undertaking the journey. The song clearly states that death is an all-too-possible outcome of unauthorized migration. As the migrant prays, he is indirectly warning other potential migrants of the physical dangers of the crossing and the danger of attack by criminals.

The corrido justifies taking the risk of unauthorized migration by stating that the migrants have no other choice, thus implying that those who stay in Mexico face greater risks, perhaps especially the risk of not being able to feed their families. The migrant's prayer for legalization implies that U.S. border policy is to blame for most of the risks of unauthorized migration.

The migrant's prayer brings to mind the important role of religion in Mexican culture. Migrants commonly rely on their religion and faith to help them cope with the risks of unauthorized migration. Thus researcher Oscar Martínez found that unauthorized migrants believed that their crossing would be successful and safe because a religious figure, Saint Lorenzo, "blinded" the U.S. Border Patrol. "I said to myself, 'Go to hell with your six months. I'm not coming back,'" one of Martínez's informants told him, "I called my sister and said, 'Those devils denied me the pasaporte. But I'm going to get back to El Paso.' I then prayed to San Lorenzo. I have a lot of faith in him. Whenever I find myself in trouble, I go to him. I said, 'San Lorencito, if you put blinders on those *viejos* [the immigration officers] I will take you some candles.' That afternoon at five I crossed at the same spot where all the viejos were. They didn't notice me. I said, 'American' and San Lorenzo helped me. I crossed without any problem."[34]

Many migrants feel they will be better protected and more likely to cross successfully if they pray. Prayer and faith may seem to be a viable risk reduction strategy because they lower migrants' perceptions of danger and break down some of the psychological barriers to migration, thus enabling the migrants to continue on their journey.

Los Tigres del Norte: Part of the "Culture" of Migration

The corridos of Los Tigres del Norte have a powerful place within migration culture. Politicians and the media talk about "illegal aliens," which dehumanizes and demonizes unauthorized immigrants.[36] By contrast, Los Tigres sing about credible characters developed from composite identities based on real life. To Los Tigres del Norte, unauthorized migrants are people who experience the consequences of their actions.

For many years, Los Tigres have responded to the risks of unauthorized migration by singing corridos based on a central character who faces adversities and becomes a hero or a martyr. They have humanized the Mexican unauthorized migrant and experiences of risk by evoking an emotional, empathetic response in their listeners. At the same time, the composite characters of their corridos blend aspects of traditional migration narratives with the news and events of the time. Embedded in the lyrics are indirect cautionary messages, such as the one about hiring "renowned" coyotes at the border in "José Pérez León," that provide some insight not only into why migrants are suffering but also into how they might avoid this suffering by making different decisions.

Over time, Los Tigres del Norte have contributed a consistent, migrant-centered perspective on the risks of unauthorized migration. They have focused on raising awareness of the risks by encouraging their audience to empathize with those who run those risks.

"Frijolero": A Molotov Cocktail Thrown into the Debate

In contrast to the corridos of Los Tigres del Norte, Molotov's song "Frijolero" is a critique of the United States' political and diplomatic relationship with Mexico. Through its popular songs, rock band Molotov presents examples of situations where U.S. attitudes and actions, including the U.S. War on Drugs and War on Terror, negatively affect unauthorized Mexican migrants. The lyrics of "Frijolero" address the broader issues affecting the diplomatic relationship between Mexico and the United States and serve to highlight the complexities of political negotiations and their effects, both direct and indirect, on migration policies.

That Molotov's gringo band member Randy Ebright wrote this severe critique of the contemporary United States is perhaps the greatest irony of "Frijolero." "The words to 'Frijolero' came to me when I was with my wife and daughter," Ebright explains, "[on our way to visit] my family in Michigan. . . . At immigration in Miami, we had to stand on separate lines, and I felt like we were being treated differently. They were looking at my daughter, like, why does she have two last names? What is this Latino name?"[37]

On one level, this song is about discrimination and migration, as experienced by the American songwriter and his Mexican wife and daughter. But Ebright has molded this incident to reflect the common Mexican experience of unauthorized migration. Other issues Ebright chooses to raise in "Frijolero" reflect his life experience. Thus Ebright's father was part of a U.S. antidrug task force, which is how the musician originally came to live in Mexico.[38] With his insider's perspective, he mocks the U.S. government and takes a stand on policies dealing with migration, drugs, oil, and war. As much as "Frijolero" is about Mexicans, it is also one U.S. citizen's critique of his country's politics.

According to band member Tito Fuentes, the word *frijolero* has special significance beyond any literal translation as "beaner." "Frijolero" is "the most disrespectful word you can call a Latin American in the United States. . . . So, it's a type of confrontational humor in the vein of Sly & the Family Stone: 'Don't Call Me Nigger, Whitey'—'Don't Call Me Beaner, Gringo.'"[39]

This bilingual name-calling is more than a dialogue between the characters in the song. The deliberate lyrical reference to Sly & the Family Stone means that Molotov subtly incorporates the commentaries of these musicians into its song. In the end, however, the song is very much Molotov's take on risk and unauthorized migration, inspired by personal experience, but informed by public debate and cultural knowledge. "Molotov is not everyone's cup of tea," writes music critic Ramiro Burr. "But on the set's lead single—the polka-rock-hued 'Frijolero,' with lyrics attacking the U.S. over Iraq and immigration—Molotov certainly has its fingers on the pulse of Mexico. The song's stance mirrors polls that show most Mexicans oppose a war with Iraq and favor open immigration to the U.S."[40]

"Frijolero" struck a chord not only with Mexicans at home but also with those living in the United States. Molotov was nominated for four Grammys at the Fourth Annual Latin American Grammy awards: Record of the Year and Best Rock Album by a Duo or Group; Best Rock Song and Best Video for "Frijolero." The band was awarded Video of the Year, Best Group or Duo, Alternative Artist, and Best Mexican Artist at the 2003 MTV Latin Music Awards.[41] The members of Molotov carefully crafted the tune, lyrics, and music video of "Frijolero" to present their perspective on unauthorized migration; the song's popularity testifies to the success of their efforts.

The Melody: Creating a Mood to Convey a Message

Just as rap music often takes snippets of tunes from previously popular songs and rearranges them into something new, so, too, Molotov took sounds and sentiments from música norteña songs and rearranged them to create "Frijolero." Based on European polka music, música norteña was introduced into Mexico in the mid-nineteenth century. It can be played at set venues, events, or, more commonly, on a "pay per song" basis, with the band (most often all men) moving along the streets of the restaurant and bar district of a town. The songs, mostly corridos, are played on the accordion, the signature instrument of música norteña, accompanied by a single standing drum, double bass, and, on occasion, additional instruments such as the guitar or clarinet.[42]

In the case of "Frijolero," by combining an accordion with an electric guitar within an alternative pop musical structure, the song invokes and refers to, without actually being, música norteña. "A mournful polka-rock that at first sounds like music by Los Tigres del Norte," writes Burr, "'Frijolero' unleashes a barrage of racial epithets directed at Americans and Mexicans."[43]

The reference to Los Tigres del Norte is significant. Because Los Tigres have long been well known for their musical commentary on border life, it is not surprising that Molotov has been influenced by them. Molotov's use of música norteña acknowledges the important role that this musical style has played in shaping Mexican society's understanding of migration issues, and pays tribute to one of the corrido genre's most successful bands.[44]

The melody of "Frijolero" is indeed mournful, with repetitive phrases that only build up energy at the chorus. It is complemented by lyrics arranged into eight verses, six in Spanish and two in English, and a chorus incorporating both English and Spanish.

The Lyrics: Speaking Out on Mexican Rights

The simple fact that some lyrics are in English and others are in Spanish is meaningful. Brad Kava even goes so far as to suggest that it is part of a "border-dissolving trend," a political strategy employed by Molotov to encourage greater connectedness between Mexicans and Americans at the border, and to reduce stereotyping and misperceptions of "other."[45]

The lyrics are delivered using not only both English and Spanish but also particular accents to portray specific characters and to convey specific messages. Thus Molotov uses gringo-accented Spanish to mimic and mock Americans.[46] Marginalized people sometimes strategically employ mimicry and mockery as an attention-seeking tool.[47] Shifting into English, the "Americans" in the song drawl.[48] Ebright's drawl characterizes "the racist" and suggests that Southerners, perhaps especially Texans, are more racist than the general U.S. population. Aaron Wherry would seem to concur, noting that "Frijolero" explores the tension between Texans and Mexican unauthorized workers.[49]

For the purposes of this discussion, all lyrics are provided in English, with those translated from the Spanish italicized. Some Spanish lyrics are sung in a strongly American-accented Spanish while some English lyrics are drawled. Molotov uses these vocal and linguistic tools strategically, to emphasize different aspects of its argument. The lyrics are discussed in the context of U.S. border policy and Mexican unauthorized migration to the United States at the time of this single's release (2003).

Verse 1 of "Frijolero" is a declaration of defiance: "*I've had it up to here with them putting a sombrero on me, / so listen when I tell you, don't call me 'beaner.'*" Mexicans are angry with Americans who characterize them as sombrero-wearing bean eaters. They demand to be listened to, rather than stereotyped. As Paul Rich and Guillermo De Los Reyes tell us, Mexicans have long felt that Americans consider them to be poor, lazy, backward, and dishonest. Indeed, the stereotypical Mexican has a firmly established place in the world's political mythology.[50] The result, as the Mexican representative to the United Nations once put it, is that Mexico is treated as "America's backyard," a dumping ground, which does not (or cannot) defend itself.[51] For Mexicans living in the United States, particularly unauthorized migrants, there are few opportunities to speak up.[52]

According to Americas Watch, because stereotyping dehumanizes and, in the case of unauthorized migrants, indirectly validates their mistreatment, it can be physically dangerous. "'Tonk' is the word used [by U.S. Border Patrol agents] to refer to an undocumented immigrant," the group's 1993 report on migration reads, "and refers to the sound of an agent's flashlight striking an immigrant's head."[53]

Labeling the migrant a "tonk" implies that you have heard the sound of a flashlight hitting a migrant, or that such a sound would be permissible within the border control culture.[54] "Frijolero" speaks out against the stereotype of the "sombrero-wearing beaner" and the potential violence that goes with it.

Verse 2 addresses the diplomatic relationship between the United States and Mexico at a foreign policy level: "*And although there is some respect and we don't interfere, / we never inflate our currency by making war with other countries.*" At the foreign policy level, there is a basic agreement between the United States and Mexico to coexist as neighbors, an understanding that neither country should interfere in the daily domestic activities of the other. This has always been a point of conflict, particularly because Mexico feels that the United States regularly shows disrespect for its autonomy. While "Frijolero" was receiving considerable airplay, these lyrics uncannily seemed to mirror events at the time, taking the message far beyond the idea originally conceived by Molotov.

As a member of the U.N. Security Council in March 2003, Mexico was required to vote on whether the proposed U.S. invasion of Iraq was justified. The vote put Mexico in an extremely difficult position. Mexico's leaders could either follow the spirit of the Mexican Constitution, which states that Mexico should not participate in wars beyond its boundaries, or support the United States, its neighbor and principal trading partner (approximately 85 percent of Mexico's exports go to the United States).[55] There was also considerable pressure from the European Union for Mexico not to support the war.[56]

Some Mexicans feared retribution if their country were to vote against the United States, in particular a backlash against unauthorized migrants, tightening of border controls, or unofficial trade sanctions.[57] In the end, Mexico did indeed vote against the United States because the Mexican public clamored against "making war with other countries," especially a war based on economic benefits for the United States.[58]

Verse 3 speaks about the complex economic interrelationship between Mexico and the United States: "*We pay interest on our debt with petroleum, / meanwhile, we don't know who ends up with the change.*" Hikes in oil prices during the 1980s raised Mexico's foreign debt to exorbitant levels.[59] The situation has been made worse by corruption within Mexico and the United States: profits from petroleum have been siphoned away into private bank accounts rather than channeled into clearing Mexican national debt.

At the economic level, some Mexican unauthorized migration to the United States can be explained in terms of "push" and "pull" factors. Poverty in Mexico as the country of origin combines with the perceived strong economy of the United States as the receiving country to "push" migrants from their homeland and "pull" them across the border.[60] In principle, unauthorized migration by Mexicans to the United States would cease if there were no disparity between the Mexican and U.S. economies.[61] Economic policy is particularly pertinent to any discussion of unauthorized migration because when U.S. policies hinder economic development in Mexico, more Mexicans are likely to migrate unauthorized to the United States, thus exacerbating the supposed U.S. migration problem.

Molotov also realizes that oil has long been a bargaining chip for migration discussions. In May of 2003, U.S. legislators wanted to trade Mexican petroleum for policy reform on unauthorized migration. Legislators suggested that if Mexico were to privatize the government petroleum company (PEMEX) to allow for U.S. investment, the United States would begin addressing the issue of unauthorized migration and rights for Mexican workers in the United States.[62] Thus U.S. legislators were treating Mexican workers as a commodity or political token, to be traded like oil.

Verse 4 is an indictment of the U.S. War on Drugs: "*Even though you give us a reputation as dealers of the drugs we grow, / It's you who are the consumers.*" Like unauthorized migrants, drugs are often considered to be an undesirable Mexican import that the U.S. government should try to keep out despite high demand for them among the U.S. population.[63] When the United States declared a War on Drugs, it put Mexico under considerable pressure to control drug-related activities even as it almost entirely ignored drug consumption and money laundering by drug dealers within its own borders. "Frijolero" berates the United States for blaming its social problems on Mexico.

Inadvertently, the U.S. War on Drugs has also exacerbated the risks that unauthorized migrants face at the border. The heightened efforts by the United States at smuggler detection along the border make it much more difficult for unauthorized migrants to successfully cross, forcing them to shift to more remote desert areas where there is less likelihood of detection, but greater risk of exposure to the elements.[64]

The chorus caricatures cross-border dialogue between Mexicans and Americans: "Don't call me gringo, you fuckin' beaner, / stay on your side of that goddamn river, / Don't call me gringo, you fuckin' beaner." / *"Don't you call me beaner, Mr. Asshole, / I'll scare you for being racist and an asshole, / Don't you call me beaner, you goddamn American asshole."* The American implies that Mexicans have no rights to be in the United States and should stay on their side of the river. This is a direct reference to the Rio Grande at the U.S.–Mexico border, renowned for unauthorized crossings by Mexicans into the United States, which gave rise to the term "wetbacks," because unauthorized migrants would arrive wet from their river crossing.[65]

The Mexican responds with machismo by threatening the American and calling him "Mr. Asshole." The juxtaposition of a term of respect (Mr.) with an insult (asshole) most likely alludes to the need for unauthorized migrants to show respect for their U.S. employers (and U.S. society) even while feeling contempt for them due to injustice and the mistreatment they have received in the United States. The Mexican then fantasizes about seeking justice, about asserting authority over the American, scaring him as a punishment for his racist behavior.

Verse 5, in English, presents the suffering of unauthorized migrants: "Now I wish I had a dime for every single time / I've gotten stared down, For being in the wrong side of town. / And a rich man I'd be if I had that kind of chips / lately I wanna smack the mouths of these racists." Racism, the verse implies, is a common experience for Mexicans in the United States. Once in the United States, unauthorized migrants, largely confined to Hispanic neighborhoods, may face either physical or psychological threats "for being in the wrong side of town." Marginalized, migrant workers are vulnerable to exploitation by employers.[66] But speaking up under these circumstances only heightens the risk of deportation.[67] Verse 6 talks about one of the commonest risks of unauthorized migration, family separation and fragmentation: *"As an outsider, can you imagine being a Mexican crossing the border, / thinking about your family as you cross, leaving everything you know behind?"* Migrants risk not seeing their families for extended periods of time because of the cost and potential consequences of the return crossing[68]—or even forever, should they die. Some migrants become trapped in border towns with no money either to cross again or to return home.

Though Verse 6 asks Americans to imagine leaving their family, language, and culture in order to get a job, to empathize with the "outsider," and to see the migration experience from a human perspective, because the verse is entirely in Spanish, it is in fact targeted at the migrants themselves. It validates their experiences by voicing their issues even when they are still not in a position to speak out on their own behalf.

Verse 7 raises the controversial issue of racial attacks on unauthorized migrants: "*If it were you who had to avoid the bullets of some American ranchers, / Would you still say* 'good-for-nothing wetback'? / *if it were you who had to start from zero?*" Paramilitary activity has increased in Arizona since Operation Gatekeeper was implemented in California. Illegal border crossings have shifted from urban centers to less patrolled sectors of the border. Although some of the attacks on migrants are carried out by locals overwhelmed by migrant numbers and wishing to protect their property, most appear to be by unsupervised militant groups or individuals who patrol remote areas along the border and take the law into their own hands.[69] In 2000, for example, it was reported that "at least two Mexicans have been killed, and seven wounded by gangs patrolling the arid badlands of Arizona's Cochise County to round up Mexicans searching for more prosperous lives. Some ranchers have declared publicly that they are 'hunting' the Mexicans 'for sport.'"[70] Evidence of these attacks is almost entirely limited to the material documented by human rights groups (government and civil society), constrained by the requirement that the unauthorized migrant victims come forward, thereby risking deportation.[71]

In a report by the Comisión Nacional de Derechos Humanos, of 23,408 unauthorized migrants surveyed from September 1988 to August 1990, nearly 14 percent said they had been physically assaulted while in the United States. The report also documented, in the same time period, 117 cases of human rights violations at the hands of U.S. law enforcement officers. Sixteen incidents resulted in death of an unauthorized migrant. The U.S. Border Patrol was implicated in almost 60 percent of the cases.[72]

U.S. Border Patrol agents have a legal right to shoot at unauthorized migrants in self-defense, but, at times, they are accused of being overzealous.[73] Americas Watch documented one case where a U.S. Border Patrol agent shot indiscriminately into a crowd of 30 migrants. It still took several other random incidents and the shooting death of an unarmed migrant for this agent to be brought to the attention of his superiors.

In some cases, there may be a fine line between the racist rancher and the overzealous law enforcement officer. This is of particular concern when, historically, the trend has been to increase the Border Patrol's law enforcement powers without increasing its accountability.[74]

Verse 7 reminds listeners that the "enemy" are Mexican workers who have left their homeland and are starting from scratch in the United States. It asks whether, having risked their lives to get a job, these Mexican should be put down as "good-for-nothing wetbacks." Although Molotov may overstate the actual risk of attacks on migrants by ranchers, the powerful image of the "redneck" attacker effectively illustrates the dehumanization of migrants at the border and the dangerous situation that migration puts them in.

Verse 8 challenges American assertions of sovereignty: "Now why don't you look down to where your feet are planted / That U.S. soil that makes you take shit for granted / If not for Santa Anna, just to let you know / That where your feet are planted would be Mexico / ¡*Correcto!*" The U.S. occupation of Mexico City in 1848 led to López de Santa Anna agreeing to sell one-third of Mexico's territory in return for the withdrawal of U.S. troops and a signed peace between the two nations. Mexico's population and the 300,000 "instant" Mexican-Americans living on the ceded land did not readily accept the resulting Treaty of Guadalupe Hidalgo. They considered Santa Anna a traitor. Not only was the treaty "imposed" after a humiliating defeat but, shortly after it went into effect, it was revealed that the United States had known there were gold deposits on the land it was to acquire and had not informed Mexico. Mexicans felt they had been tricked into "giving" their gold to the United States.[75]

Even though the land was ceded more than a century ago, some Mexicans and Mexican Americans do not accept the treaty as legitimate. They argue that unauthorized migrants are not "illegal" and that all Mexicans have an intrinsic right to inhabit what is now the southwestern portion of the United States.[76] Verse 8's "¡Correcto!" (Right!) suggests that Molotov thinks this view is correct, that only by an unfair twist of fate does the United States "own" the land that many Mexicans struggle to reach.

Overall, the lyrics of "Frijolero" present Mexico's struggle to gain respect in the eyes of Americans. Though angry at being dehumanized by racist stereotyping, Mexicans feel powerless to stand up for their rights because they are economically dependent on the United States, both as resident unauthorized migrants and in Mexico, where they must pay back the debt their country owes the Americans. In emphasizing that

Mexico does not interfere with U.S. domestic policy, Molotov implies that the reverse is clearly not true.

The Music Video: Visual Messages and Complex Meanings

There is one additional tool that visually represents the music and lyrics, contributing to the audience's overall understanding of the song—the music video.[77] Filmed in Austin, Texas, the original digital video images of "Frijolero" were then converted into a cartoonlike format so the people would appear as caricatures.[78] Presenting musicians as characters in a fantasy world has been a successful trend in music videos.[79] Besides attracting attention, entertaining, promoting the song, and earning MTV and Latin Grammy awards, Molotov's music video helped clarify the more complicated concepts in "Frijolero."

The video begins with an image of the Mexican flag overlaid with the word *Molotov* and the tattooed buttocks of a young woman wearing a G-string (scene 1). The camera zooms in on the tattoo and it begins to move. The moving image fills the screen and becomes Molotov (all four members side by side) waking up and getting out of a large bed (scene 2).

The camera is drawn into the eye of one band member, Paco Ayala, and comes out the eye of another, Tito Puentes, wearing a cowboy hat and sitting in a pickup truck. Cowboy Puentes approaches the U.S. side of the border wall, where three Mexicans—the other members of Molotov—are depicted in the colors of the Mexican flag (red, white, and green). The cowboy sticks his hand out the window of his pickup truck and, using his fingers, signals for the Mexicans to join him (scene 3).

The three jump in the back of his pickup truck, where they begin to sing the song's lyrics and play the guitar and the accordion (scene 4). Little by little, viewers see more of the landscape around the moving pickup truck. There are two hills with defined peaks that appear to be women's breasts (scene 5).

Rising up between the "hills" is Mexican President Fox in a suit, followed by the Devil and George W. Bush (both of whom are wearing nothing but Y-front underwear). They all proceed to hug, as American flags, dollar sign–emblazoned red, white, and blue missiles, and then oil barrels fall toward the ground (scene 6). The camera then returns to the three Molotov Mexicans singing and playing their instruments in the back of the pickup truck (scene 7).

A green U.S. Border Patrol wagon pulls alongside the cowboy's pickup. The officer at the wheel, who is wearing dark sunglasses and has a mustache, proceeds to sing the English part of the chorus (scene 8). All four members of Molotov then sing the Mexican response as children on bicycles, giving the finger to the U.S. Border Patrol officer as they ride by a colonial-style Catholic Church. A choir of identical schoolgirls fills the screen and sings the rest of the chorus. Suddenly, a piñata with band member Ayala's face on it drops down in front of the schoolgirls. As the girls are about to take a swing at it, the piñata swears (scene 9).

Molotov is seen standing by the border wall again, its members all in Mexican colors (scene 10). Four U.S. Border Patrol agents chase them along the border wall into a town, where a man is walking down the street. As they run along a brick wall with a large red high heel shoe painted on it, a skull drives by them in a car (scene 11).

The U.S. Border Patrol apprehends Molotov against the border wall, but, as the camera zooms out, the backdrop changes to a "Caution" sign showing people running (scene 12). Three members of Molotov change into silhouettes in the colors of the Mexican flag with their hands tied behind them. They get into a U.S. Border Patrol wagon, where the fourth band member, Micky Huidobro, dressed as General Santa Anna with his hands also tied, has already been detained (scene 13).

The officers in the U.S. Border Patrol wagon then sing the English chorus while driving by a row of women in military uniform doing the can-can. These women turn into Molotov doing the can-can in front of the U.S. Border Patrol vehicle (scene 14). The camera cuts to the faces of Molotov on a can bearing a picture of refried beans but labeled "Refried Molotov." It is only one of many cans stacked in a supermarket. A customer in a gas mask and protective outfit puts several cans into a shopping cart. The wire in the shopping cart changes into a wire fence, presumably along the border (scene 15).

A U.S. Border Patrol officer is patrolling the border on horseback. Behind him is the image of a setting sun and, superimposed on it, the image of Molotov band members playing their instruments (scene 16). At a broken part of the border fence (presumably in Mexico), Molotov reappears, doing the can-can with the military girls as a plane tows an unreadable message across the sky (scene 17). The camera then focuses on the band members changing again and again into different people and iconic images—the U.S. Border Patrol, the shopper in the gas mask, the little choirgirls, the Day of the Dead skull, the Devil, and, finally, a balloon—before coming back as the caricatures of themselves giving the finger (scene 18). The camera zooms out, returning to the woman's buttocks. She pulls up her pants and the Mexican flag appears with "Molotov" written in the middle of it (scene 19).

The music video's principal narrative is combined with images that provide contextual information, like parentheses in language, although there are also some that do not build toward an overall conceptual understanding of "Frijolero." The video exhibits the characteristics of most successful, that is, most highly popular, ones: combining a performance by the musicians with a narrative, it also includes perplexing images that are designed to maintain the interest of the audience beyond the first viewing.[80] Our discussion focuses on key facets of the principal narrative and on images that serve as contextual parentheses, passing over those designed only to hold the viewers' attention (the tattoo on the woman's buttocks, the "hills" that mimic a woman's breasts, the plane towing an unreadable message across the sky, the military can-can women), but which are not relevant to their understanding of Molotov's message on Mexican unauthorized migration.

In the principal narrative (comprising scenes 2, 3, 4, 10, 11, 12, 13, and 17), unauthorized migrants (played by Molotov) work illegally in the United States, are spotted by the U.S. Border Patrol, apprehended, and deported back to Mexico. In the United States, it is common practice for day laborers to gather at unofficial sites, where they wait for employers to drive by and offer them a day's work. Scenes 2, 3, and 4 of the video depict a typical day for an unauthorized migrant. The members of Molotov wake up and gather where U.S. employers regularly hire unauthorized migrant workers. Offered work, like ordinary day laborers, they leave with an employer, who drives them to his farm for a day of work. This unregulated source of work is a popular choice for unauthorized migrant workers, who cannot legally enter the formal labor market.[81]

In scene 10, the members of Molotov are back at the wall waiting to be employed again, but, this time, they are spotted by the U.S. Border Patrol. They run away, as would any migrant with no legal right to be in the United States and therefore at risk of being deported back to Mexico. Molotov is chased (scene 11), apprehended (scene 12), and put inside the U.S. Border Patrol wagon (scene 13). The narrative resumes in scene 17 at a broken part of the border fence, where, back in Mexico after being processed and deported, the members of Molotov tease a lone U.S. Border Patrol officer and give the finger to America.

The principal narrative contrasts the complicity of the U.S. employer with the strict law enforcement of the U.S. Border Patrol. It implies that Mexicans will work illegally in the United States as long as Americans are willing to employ them. This is the video's take on Molotov's principal message: Americans say one thing but do another. In the lyrics, this same idea is expressed in the ironic statement "Don't call me gringo, you fuckin' beaner."

Visual parentheses (scenes 6, 8, 9, 11, 12, 13, 15, 16, 17, and 18) contain discrete ideas not obviously interlinked with the principal narrative or each other that help Molotov clarify its message and establish a common meaning for its audience. Thus, in dreamlike scene 6, Mexico's President Fox rises from behind the hills into the sky, where he is joined by U.S. President Bush and the Devil. The lyrics tell viewers about U.S. economic strategies based on war and oil, while the visuals show a friendship—an alliance—between Fox and Bush. Fox and Bush are then seen hugging the Devil.

Indeed, Presidents Fox and Bush had a close friendship that was well established before either of them took presidential office. At the Americas Summit in Mexico in January 2004, Bush stated, "Vicente Fox is a good friend, and he can tell me his opinion without losing our friendship."[82]

At times, the Mexican public has been suspicious that this friendship might have enabled the United States to take advantage of Mexico. The implication of Fox and Bush hugging the Devil is that neither man has good intentions or, at least, are not working together to achieve positive outcomes. Certainly, in terms of unauthorized migration, there has been little bilateral cooperation to address this issue. For more than sixty years, the migration of Mexicans to the United States has been a sensitive, but mostly avoided, issue on the bilateral agenda.[83] Daniel James goes so far as to call it a "conspiracy of silence," with neither the United States nor Mexico really addressing the issue.[84]

In scene 8 and again in scene 17, Molotov's drawled American lyrics become the voice of a U.S. Border Patrol officer. Allan Wall, like some other Americans, resented Molotov's presentation of the U.S. Border Patrol officer as an aggressive racist.[85] That said, as noted above, the U.S. Border Patrol has been repeatedly implicated in violating the human rights of unauthorized migrants.[86]

In scene 9, Molotov band members are depicted as children on bicycles taunting the U.S. Border Patrol officer (who is now off camera), with the iconic image of a Spanish colonial Catholic church behind them. The Catholic Church, as an institution, is fundamental to the Mexican way of life.[87] Nevertheless, the Church in Mexico neither condemns unauthorized migration as "illegal" behavior nor condones it; nor does it lobby against border policies that risk human life.[88] In contrast, the Church in the United States has been outspoken on migration and protecting the human rights of unauthorized migrants.[89]

In scene 11, a man, to all appearances an average American, is walking down the street while the U.S. Border Patrol chases the unauthorized migrants. That the man does not seem to notice the drama going on around him suggests that average Americans do not notice, or do not pay attention to, migration events within their communities. The video image jibes with the lyrics, which challenge Americans to imagine the plight of the unauthorized migrant. At the same moment, a skull drives by in a car. The skull motif is linked to the Mexican Day of the Dead, which commemorates and celebrates family members and friends who have died.[90] The lyrics talk about migrants risking a border crossing while thinking about their families. The skull is a visual reminder that not all migrants make it safely to the United States or, on their return, to their families back home.

In scene 12, the Molotov band members are apprehended against a large "Caution" sign, which reproduces a controversial San Diego highway sign near the border. Showing a man, woman, and child running, the sign is intended to warn drivers that unauthorized migrants may cross in front of them when attempting to enter the United States or to escape the U.S. Border Patrol. This widely reproduced border image appears on the album cover of *Pacto de sangre* and also on the replica border wall in Coyoacán, described in chapter 4 (see fig. 5.1). One Canadian reporter describes it as "similar to [traffic signs] alerting motorists to watch for playing children, wandering moose or fallen rocks. This one depicts a man, woman, and child fleeing. It is unclear whether the sign is meant to protect illegal migrants from speeding cars or motorists from denting their bumpers."[91] The image conveys a strong message of caution to the video's viewers. You, too, will be dehumanized, detained, or both if you decide to try to migrate to the United States.

When, in scene 13, three band members are put into the back of a U.S. Border Patrol vehicle with their hands tied, they encounter their fourth member, dressed as General Santa Anna and also with his hands tied. The implication, from the accompanying lyrics, is that Santa Anna

Figure 5.1 A depiction of a highway sign in use at San Ysidro on the replica border wall in Coyoacán.

metaphorically had his hands tied when dealing with the United States on the Treaty of Guadalupe Hidalgo, under which Mexico handed over much of what is today the U.S. Southwest.

By showing an American in a gas mask buying tins of "Refried Molotov," scene 15 mocks the large number of Americans buying safety equipment and stocking up after the terrorist attacks of September 11, 2001.[92] That the American is buying what looks like refried beans is a none-too-subtle allusion to the Mexicanization of the United States. Indeed, the dilemma for U.S. policy on Mexican migrants is that anti–Mexican migrant sentiments coexist with pro–Mexican food and culture sentiments, most notably in U.S. border communities.[93]

In the musical interlude, scene 16, reminiscent of the "lone cowboy" icon in American culture, a lone U.S. Border Patrol officer on horseback is patrolling the frontier, an apparently peaceful landscape. The scene suggests that decision makers in distant capital cities have little experience of border life and manage the border with romantic notions of the yesteryear rather than with current experience.[94]

In scene 18, the members of Molotov change into a series of "other" iconic stereotypes, including U.S. Border Patrol officers. With Molotov's cross-border name-calling lyrics in the background, the scene implies that these stereotypes, however interchangeable they might be, are of little help when addressing border management issues.

"Frijolero": The Human Consequences of U.S.–Mexico Politics

The name "Molotov" immediately evokes the notorious gasoline grenade first widely used by Soviet soldiers in World War II. Indeed, "Frijolero" is a "grenade" hurled into the debate over the escalating risks of unauthorized migration to the United States. Its lyrics are hard hitting; they criticize U.S. and Mexican politicians, U.S. law enforcement officers, and average Americans bluntly and harshly. They reflect Mexico's general discontent with the United States. Through its choice of música norteña, which is closely aligned with the Mexican migration experience, Molotov suggests that the racism Mexicans experience parallels that experienced by African Americans, with Sly & the Family Stone's "Don't Call Me Nigger, Whitey" replaced with "Don't call me gringo, beaner." Far from being a simple pop song, Molotov's "Frijolero" is a critical commentary on border politics and policies that focus on economic issues rather than on the risks and human consequences of the situations these policies create.

Music and the Risks of Migration

In 1998, Latin American music generated a profit of $570.8 million, one-third from within the United States.[95] Music has become a medium of communication between the Mexican homeland and Mexican migrant society in the United States. Successive generations of Mexican migrants in the United States share hybrid music with the homeland, for example, the urban bilingual rap that comes out of Los Angeles, music that reflects their Mexican, Chicano, and American culture. According to Deborah Pacini Hernández, "U.S. Latino musicians have rendered national borders irrelevant by routinely marketing their recordings and live performance tours to their ethnic/national cohorts no matter where they live. More importantly, fusing their 'home' communities' traditional genres with others they have encountered in their host society, some of which are themselves transplants."[96]

Music promotes shared cultural experiences beyond national boundaries. Migration is a defining point in an individual migrant's personal history. Cut off from the everyday life and the culture of their homeland, migrants establish a hybrid culture as they adjust to their host country. Eventually, they have little common experience with the homeland, which has changed and evolved without them.[97]

Sound has a unique capacity to provoke shared emotional reactions and establish common meaning at a basic level.[98] Music can maintain cultural identity, particularly for ethnic subcultures coexisting with a dominant foreign culture.[99] For Mexicans residing in the United States, music can promote stronger cultural ties with Mexico by providing insights into all facets of Mexican life. Moreover, a song that is popular in both Mexico and the United States becomes part of the collective cultural memory of Mexicans in both countries.

Intentionally or not, Molotov and Los Tigres del Norte form part of a musical cultural movement. They feed into the cross-border community dialogue on unauthorized migration. Though their message may have ideological implications, Los Tigres create awareness of the everyday issues that Mexicans face in the north. And though the political players in Mexico City may not even listen, their music speaks to the community and informs the potential migrants of the risks they will face if they make the journey to the United States. In contrast, by debating U.S.–Mexico foreign relations, with references ranging from the Treaty of Guadalupe Hidalgo to the War on Drugs and the War on Terror, Molotov's "Frijolero" is a message from Mexico's political hub, Mexico City, not only to northern Mexicans and Mexican migrants in the United States but also to ordinary Americans, at least in principle.

This, in part, explains the different approaches of Molotov and Los Tigres del Norte to the migration issue. The songs of Los Tigres slip into the homes of Mexicans with pleasant, often danceable, tunes. Once there, Los Tigres present options as to how the situation could improve; they draw attention to an issue. This is not to say they are not controversial; indeed, some of their music has been banned by the Mexican government. But Los Tigres focus on establishing empathy, rather than controversy, to promote change.[100] *Pacto de sangre* is an invitation to take action, to follow the advice they offer in their music, to advance a common meaning and the common goal of reducing the violence and death associated with unauthorized migration at the border.

In contrast, Molotov's "Frijolero" is explosive, creates awareness, and provokes debate. Although Molotov makes controversial statements on U.S.–Mexico relations, it does not make suggestions for change or resolution of the issues. Molotov highlights the inconsistencies of unauthorized migration, namely, the United States taking a tough stand against something it wants and permits. There is a War on Drugs, but it is against the suppliers and not the consumers. There is almost a "War on Unauthorized Migration," but, again, it is focused on the migrant workers and not on the employers who hire them. "Frijolero" is an angry retort against this hypocrisy.

The music of both Los Tigres del Norte and Molotov represents the psychological and physical risks of unauthorized migration to the United States: the risk of death ("José Pérez León"), of physical violence ("Frijolero"), of racial vilification ("Frijolero"), of family fragmentation ("Niño de la calle," "José Pérez León"), and of exposure to the elements ("El santo de los mojados"). Molotov's "Frijolero" identifies the U.S. government as the primary culprit for the risks experienced by Mexican migrants. Los Tigres del Norte's "El santo de los mojados" implies that the United States is the cause of suffering, and presents legalization of migrants by the United States as the solution. In contrast, "José Pérez León" implies that the coyote may be to blame because he trapped the migrants in a confined space, leading to their asphyxiation.

Overall, Los Tigres del Norte believe that, when people identify with, or are touched by, a personal experience and then make grassroots efforts, they can be a powerful force for change. In contrast, Molotov takes an ideological approach to unauthorized migration in "Frijolero," a critique of U.S.–Mexico relations intended to promote change at a national political level. Both groups of musicians aim to reduce risks for Mexican workers crossing into the United States in search of work and a better life.

Conclusion

Based on extensive fieldwork in 2003 and 2004, this study determined that the degree of risk experienced by unauthorized migrants depends on the effectiveness of their respective families' practical risk management strategies. It also found that migrants' responses to the escalating level of risk were varied and affected by various sectors of Mexican society, including government, civil society, the news media, artists, and musicians.

Mexican Migrant Management of Risk

Rather than blaming U.S. government policy, the migrant participants in my study tended to get on with managing the risks of their migration journey to ensure that they reached the United States safely and successfully.

Risk as a Factor in Unauthorized Migration

Without a doubt, unauthorized Mexican migrants have responded to changes in U.S. border policy and the barriers put in place to block their entry into the United States. However, their responses have not been in line with the expectations of U.S. policy makers. Whereas the United States expected that increasing levels of risk would reduce the number of unauthorized migration attempts, in reality, it has not. But as the policies and practices of U.S. border management have become stricter, opportunities for a safe crossing have diminished, and more Mexican migrants have experienced physical injury, psychological trauma, or even death.

According to Everette Lee, a person's predisposition to migrate is determined by the conditions in the country of origin (push), the state of affairs in the receiving country (pull), intervening obstacles (barriers), and personal circumstances (beliefs, perceptions).[1] Although my study found that migration was motivated by strong, primarily economic push-pull factors, it also found that risk did not constitute an intervening obstacle to migration, largely because "personal circumstances" tended to offset the risk. Not only were migrants motivated to migrate by family members, but many families also had well-established social networks that could facilitate the whole migration process, from raising funds to undertaking the logistics of travel. Indeed, even though individual migrants tended not to undertake pretrip risk assessment, their families did, in often sophisticated, albeit informal, ways.

The Family as Integral to Risk Management

Without a doubt, the number one risk management tool for unauthorized Mexican migrants is family. According to the migrant participants in this study, the closer the kinship relationship of the migrant to the human trafficker, the better the chances for a safe, successful crossing into the United States. Chances are better still if the migrant can afford to pay the trafficker more: the higher the fee, the more sophisticated the strategy, and the safer the journey. This is why male migrants often cross first into the United States to raise money to fund safer journeys for their wives and children.

Again, according to my study's migrant participants, the best, safest option is to cross at an official port of entry using, in order of preference, an original citizenship or permanent resident document (either borrowed or stolen), a false document, or an original document altered to include the migrant's own photo. The second best option is to be smuggled across the border in a vehicle at night through an official port of entry or to cross nearby because, even though the chances of being caught may be higher, the risk of assault is lower. The worst, most dangerous, but also most economical option is to cross in a less secure, remote area, where migrants are often exposed to extreme climatic conditions or to attack either by other traffickers or, on the U.S. side of the border, by individuals with antimigrant sentiments.

As conditions at the border have become more treacherous, study participants have chosen to stay longer in the United States to avoid frequent border crossings. As a result, they have also chosen to cross all their family members, rather than just the male worker. Many were prepared to remain for long periods of time in the United States to ensure that their children would be born and raised as U.S. citizens, entitled to move freely between the United States and Mexico. This greater migration of

Mexican women and children to the United States has long-term demographic implications for the United States, an unintended consequence of U.S. efforts to tighten border security.

Risk Management as Reflected in Experiences of Risk

As others have reported and my study participants have confirmed, most unauthorized migrants actually make it to the United States and, once there, are able to achieve many of their personal goals, in particular, to earn enough to purchase land and build a house in Mexico. For them, this reward is worth the risk of unauthorized migration and living as an "illegal" for extended periods of time in the United States.

A consequence of women and children crossing in growing numbers is that more are being exposed to the risk and trauma of unauthorized migration. On the other hand, the greater incidence of women and children migrating has considerably reduced family fragmentation. Today, if all members are able to migrate successfully, families can live together, whereas, in the past, working males lived away from home for extended periods of time.

On their actual migration journey, the migrant participants in my study experienced mainly psychological trauma rather than physical injury. Their growing level of trauma was closely associated with the growing level of difficulty they faced in the years since the early 1990s, especially since the implementation of Operation Gatekeeper and ever stricter U.S. border controls.

When I compared the participants' experiences with those reported in the Mexican print media, it quickly became clear that migrants most at risk of death or physical injury were those trying to negotiate the complexities of migration without family support. Migrants who did not have family to help them choose a human trafficker were much more likely to hire one associated with organized crime, who felt no sense of duty to the migrant, or who, to secure a commission, would downplay risks of the migration journey, thus leaving the migrant unprepared for the journey.

Even with a reliable trafficker, study participants were still exposed to some of the risks reported in the print media. Nevertheless, the participants believed their overall chances of survival had been good because of the sense of responsibility that their trafficker had felt toward them. They believed that their trafficker had reduced any unnecessary risk and had successfully managed the inherent risks of unauthorized migration.

My study's migrant participants had encounters with law enforcement and, in particular, with the U.S. Border Patrol, encounters that were often traumatic, not because of the nature of detention but because of the attitudes of the law enforcement officers. By putting into place better human rights training for Border Patrol officers, the U.S. government could avoid most of these unnecessary incidents.

That the informal risk management strategies of family networks were effective in reducing the risk that the migrant participants endured during their migration journey was clear from both the individual and the Hernández Cruz family cases. These strategies were also informed by the social and cultural environment surrounding the migrants, including the government, civil society, the news media, and popular music and art.

Mexican Society's Responses to Risk

During the course of my research, it became clear that Mexicans respond to, rather than effectively influence, U.S. border management and unauthorized migration policies. Various sectors of Mexican society—government, civil society, the news media, artists, and musicians—have all, in their own ways, decried or denounced the escalating risks of migration, whereas the migrants themselves have simply managed them.

Thus the Mexican government has initiated a series of programs, from establishing a better diplomatic dialogue with the United States to developing a migrant protection and rescue strategy, yet both the actual intent and effectiveness of its initiatives are questionable. Moreover, what genuine assistance the government could provide has been given mostly to returning, better-off migrants rather than to the poorer, more vulnerable migrants on their way north.

In contrast, civil society organizations have used the news media to project their events and messages all over the United States and Mexico. Political lobbying, combined with the documenting of human rights infringements, has created some political pressure for policy change while also contributing to greater awareness in the United States and Mexico of the dangers facing migrants at the border.

In their coverage of migration-related incidents, the Mexican print media have tended to single out human traffickers, criminals, or overzealous law enforcement officers, rather than to address inherent policy problems. They seem to have accepted the risks that migrants face as inevitable, except when it comes to the migration of children. Here they have voiced their strong opposition and advised unauthorized migrant parents to leave their children in Mexico, despite the likelihood of family fragmentation for the long term.

Many of Mexicans' underlying beliefs and attitudes toward migration are reflected in border art, one of the few sectors of Mexican society that critiques the causes, risks, and negative outcomes of migration. Tijuana's border art mural *Bienvenido paisano al sueño americano*, for example, encourages potential migrants to rethink their underlying premises for crossing the border. Yet border art neither offers nor promotes strategies for safer migration. In contrast, my analysis of migration-centered popular music revealed that songs often conveyed helpful messages about pitfalls for potential migrants to avoid, even though the musicians themselves were frustrated by government apathy and inaction on both sides of the border.

Final Thoughts

The unauthorized migration of Mexicans to the United States will continue until there is sufficient economic development in Mexico to provide better employment opportunities and living wages. If the United States continues to raise risk to discourage migration, Mexicans will continue to die unnecessarily. Raising the risk to migrants simply does not reduce unauthorized migration to the United States.

As long as Mexicans can escape poverty in Mexico by working in the United States, they will respond to and manage the risks of the unauthorized crossing. They will do what is necessary to reach the United States. This book has identified a range of responses to the risks of unauthorized migration and to the death of migrants, some responses spontaneous and heartfelt, others political and strategic—from apathy to effective political pressure. That said, no matter the level or type of response, Mexicans have little influence over the United States. It is U.S. border policies, together with the actions of individuals charged with their implementation, that determine the level of exposure of migrants to risk. Unfortunately for Mexicans, effective control over risk is in the hands of the United States.

Mexicans determined to reach the United States have developed sophisticated, informal strategies to manage the migration process. In the short term, they reduce risk for themselves by accessing information from their family networks, the news media, and popular art and music.

In the long term, many migrants ensure that future generations will be able to pass safely to and from the United States and will have access to work there by seeing that their children are born in the United States, although the trade-off for these new U.S. citizens will be detachment from Mexico and from certain aspects of its culture. More than anything else, however, my research has shown that Mexican migrants are quick to acquire knowledge through their social networks and to apply it to their everyday lives with dynamism, with creativity, and often with great personal success.

Glossary

American Border Patrol. Anti–unauthorized migration membership organization coordinated by Glen Spencer. See also Web site at http://www.american patrol.com/.

American Friends Service Committee. Quaker organization that includes people of various faiths committed to social justice, peace, and humanitarian service. See also Web site at http://www.afsc.org/.

Americas Watch. Subdivision of Human Rights Watch, an organization dedicated to protecting the human rights of people around the world. See also Web site at http://www.hrw.org/.

bajadero **(badlander).** Criminal who kidnaps migrants from their coyote once they have crossed into the United States, collecting the coyote's fee without taking any of the risks associated with crossing unauthorized migrants.

beaner. Derogatory term for a Mexican.

Border Angels. Nonprofit volunteer organization founded and coordinated by Enrique Morones dedicated to preventing the deaths of migrants traveling through desert and mountain areas near the U.S.–Mexico border and surrounding San Diego County. See also Web site at http://www.borderangels.org/.

California Rural Legal Assistance Foundation. Nonprofit organization dedicated to defending migrants' human and legal rights. See also Web site at http://www.crlaf.org/.

campesinos **(peasants).** Rural farmworkers.

"Carter Curtain." Reference to ex-President Carter's proposal to build walls between the United States and Mexico.

Casa del Migrante en Tijuana (Tijuana Migrant Hostel). Migrant hostel run by the Scalibrini Catholic religious order. See also Web site at http://www .migrante.com.mx/.

Centro Binacional de Derechos Humanos (Binational Center for Human Rights). Nonprofit human rights organization founded and coordinated by Victor Clark Alfaro and based in Tijuana.

chicano. Mexican American; U.S. citizen of Mexican descent.

Comisión Nacional de Derechos Humanos (National Commission for Human Rights. Mexican government organization dedicated to the protection of human rights in Mexico. See also Web site at http://www.cndh.org.mx/.

corrido **(ballad).** Genre of traditional Mexican music.

coyote. Colloquial Mexican term for human trafficker. The coyote coordinates migration strategies and often employs a guide to actually cross the unauthorized migrants.

Día de los muertos (Day of the Dead). Mexican folk holiday commemorating deceased ancestors, celebrated in November and combined with the Catholic Church's All Souls Day.

documented unauthorized migrant. Unauthorized migrant who enters or remains within a foreign country contrary to the terms of valid documents or by using borrowed, stolen, or false documents.

frijolero. See beaner.

gringo/a. Colloquial, often derogatory Mexican term for an American, particularly a Caucasian American.

Grupo Beta (Beta Group). Subdivision of the Instituto Nacional de Migración dedicated to rescuing distressed migrants in Mexican territory.

guide. Person employed by a coyote to accompany unauthorized migrants on the border crossing.

illegal alien. Official U.S. government term for unauthorized migrant.

Immigration Reform and Control Act. U.S. legislation implemented in 1986 that legalized an existing unauthorized migrant population while tightening U.S. border controls.

Instituto Nacional de Migración (National Migration Institute). Mexican government entity dedicated to managing foreign nationals on Mexican territory and to discouraging Mexican migration to the United States. See also Web site at http://www.inami.gob.mx/.

jus soli. Legal precept that citizenship of a child is determined by its place of birth.

la migra. Colloquial Mexican term for the U.S. Border Patrol.

migrant. Person who leaves one place for another.

mojado **(wetback).** Colloquial Mexican term for an unauthorized migrant in the United States, particularly one who has crossed the Rio Grande.

música norteña **(northern music).** Style of music traditional to northern Mexico.

narcos. Colloquial term for drug or narcotic traffickers.

North American Free Trade Agreement (NAFTA). Agreement between Canada, the United States, and Mexico, concluded in 1994, to reduce trade barriers between their countries.

Operation Blockade—Hold the Line. U.S. border management strategy to prevent unauthorized migration, implemented in the El Paso region in 1993.

Operation Gatekeeper. U.S. border management strategy to prevent unauthorized migration, implemented in California in 1994.

el otro lado **(The other side).** Colloquial Mexican term for the other side of the border, the United States; more specifically, the region adjacent to the border.

piñata. Papier-mâché figure filled with candy, held aloft by a rope and hit with a stick by blindfolded children until it bursts and sprinkles them with sweets.

pollero. See *coyote.*

pueblo (village). Term used in Mexican Spanish to describe a village or the place of one's origin.

Raza Rights Coalition. San Diego–based organization dedicated to creating awareness of human rights violations against Mexican migrant workers.

redneck. Colloquial derogatory term for an uneducated or racist Caucasian American who resides in a rural area.

seasonal worker program. Program that facilitates the issuing of temporary visas to foreign migrants to enter a country for the purposes of work.

Secretaría de Relaciones Exteriores (Department of Foreign Affairs). Mexican government entity charged with managing diplomatic relations between Mexico and other nations and with protecting Mexican nationals residing in foreign countries.

Southern Plan. Mexican government border management policy designed to reduce unauthorized migration into Mexico from Central America and implemented to gain bargaining power with the United States in the unauthorized migration debate.

TJ. Colloquial shorthand term used by the residents of Tijuana to refer to their city.

"Tortilla Curtain." Colloquial term referring to the border wall constructed at the U.S.–Mexico border at San Diego–Tijuana.

Treaty of Guadalupe Hidalgo. Peace treaty signed in 1848 under which Mexico ceded a large portion of its territory to the United States.

unauthorized migration. Migration from one country to another without the formal permission of either or contrary to the terms of that permission.

undocumented unauthorized migrant. Unauthorized migrant who enters a foreign country without valid documents.

U.S. Border Patrol. Field division of the U.S. Department of Homeland Security responsible for preventing the smuggling of "illegal" goods and unauthorized migrants into the United States.

wetback. See *mojado.*

Notes

Chapter 1. Mexican Experiences, Responses, and Management of Migration Risks

1. Stalker, *No-Nonsense Guide*, 8–9; statistics on migrants are from page 15.
2. Ibid.
3. Nevins, *Operation Gatekeeper*, 7, 16, 25.
4. Hall, "Cultural Identity," 292, 293, citing Schwarz, "Conservatism, Nationalism."
5. Hall, "Cultural Identity," 292.
6. Stalker, *No-Nonsense Guide*, 8–9.
7. Ibid., 21.
8. Ibid., 22.
9. Ibid.
10. Ibid.
11. Lee, "Theory of Migration," as cited in Heer, *Undocumented Mexicans*, 8.
12. Bustamente, "Undocumented Immigration"; Cornelius, "Mexican Labor"; Maciel and Herrera Sobek, *Culture across Borders*; Valenzuela Arce, *Nuestros piensos*; Fox, *Fence and River*; Vila, *Crossing Borders*; and Mains, "Contested Spaces."
13. Maciel and Herrera Sobek, "Introduction."
14. Nevins, *Operation Gatekeeper*, 12, 177.
15. See Douglas, *Risk and Blame*; and Gilpin, *Environmental Impact Assessment*. Anthropologist Mary Douglas explores risk as a social construct; Alan Gilpin, a risk management practitioner, complements this discussion with a pragmatic stance on the social politics of blame, the attribution of responsibility for the negative outcomes of a risky situation.
16. Thompson et al., "Aviation Risk Perception," 1590.
17. Davidson and Freudenburg, "Gender and Environmental Risk, 302–39, as cited in Siegrist, Keller, and Kiers, "Perception of Hazards."
18. Douglas, *Risk and Blame*, 12.
19. Martin, "New Migrants," 182.
20. Egan, "Border desert," A1.
21. Ibid.
22. Stalker, *No-Nonsense Guide*, 24.

23. Grimes, *Changing Social Identities,* chap. 11.

24. Lorey, *U.S.–Mexican Border,* 168–69.

25. Rohter, "Brazilians Streaming," A3.

26. American Immigration Lawyers Association Web site, http://www.aila .org/ (accessed May 31, 2008); and Federation for American Immigration Reform Web site, http://www.fairus.org/ (accessed May 31, 2008).

27. Orozco, González, and Díaz de Cossio, *Organizaciones mexicano-americanas,* 73; Bean et al., "Quantification of Migration," 1:61.

28. Lorey, *U.S.–Mexican Border,* 2–3.

29. Orozco, González, and Díaz de Cossio, *Organizaciones mexicano-americanas,* 32.

30. González, *History of Mexicans,* 225.

31. Stalker, *No-Nonsense Guide,* 27.

32. Orozco, González, and Díaz de Cossio, *Organizaciones mexicano-americanas,* 9, 78.

33. Preston, "Fewer Sending Money," A10.

34. Thompson, "Mexico's Migrants Profit," A1.

35. See U.S. Commission on Immigration Reform and Secretaría de Relaciones Exteriores, *Migration;* and Bean et al., "Introduction."

36. Heer, *Undocumented Mexicans,* 194.

37. See Stalker, *No-Nonsense Guide;* and Martin, "New Migrants."

38. *El Vigia,* "Mueren migrantes," 9. Translation of quotations from this and all other Spanish-language sources, including study participants, is mine unless otherwise noted.

39. Berestein and de la Vega, "Absentees Are Scarce," B1; and Groginsky, "Migration Policy," 9–13.

40. Vann, "Migrant Workers Die."

41. Santibáñez Romellón, "Guerra y frontera," 13.

42. Kammer, "Two Presidents Failed," A23.

43. See Santibáñez Romellón, "Guerra y frontera," 13; Campa, "Diplomacia agónica," 4A; Campa and Esquivel, "Cumbre artificial," 4A; Alos, "Ajedrez político," 2A; and Beltrán del Río, "Acuerdo migratorio," 4A.

44. Heer, *Undocumented Mexicans,* 80, citing North and Houstoun, *Illegal Aliens,* 22, and also Cornelius, "*Mexican Labor,*" 26.

45. Binford, "Generation of Migrants," 34.

46. Maram, "Hispanic Workers," as cited in Heer, *Undocumented Mexicans,* 80.

47. Orozco, González, and Díaz de Cossio, *Organizaciones mexicano-americanas,* 73.

48. Ibid., 23.

49. Lightfoot, *Adolescent Risk-Taking,* chap. 2.

50. Sánchez Zambrano, "Pegueros," 6.

51. Vila, "Introduction," x.

52. Hobsbawm, "Inventing Traditions," 1.

53. Maciel and Herrera Sobek, "Introduction," 17–18.

54. See Crosthwaite, William, and Byrd, *Puro Border*; Maciel and Herrera Sobek, "Introduction"; Vila, *Ethnography at the Border*; and Vila, *Crossing Borders*.

55. García, *Operation Wetback*, 96–100.

56. Martin and Teitelbaum, "Guest Workers," 130.

57. Lorey, *U.S.–Mexican Border*, 29.

58. See Griswold del Castillo, "Treaty of Guadalupe Hidalgo."

59. James, *Illegal Immigration*, 16.

60. Ibid.

61. Nevins, *Operation Gatekeeper*, chap. 2.

62. Gobierno del Estado de Baja California, "Problema migratorio."

63. Heer, *Undocumented Mexicans*, 11.

64. Lorey, *U.S.–Mexican Border*.

65. Stalker, *No-Nonsense Guide*, 41.

66. Heer, *Undocumented Mexicans*, 11.

67. Gobierno del Estado de Baja California, "Problema migratorio."

68. Heer, *Undocumented Mexicans*, 4.

69. Cardenas, "Impact of Immigration."

70. Heer, *Undocumented Mexicans*, 196.

71. Ibid., 4, 200.

72. Magaña, *Straddling the Border*; and González, *History of Mexicans*.

73. Cockcroft, *Outlaws in the Promised Land*.

74. Lorey, *U.S.–Mexican Border*, 163–64.

75. Martin and Teitelbaum, "Guest Workers."

76. González, *History of Mexicans*, 23.

77. Ledesma, "Undocumented Crossings," 67.

78. Sorell, "Telling Images."

79. Magaña, *Straddling the Border*, 20.

80. González, *History of Mexicans*, 230.

81. Nevins, *Operation Gatekeeper*, chap. 4.

82. Orozco, González, and Díaz de Cossio, *Organizaciones mexicano-americanas*, 76.

83. Heer, *Undocumented Mexicans*, 5.

84. González, *History of Mexicans*, 228.

85. Nevins, *Operation Gatekeeper*, 75; González, *History of Mexicans*, 225.

86. Nevins, *Operation Gatekeeper*, 78.

87. Nevins, *Operation Gatekeeper*; and González, *History of Mexicans*.

88. Wheaton, "Huckabee Immigration Plan"; and Thompson, "Mexican Leader Condemns U.S.," A6.

89. Nevins, *Operation Gatekeeper*, 72.

90. Ibid., 79–80.

91. Spener, "Controlling the Border."
92. Nevins, *Operation Gatekeeper*, 90.
93. Spener, "Controlling the Border."
94. Martínez, "Introduction."
95. Durand, Malone and Massey, *Beyond Smoke and Mirrors*, 2.
96. Hall, "Cultural Identity."
97. González, *History of Mexicans*, 231.
98. Nevins, *Operation Gatekeeper*, 4.
99. Ibid.
100. Ibid.
101. Berestein, "Migrants Push East," A1.
102. Magaña, *Straddling the Border*, 1.
103. *El Vigia*, "Migrantes muertos," 3.
104. Nevins, *Operation Gatekeeper*, 145.
105. Berestein, "Grim Record," A3.
106. Egan, "Border Desert," A1.
107. Nevins, *Operation Gatekeeper*, chap. 6.
108. Lezon and Rice, "Trailer Survivors," B1.
109. Reuters, "Illegal Aliens," 26.
110. Nevins, *Operation Gatekeeper*, chap. 6.
111. *Washington Post*, "Peso Crisis Spurs Migrants," A1.
112. Nevins, *Operation Gatekeeper*, chap. 6.
113. Vann, "18 Migrant Workers Die."
114. Nevins, *Operation Gatekeeper*, 125–26.
115. Strickland and Gold, "17 Found Dead," A2.
116. Douglas, *Risk and Blame*, 3–21.
117. Frith, *Performing Rites*, 159.
118. Vila, *Ethnography at the Border*, ix–xxxiii.
119. See Davidson, *Lives on the Line*.
120. Lewis, *Five Families*, 62–63.
121. Taplin, Scheld, and Low, "Rapid Ethnographic Assessment."
122. See Rodríguez, *Mito, identidad*; and Oktavec, *Answered Prayers*.
123. Oktavec, *Answered Prayers*, xv–xxi.
124. Nevins, *Operation Gatekeeper*, 80, 131.
125. See Maciel and Herrera Sobek, "Introduction"; and Crosthwaite, William, and Byrd, *Puro Border*.
126. See Vila, *Ethnography at the Border*; and Vila, *Crossing Borders*.
127. Douglas, *Risk and Blame*, 3–21.
128. Marcus and Fischer, *Anthropology as Cultural Critique*, 77.
129. Becker, "Whose Side?" 239–47, as cited in Taylor and Bogdan, *Qualitative Research Methods*, 20.
130. Strauss and Corbin, "Grounded Theory Methodology."

131. Arias, "Migratory Tradition."

132. Nevins, *Operation Gatekeeper*, 6.

133. Ibid., 9. Nevins points out that "many terms employed historically . . . such as . . . 'illegal aliens' . . . are often pejorative due to the images of the immigrant they suggest and the ideas of the undesirable 'other' they embody. The frequently used term 'illegal,' for example, implies that unsanctioned immigrants are criminals. . . . [There are] less politically charged terms, such as authorized and unauthorized, to describe unsanctioned immigrants or immigration."

134. My use of these terms is in accordance with U.S. Commission on Immigration Reform and Secretaría de Relaciones Exteriores, *Migration*, 6: "Unauthorized migrants includes individuals who enter [the United States] without permission, through use of fraudulent documents, or with permission but who violate the terms of their visas."

Chapter 2. Delving into the Migrant's World

1. Irapuato municipal Web site, http://www.irapuato.gob.mx/ (accessed April 3, 2005).

2. Nevins, *Operation Gatekeeper*, 129.

3. Reichart, "Town Divided," 420–21, as cited in Mooney, "Migrants' Social Capital," 46–47.

4. Patricia's behavior matches the social network patterns identified by Martin in "New Migrants."

5. Stalker, *No-Nonsense Guide*, 45–46.

6. Nevins, *Operation Gatekeeper*, 33–36, 53–54.

7. Orozco, González and Díaz de Cossio, *Organizaciones mexicano-americanas*, 72.

8. Donato and Patterson, "Women and Men on the Move," 114.

9. Nevins, *Operation Gatekeeper*, 79.

10. Ibid.

11. Spener, "Controlling the Border," 188.

12. Ibid.

13. Nevins, *Operation Gatekeeper*, 92.

14. Lipton, "U.S. Failing on Overstays," A13.

15. San, "Llegar a E.U.," 11.

16. Nevins, *Operation Gatekeeper*, 142, citing Ortiz Pinchetti, "Como si fueran criminals," 18–24.

17. Martínez, "Kindness of Strangers," A19.

18. Cornelius, "Ambivalent Reception."

19. González, *History of Mexicans*, 229.

20. Heer, *Undocumented Mexicans*, 200.

21. Lightfoot, *Adolescent Risk-Taking*, chap. 2.

22. Nevins, *Operation Gatekeeper*, 169.

23. Lorey, *U.S.–Mexican Border*, 163.

24. Nevins, *Operation Gatekeeper*, 128, citing Cornelius, "Mexican Immigrant Labor," 130.

25. Ibid.

26. Lightfoot, *Adolescent Risk-Taking*, chap. 2.

27. Donato and Patterson, "Women and Men on the Move," 114–15.

28. Lorey, *U.S.–Mexican Border*, 166–67.

29. Spener, "Controlling the Border," 187.

30. Ibid.

31. Orrenius, "Effect of U.S. Border Enforcement," 287.

Chapter 3. Government, Civil Society, and Print Media Responses

1. U.S. Commission on Immigration Reform and Secretaría de Relaciones Exteriores, *Migration*, 4.

2. Ibid., 57.

3. Martin and Teitelbaum, "Guest Workers"; Berestein and de la Vega, "Absentees Are Scarce"; and Groginsky, "Migration Policy."

4. Comisión Nacional de Derechos Humanos, *Derechos humanos*.

5. Lorey, *U.S.–Mexican Border*, 162.

6. Heer, *Undocumented Mexicans*, 194.

7. U.S. Commission on Immigration Reform and Secretaría de Relaciones Exteriores, *Migration*.

8. Vann, "Migrant Workers Die"; and Santibáñez Romellón, "Guerra y frontera," 13.

9. Stalker, *No-Nonsense Guide*, 132.

10. Secretaría de Relaciones Exteriores, "Guía del migrante mexicano."

11. LeDuff and Flores, "Everymigrant's Guide," A16.

12. Ibid.

13. Ibid.

14. Groginsky, "Migration Policy"; and Berestein and de la Vega, "Absentees Are Scarce."

15. Valenzuela, "Programa Beta."

16. Mohar and Alcaraz, "U.S. Border Controls," 145.

17. *El Mexicano*, "Apoyará C.N.D.H.," 5C.

18. *La Opinión*, "Auxilio fronterizo," 4A.

19. Nevins, *Operation Gatekeeper*, 133.

20. Instituto Nacional de Migración, "Guía paisano 2003."

21. Ibid., 29.

22. Revelli, "Devourer of Migrants."

23. Katel, "Mexico's Other Border," 6.

24. Thompson, "Mexico Worries," A1.

25. Centre for Civil Society, "What Is Civil Society?"

26. Nevins, *Operation Gatekeeper*, 124.

27. Sterngold, "Urge Change," 10.

28. McDonald, "Border Fence," B2.

29. Moran, "Border Watch," B2.

30. Americas Watch, *U.S. Frontier Injustice*, 3.

31. Nevins, *Operation Gatekeeper*, 125.

32. Rozemberg, "Migrant Aid."

33. *Frontera*, "Extiende O.N.G apoyo," 13.

34. Rozemberg, "Migrant Aid."

35. Douglas, *Risk and Blame*, 3–21.

36. *Frontera*, "Sufren migrantes," 12.

37. *El Vigia*, "Arrestan torturador," 8.

38. *El Mexicano*, "Rescataron a mas de 100 ilegales."

39. Landesman, "Tráfico de sexo," 2.

40. Ortiz, "Migrantes hacen sudar," 15.

41. *Frontera*, "Sufren migrantes," 12.

42. *El Mexicano*, "Detectan 17 indocumentados," 7A.

43. Blanco, "Mueren 4 ilegales," 1A.

44. Murillo, "Mueren 4 migrantes," 1.

45. Limon, "Dispara border," 13.

46. *El Mexicano*, "Conceden a 40 indocumentados," 3C.

47. Strickland and Gold, "17 Found Dead," A2.

48. *El Mexicano*, "Descubren a mas ilegales," 1C.

49. Viana et al., "Sufren niños," 15.

50. Bojorquez, "Ilegales centroamericanos," 1–2.

51. *El Mexicano*, "Mueren tres migrantes," 2C.

52. LeDuff, "Nueva clase," 1.

53. Viana et al., "Sufren niños," 15.

54. San, "Llegar a E.U.," 11.

55. Viana et al., "Sufren niños," 15.

56. *El Mexicano*, "Retienen a cinco niños," 4C; Thompson, "Littlest Immigrants" A1.

57. Viana et al., "Sufren niños," 15.

58. Ortiz, "Migrantes hacen sudar," 15.

59. *El Mexicano*, "Murieron cinco migrantes," 6C.

60. *El Vigia*, "Campaña para indocumentados," 4.

61. Ortiz, "Migrantes hacen sudar," 15.

62. *El Vigia*, "Rescatan del frio," 11.

63. *El Mexicano*, "Hallan 35 migrantes," 1C.

64. *El Mexicano*, "Abusos en fronteras," 7A.

65. LeDuff, "Nueva clase," 1.
66. Vásquez, "Piden por migrantes," 16.
67. *El Mexicano*, "Afirman haberlo 'confundido,'" 2C.
68. *El Vigia*, "Matan a inmigrantes," 4.
69. Smith, "Border Enforcement," 111.
70. Loret de Mola, "Desafío," 10A; Cearley, "Vigilance Stepped Up," B5; and *El Vigia*, "Mojados a terroristas," 1.
71. Gutiérrez, "Niños deportados," 4A.
72. Martínez, "Persiguen a ilegales," 1A–2A.

Chapter 4. Mexican Border Art as Activism

1. Chávez and Grynztejn, "Introduction."
2. Eraña, "Canyons and Sand."
3. González, *History of Mexicans*, 228.
4. Eraña, "Canyons and Sand," 96.
5. Nevins, *Operation Gatekeeper*, 72–79.
6. McCaughan, "Gender, Sexuality," 99.
7. Cockcroft and Barnet-Sanchez, "Introduction."
8. Lorey, *U.S.–Mexican Border*, 144–45.
9. Ibid., 178.
10. Herbst, "Politics, Expression," 17.
11. Villoro, "Nothing to Declare," 198.
12. Nevins, *Operation Gatekeeper*, 119.
13. Chaffee, "Political Graffiti."
14. Kellehear, *Unobtrusive Researcher*, vii.
15. Gruzinski, *Aztecs*, 19–20.
16. Edwards, *Painted Walls*, 7–9.
17. According to Goldman, "Chicano Murals," 23–53, indigenous heritage has experienced a renaissance in the United States, particularly in Chicano-influenced art.
18. Schele and Miller, *Blood of Kings*, 265–87.
19. Goldman, "Chicano Murals."
20. U.S. Conference of Catholic Bishops, *Welcoming the Stranger*, 15.
21. Spellman, *Holy Bible*, 108.
22. Umphlett, *Mythmakers*; and Guimond, *American Photography*.
23. Hochschild, *American Dream*, 16, 253.
24. Hartz, *New Societies*, chaps. 1 and 2.
25. Goldman, "Chicano Murals."
26. Ibid.
27. Alcántara and Egnolff, *Kahlo and Rivera*, 26.
28. Goldman, "Chicano Murals."

29. McCaughan, "Gender, Sexuality."
30. Eraña, "Canyons and Sand."
31. Goldman, "Chicano Murals," 23–53.
32. Anzaldúa, *Borderlands*, 3, as cited in Sorell, "Telling Images," 99.
33. Nevins, *Operation Gatekeeper*, 170.
34. Lubrano, "Operation Gatekeeper."
35. Jenkins, "Range of Emotions," B2.
36. Sifuentes, "Experts, Advocates."
37. Berestein, "Migrants Push East," A1.
38. Nevins, *Operation Gatekeeper*, 124–25.
39. Villegas, "Gritan creativos," 1.
40. Blake, "Reconoce logros culturales," 5.
41. Ríos Navarrete, "Grito creativo."
42. Ibid., 77.
43. Ibid.
44. Ibid.
45. Ibid.
46. Ibid.
47. Lizárraga, "Popular Expression," 3.
48. Ibid., 10.
49. Villegas, "Gritan creativos."
50. Durand, "Art and Politics I," 32.
51. Alberro, "Retablos."
52. Goldman, "Chicano Murals"; and Ybarra-Frausto, "Arte chicano."
53. Nevins, *Operation Gatekeeper*, 79–80.
54. Sorell, "Telling Images," 111.
55. Nevins, *Operation Gatekeeper*, 166.
56. Eraña, "Canyons and Sand."
57. Nevins, *Operation Gatekeeper*, 170.
58. Villegas, "Gritan creativos."

Chapter 5. The Migrant's Voice in Popular Song

1. Gebesmair, "Introduction."
2. Lewis, "Pistola y corazón."
3. Valenzuela, "Música en cultura popular."
4. Lozano, *Prensa, radiodifusión*, 33.
5. Lorey, *U.S.–Mexican Border*, 144.
6. Los Tigres del Norte, *Pacto de sangre*; and Molotov, *Dance*.
7. Valenzuela, "Música en cultura popular."
8. Frith, "Aesthetic of Popular Music," 134–35.
9. Cobo, "Music with a Social Conscience."

10. Ibid.

11. Lewis, "Pistola y corazón."

12. Ibid., 63.

13. Valenzuela, "Música en cultura popular."

14. Cobo, "Music with a Social Conscience," 85.

15. Ibid.

16. Cobo, "Stories from Real Life."

17. Pérez, *Diary of Migrant,* 40.

18. Emerick, "Blood Ties to Homeland," M1.

19. Cobo, "Stories from Real Life."

20. Ibid., 77.

21. Emerick, "Blood Ties to Homeland," M1.

22. Prieto, "Corrido de reflexión."

23. Grimes, *Changing Social Identities,* 83.

24. See Conover, *Coyotes.*

25. Cobo, "Music with a Social Conscience."

26. Jordan and Sullivan, "Migrants' Deaths Reverberate," A1.

27. Ibid.

28. Lozano, "Boy's Death."

29. Emerick, "Blood Ties to Homeland," M1.

30. Jordan and Sullivan, "Migrants' Deaths Reverberate," A1.

31. Halsell, *Illegals,* 18.

32. González, *History of Mexicans,* 228.

33. Los Tigres del Norte, *Pacto de sangre.*

34. *El Mexicano,* "Retienen en Arizona," 4C; Thompson, "Littlest Immigrants," A1.

35. Martínez, *Border People,* 168.

36. Marmon Silko, "Border Patrol State."

37. Kava, "Mexican Rockers," 1E.

38. Wall, "Frijolero."

39. Hernández, "Spotlight: Molotov," M1.

40. Burr, "Dance," 30.

41. See Molotov, "Nominations for Molotov"; and Wiederhorn, "Molotov Explodes."

42. González, *History of Mexicans,* 257.

43. Burr, "Molotov's 'Dance,'" 7.

44. Wall, "Frijolero."

45. Kava, "Mexican Rockers," 1E.

46. Castañeda, "Recupera Molotov."

47. Herbst, "Politics, Expression."

48. Burr, "Molotov's 'Dance.'"

49. Wherry, "Short File Festival."

50. Rich and De Los Reyes, "Mexican Caricature," 138.
51. *El Mexicano*, "México, 'Patio trasero de E.U.,'" 1C.
52. Heer, *Undocumented Mexicans*, 3.
53. Americas Watch, *U.S. Frontier Injustice*, 11.
54. Ibid.
55. Gortazar Rodríguez, "Afectará guerra," 1A.
56. Schmitt and Preston, "Threats and Responses." A1.
57. Del Monte, "Voto de México," 12.
58. *El Mexicano*, "Decepciona Fox a E.U.," 1C; Campa, "México cómplice," 2C.
59. Heer, *Undocumented Mexicans*, 192.
60. Stalker, *No-Nonsense Guide*, 22.
61. See González, *History of Mexicans*; and James, *Illegal Immigration*.
62. Quintana, "¿Abrir Pemex?" 15A; and *El Mexicano*, "Pemex no se vende," 1C.
63. Martínez, *Border People*, 194.
64. Nevins, *Operation Gatekeeper*, 125–26.
65. See Halsell, *Illegals*; and James, *Illegal Immigration*.
66. Orozco, González and Díaz de Cossio, *Organizaciones mexicano-americanas*, 76.
67. U.S. Conference of Catholic Bishops, *Welcoming the Stranger*, 10–12.
68. See Conover, *Coyotes*.
69. See Nevins, *Operation Gatekeeper*, 125, 171.
70. Megirk, "'Posses' Hunting Migrants," 17.
71. Nevins, *Operation Gatekeeper*, 173–74.
72. Comisión Nacional de Derechos Humanos, *Derechos humanos*, 58.
73. Martínez Serrano, "Emplean balas," 1.
74. Americas Watch, *U.S. Frontier Injustice*.
75. González, *History of Mexicans*, 79–85.
76. Halsell, *Illegals*, 6–8.
77. Roe and de Meyer, "One Planet—One Music?"
78. Wall, "Frijolero."
79. Gow, "Music Video."
80. Ibid.
81. Toma and Esbenshade, "Day Laborer Hiring."
82. Melgar, "Fox y Bush," 2A.
83. García y Griego, and Campos, "Colaboración sin concordancia."
84. James, *Illegal Immigration*, 116–29.
85. Wall, "Frijolero."
86. See Comisión Nacional de Derechos Humanos, *Derechos humanos*; and Americas Watch, *U.S. Frontier Injustice*.
87. González, *History of Mexicans*, 243.

88. Wall, "Frijolero."

89. U.S. Conference of Catholic Bishops, *Welcoming the Stranger*, 10–11.

90. Griffith, *Folklife in the Borderlands*, 15.

91. Gessell, "Bleak Divide," D7.

92. *New York Times*, "Traces of Terror"; Arnoldy, "Gas Mask 101."

93. Lorey, *U.S.–Mexican Border*, 140.

94. Ibid., 178–79.

95. Pacini Hernandez, "Race, Ethnicity."

96. Ibid., 70.

97. Hartz, *New Societies*, chaps. 1 and 2.

98. Meyer, *Emotion and Meaning in Music*, 257–60.

99. Smith, "Rural Place Attachment."

100. Simonett, "Narcocorridos."

Conclusion

1. Heer, *Undocumented Mexicans*, 8, citing Lee, "Theory of Migration," 47–57.

Bibliography

Alberro, Solange. "Retablos and Popular Religion in Nineteenth-Century Mexico." In *Art and Faith in Mexico: The Nineteenth-Century Retablo Tradition*, edited by Elizabeth Zarur and Charles Lovell, 57–67. Albuquerque: University of New Mexico, 2001.

Alcántara, Isabel, and Sandra Egnolff. *Frida Kahlo and Diego Rivera*. Munich: Prestel, 1999.

Alos, Gabriel. "Ajedrez político: Defiende Fox a Bush." *El Mexicano*, January 16, 2004, 2A.

Americas Watch. *United States Frontier Injustice: Human Rights Abuses along the U.S. Border with Mexico Persist amid Climate of Impunity*. New York, 1993.

Anzaldúa, Gloria. *Borderlands = La Frontera: The New Mestiza*. San Francisco: Spinsters/Aunt Lute, 1987.

Arias, Patricia. "Old Paradigms and New Scenarios in a Migratory Tradition: U.S. Migration from Guanajuato." In *Crossing the Border: Research from the Mexican Migration Project*, edited by Jorge Durand and Douglas Massey, 171–83. New York: Russell Sage Foundation, 2004.

Arnoldy, Ben. "Gas Mask 101." *Christian Science Monitor*, March 13, 2003, 25.

Bean, Frank, Rodolfo Corona, Rodolfo Tuirán, and Karen A. Woodrow-Lafield. "The Quantification of Migration between Mexico and the United States." In *Migration Between Mexico and the United States: Binational Study*. Vol. 1: *Themactic Chapters*. Mexico City: Ministry of Foreign Affairs, 1998.

Bean, Frank, Rodolfo de la Garza, Brian Roberts, and Sidney Weintraub. "Introduction." In *At the Crossroads: Mexico and U.S. Immigration Policy*, edited by Bean, de la Garza, Roberts, and Weintraub, 1–10. Lanham, Md.: Rowman & Littlefield, 1997.

Beltrán del Río, Pascal. "El acuerdo migratorio: Una invención mexicana." *El Mexicano*, November 9, 2003, 4A.

Berestein, Leslie. "A Grim Record at the Border: The Year Likely to Be Worst in Migrant Deaths." *San Diego Union-Tribune*, August 10, 2005, A3.

———. "Migrants Push East to Avoid Fortified Border, with Tragic Results." *San Diego Union-Tribune*, September 29, 2004, A1

Berestein, Leslie, and Norma de la Vega. "Absentees Are Scarce for Mexico's '06 Vote." *San Diego Union-Tribune*, November 3, 2005, B1.

Binford, Leigh. "A Generation of Migrants: Why They Leave, Where They End Up." *NACLA Report on the Americas* 39, no. 1 (2005): 31–39.

Blake, Patricia. "Reconoce logros culturales." *Frontera*, April 21, 2004, 5.

Blanco, Marco. "Mueren 4 ilegales en Volcadura." *El Mexicano*, September 30, 2003, 1A.

Bojorquez, Martin. "Rescatan a ilegales centroamericanos." *El Mexicano*, June 24, 2003, 1–2.

Burr, Ramiro. "Album Review: Dance and Dense Denso." *Billboard*, February 22, 2003, 30.

———. "Molotov's 'Dance' Incendiary, with No Apologies." *Houston Chronicle*, February 17, 2003, 7.

Bustamente, Jorge. "Impact of Undocumented Immigration from Mexico on the U.S.–Mexican Economies." Paper presented at the Fronteras 1976 San Diego / Tijuana: The International Border in Community Relations, San Diego, November 19–20, 1976.

Campa, Homero. "Diplomacia agónica." *El Mexicano*, August 17, 2003, 4A.

———. "México cómplice por temor." *El Mexicano*, April 6, 2003, 2C.

Campa, Homero, and Jesús Esquivel. "Cumbre artificial." *El Mexicano*, January 11, 2004, 4A.

Cardenas, Gilbert. "The Impact of Immigration in the Ethnic Enterprise." In *Chicano-Mexicano Relations*, edited by Tatcho Mindiola and Max Martinez, 60–72. Houston: University of Houston, 1992.

Castañeda, Eduardo. "Recupera Molotov el humor." *El Norte*, January 31, 2003. http://www.mural.com/ (accessed January 31, 2003).

Cearley, Anna. "Baja Officials Say Vigilance Stepped Up along Border." *San Diego Union-Tribune*, March 22, 2003, B5.

Centre for Civil Society. "What Is Civil Society?" London School of Economics and Political Science, March 2004. http://www.lse.ac.uk/collections/CCS/whatis_civil_society.htm/ (accessed December 30, 2005).

Chaffee, Lyman. "Political Graffiti and Wall Painting in Greater Buenos Aires: An Alternative Communication System." *Studies in Latin American Popular Culture* 8, no. 8 (1989): 37–60.

Chávez, Patricio, and Madeleine Grynztejn. "Introduction." In *La Frontera: Art about the Mexico–United States Border Experience*, edited by Patrick Chavez and Madeleine Grynztejn, xvii–xxi. San Diego: Centra Cultural de la Raza, 1993.

Cobo, Leila. "Los Tigres del Norte: Music with a Social Conscience." *Hispanic* 17, nos. 7–8 (2004): 84–86.

———. "Los Tigres Take Their Stories from Real Life." *Billboard*, April 17, 2004, 5, 77.

Cockcroft, Eva, and Holly Barnet-Sanchez. "Introduction." In *Signs from the Heart: California Chicano Murals*, edited by Cockcroft and Barnet-Sanchez, 5–21. Albuquerque: University of New Mexico Press, 1999.

Cockcroft, James. *Outlaws in the Promised Land*. New York: Grove Press, 1986.

Comisión Nacional de Derechos Humanos. *Informe sobre las violaciones de los derechos humanos de los trabajadores migratorios mexicanos en su tránsito hacia la frontera*. Mexico City, 1991.

Conover, Ted. *Coyotes*. New York: Random House, 1987.

Cornelius, Wayne. "Ambivalent Reception: Mass Public Responses to the "New" Latino Immigration to the United States." In *Latinos: Remaking America*, edited by Marcelo Suárez-Orozco and Mariela Páez, 165–89. Berkeley: University of California Press, 2002.

———. "The U.S. Demand for Mexican Labor." In *Mexican Migration to the United States: Origins, Consequences, and Policy Options*, edited by Wayne Cornelius and Jorge Bustamante, 25–47. San Diego: University of California, 1989.

Crosthwaite, Luis Humberto, John William Byrd, and Bobby Byrd, eds. *Puro Border: Dispatches, Snapshots and Graffiti from La Frontera*. El Paso: Cinco Puntos Press, 2003.

Davidson, Miriam. *Lives on the Line: Dispatches from the U.S.–Mexico Border*. Tucson: University of Arizona Press, 2000.

Del Monte, Fernando. "El voto de Mexico." *Frontera*, March 2, 2003, 12.

Donato, Katharine, and Evelyn Patterson. "Women and Men on the Move: Undocumented Border Crossing." In *Crossing the Border: Research from the Mexican Migration Project*, edited by Jorge Durand and Douglas Massey, 111–30. New York: Russell Sage Foundation, 2004.

Douglas, Mary. *Risk and Blame: Essays in Cultural Theory*. London: Routledge, 1992.

Durand, Jorge, Nolan Malone, and Douglas Massey. *Beyond Smoke and Mirrors: Mexican Immigration in an Era of Economic Integration*. New York: Russell Sage Foundation, 2003.

Durand, Mark. "Art and Politics I: Activist Art in the Shadow of Rebellion." *Arts in America* 80, no. 7 (1992): 31–35.

Edwards, Emily. *Painted Walls of Mexico*. Austin: University of Texas Press, 1966.

Egan, Timothy. "Border Desert Proves Deadly for Mexicans." *New York Times*, May 23, 2004, A1.

Emerick, Laura. "Blood Ties to Homeland, a 'Pacto de Sangre.'" *Chicago Sun-Times*, April 4, 2004, M1.

Eraña, Maria. "From a Border of Canyons and Sand." In *La Frontera: Art about the Mexico–United States Border Experience*, edited by Patricio Chávez and Madeleine Grynztejn, 95–99. San Diego: Centro Cultural de la Raza, 1993.

Fox, Claire. *The Fence and the River: Culture and Politics at the U.S.–Mexico Border*. Minneapolis: University of Minnesota Press, 1999.

Frith, Simon. *Performing Rites: On the Value of Popular Music*. Cambridge: Harvard University Press, 1996.

Frith, Simon. "Towards an Aesthetic of Popular Music." In *Music and Society*, edited by Richard Leppert and Susan McClary, 132–49. Cambridge: Cambridge University Press, 1987.

Frontera. "Extiende O.N.G. apoyo hacia B.C. para migrantes." July 27, 2004, 13.

———. "Sufren los migrantes de constantes asaltos." May 2, 2004, 12.

García, Juan Ramón. *Operation Wetback: The Mass Deportation of Mexican Undocumented Workers in 1954*. Westport, Conn.: Greenwood Press, 1980.

García y Griego, Manuel, and Mónica Verea Campos. "Colaboración sin concordancia: La migración en la nueva agenda bilateral Mexico–Estados Unidos." In *Nueva agenda bilateral en la relación México–Estados Unidos*, edited by Varea Campos, Rafael Fernandez de Castro, and Sidney Weintraub, 107–34. Mexico City: Instituto Tecnológico Autónomo de México, 1998.

Gebesmair, Andreas. "Introduction." In *Global Repertoires: Popular Music within and beyond the Transnational Music Industry*, edited by Andreas Gebesmair and Alfred Smudits, 1–6. Hants, U.K.: Ashgate, 2001.

Gessell, Paul. "Running Fence Captures Bleak Divide: Geoffrey James' Photos of 23-Kilometre Fence along the California–Mexican Border Tell a Sad Tale." *Ottawa Citizen*, March 1, 1999, D7.

Gilpin, Alan. *Environmental Impact Assessment: Cutting Edge for Twenty-First Century*. Cambridge: Press Syndicate of the University of Cambridge, 1995.

Gobierno del Estado de Baja California. "Un enfoque del problema migratorio en Baja California." Mexicali, 1997.

Goldman, Shifra. "How, Why, Where and When It All Happened: Chicano Murals of California." In *Signs from the Heart: California Chicano Murals*, edited by Eva Cockcroft and Holly Barnet Sánchez, 23–53. Albuquerque: University of New Mexico Press, 1999.

González, Manuel. *Mexicanos: A History of Mexicans in the United States*. Bloomington: Indiana University Press, 2000.

Gortazar Rodríguez, Iciar. "Afectará la guerra a la mano de obra." *El Mexicano*, March 27, 2003, 1A.

Gow, Joe. "Music Video as Communication: Popular Formulas and Emerging Genres." *Journal of Popular Culture* 26, no. 2 (1992): 41–70.

Griffith, James. *A Shared Space: Folklife in the Arizona-Sonora Borderlands*. Logan: Utah State University Press, 1995.

Grimes, Kimberly. *Crossing Borders: Changing Social Identities in Southern Mexico*. Tucson: University of Arizona Press, 1998.

Griswold del Castillo, Richard. "The Treaty of Guadalupe Hidalgo." In *U.S.–Mexico Borderlands: Historical and Contemporary Perspectives*, edited by Oscar Martínez, 1–9. Wilmington, Del.: Scholarly Resources, 1996.

Groginsky, V. "Migration Policy: The Inevitable U.S.–Mexico Clash." *Defense & Foreign Affairs' Strategic Policy* 33, no. 3 (2005): 9–13.

Gruzinski, Serge. *The Aztecs: Rise and Fall of an Empire.* New York: H.N. Abrams, 1992.

Guimond, James. *American Photography and the American Dream.* Chapel Hill: University of North Carolina, 1991.

Gutiérrez, Alejandro. "Niños deportados." *El Mexicano,* September 14, 2003, 4A.

Hall, Stuart. "The Question of Cultural Identity." In *Modernity and Its Futures,* edited by Hall, David Held, and Tony McGrew, 291–99. Cambridge: Polity Press, 1992.

Halsell, Grace. *The Illegals.* New York: Stein and Day, 1978.

Hartz, Louis. *The Founding of New Societies.* New York: Harcourt, Brace & World, 1964.

Heer, David. *Undocumented Mexicans in the United States.* Cambridge: Cambridge University Press, 1990.

Herbst, Susan. "Politics, Expression and Marginality." In *Politics at the Margin,* 8–32. Cambridge: Cambridge University Press, 1994.

Hernández, Raoul. "Spotlight: Molotov." *Austin Chronicle,* March 14, 2003, M1.

Hobsbawm, Eric. "Introduction: Inventing Traditions." In *The Invention of Tradition,* edited by Hobsbawm and Terence Ranger. Cambridge: Cambridge University Press, 1995.

Hochschild, Jennifer. *Facing up to the American Dream.* Princeton, N.J.: Princeton University Press, 1995.

Instituto Nacional de Migración. "Guía paisano 2003." Mexico City, 2003.

James, Daniel. *Illegal Immigration: An Unfolding Crisis.* Washington, D.C.: University Press of America, 1991.

Jenkins, Logan. "Illegal Immigration Stirs up a Range of Emotions." *San Diego Union-Tribune,* September 27, 2004, B2.

Jordan, Mary, and Kevin Sullivan. "Migrants' Deaths Reverberate at Home; Friends, Relatives in Mexico Know Risks of Border Crossing." *Washington Post,* May 16, 2003, A1.

Kammer, Jerry. "Two Presidents Failed to Grasp Complexity of Immigration Issue." *San Diego Union-Tribune,* November 17, 2002, A23.

Katel, Peter. "A Bus Ride across Mexico's Other Border." *Time* 158, no. 6 (2001): 6.

Kava, Brad. "Mexican Rockers Throw Down Gauntlet against Racism and Imperialism." *San Jose Mercury News,* April 2, 2003, 1E.

Kellehear, Allan. *The Unobtrusive Researcher: A Guide to Methods.* St Leonards: Allen & Unwin, 1993.

Landesman, Peter. "Tráfico de sexo: Un negocio lucrativo." *El Vigía* 2004, 2.

Ledesma, Alberto. "Undocumented Crossings: Narratives to Mexican Immigration to the United States." In *Culture across Borders: Mexican Immigration and Popular Culture,* edited by David Maciel and María Herrera Sobek, 67–98. Tucson: University of Arizona Press, 1998.

LeDuff, Charlie. "Nueva clase de criminal emerge en la frontera." *Enlace*, November 15, 2003, 1.

LeDuff, Charlie, and Emilio Flores. "The Everymigrant's Guide to Crossing the Border Illegally." *New York Times*, February 9, 2005, A16.

Lee, Everette. "A Theory of Migration." *Demography* 3 (1966): 44–57.

Lewis, George. "La pistola y el corazón: Protest and Passion in Mexican-American Popular Music." *Journal of Popular Culture* 26, no. 1 (1992): 51–67.

Lewis, Oscar. *Five Families*. New York: New American Library, 1959.

Lezon, Dale, and Harvey Rice. "Trailer Survivors Tell Tales of Death." *Houston Chronicle*, March 11, 2005, B1.

Lightfoot, Cynthia. *The Culture of Adolescent Risk-Taking*. New York: Guilford, 1997.

Limon, Beatriz. "Dispara border a una camioneta con migrantes." *El Vigia*, May 15, 2004, 13.

Lipton, Eric. "Report Finds U.S. Failing on Overstays of Visas." *New York Times*, October 22, 2005, A13.

Lizárraga, Maximiliano. "The Wall as a Means of Popular Expression." La Universidad Iberoamericana del Noroeste, 2000.

Loret de Mola, Rafael. "Desafío: Terrorismo de estado—la relación con Bush." *El Mexicano*, August 11, 2003, 10A.

Lorey, David. *The U.S.–Mexican Border in the Twentieth Century*. Wilmington, Del.: Scholarly Resources, 1999.

Lozano, José Carlos. *Prensa, radiodifusión e identidad cultural en la frontera norte*. Tijuana: El Colegio de la Frontera Norte, 1991.

Lozano, Juan. "Boy's Death Crucial to Smuggling Trial." *Victoria Advocate*, 2004. http://www.thevictoriaadvocate.com/local/state/story/2448011p-2834945c .html/ (accessed December 24, 2004).

Lubrano, Gena. "Looking at Operation Gatekeeper." *San Diego Union-Tribune*, October 11, 2004, B7.

Maciel, David, and María Herrera Sobek. "Introduction: Culture across Borders." In *Culture across Borders: Mexican Immigration and Popular Culture*, edited by Maciel and Herrera Sobek, 3–26. Tucson: University of Arizona Press, 1998.

———, eds. *Culture across Borders: Mexican Immigration and Popular Culture*. Tucson: University of Arizona Press, 1998.

Magaña, Lisa. *Straddling the Border: Immigration Policy and the I.N.S.* Austin: University of Texas Press, 2003.

Mains, Susan. "Contested Spaces: Representing Borders and Immigrant Identities between the United States and Mexico." Ph.D. diss., University of Kentucky, 2000.

Maram, Sheldon L. "Hispanic Workers in the Garment and Restaurant Industries in Los Angeles County." With the assistance of Stewart Long and

Dennis Berg. Program in U.S.–Mexican Studies, University of California at San Diego, 1980.

Marcus, George, and Michael Fischer. *Anthropology as Cultural Critique: An Experimental Moment in the Human Sciences.* Chicago: University of Chicago Press, 1986.

Marmon Silko, Leslie. "The Border Patrol State." In *Puro Border: Dispatches, Snapshots and Graffiti from La Frontera,* edited by Luis Humberto Crosthwaite, John William Byrd, and Bobby Byrd, 72–78. El Paso: Cinco Puntos Press, 2003.

Martin, Chris. "The New Migrants: Flexible Workers in a Global Economy." In *Culture and Global Change,* edited by Tracey Skelton and Tim Allen, 180–89. London: Routledge, 1999.

Martin, Philip, and Michael Teitelbaum. "The Mirage of Mexican Guest Workers." *Foreign Affairs* 80, no. 6 (2001): 117–31.

Martínez, Aldo. "Persiguen y detienen a ilegales." *El Mexicano,* November 12, 2003, 1A–2A.

Martínez, Oscar. *Border People: Life and Society in the U.S.–Mexico Borderlands.* Tucson: University of Arizona Press, 1994.

———. "Introduction." In *U.S.–Mexico Borderlands: Historical and Contemporary Perspectives,* edited by Martínez, xiii–xix. Wilmington, Del.: Scholarly Resources, 1996.

Martínez, Rubén. "The Kindness of Strangers." *New York Times,* December 24, 2004, A19.

Martínez Serrano, Pedro. "Emplean balas expansivas para matar a migrantes." *El Mexicano,* August 14, 2003, 1.

McCaughan, Edward. "Gender, Sexuality and Nation in the Art of Mexican Social Movements." *Nepantla: Views from South* 3, no. 1 (2002): 99–143.

McDonald, Jeff. "Death and 10 Years of Border Fence: Seminar, Protest Oppose Gatekeeper." *San Diego Union-Tribune,* October 3, 2004, B2.

Megirk, Jan. "Mexico Asks for Help to Stop Ranch 'Posses' Hunting Migrants." *Independent,* May 20, 2000, 17.

Melgar, Ivonne. "Fox y Bush, mas aliados." *El Mexicano,* January 13, 2004, 1A–2A.

El Mexicano. "Abusos en fronteras de Arizona y Texas." May 29, 2003, 7A.

———. "Afirman haberlo 'confundido' con un jabalí 'Cazan' a ilegal." June 4, 2003, 2C.

———. "Apoyará C.N.D.H. a los migrantes en fronteras." December 30, 2002, 5C.

———. "Conceden a 40 indocumentados permiso para vivir y trabajar en E.U." October 7, 2003, 3C.

———. "Decepciona Fox a E.U." March 19, 2003, 1C.

———. "Descubren a mas ilegales en Texas." May 17, 2003, 1C.

———. "Detectan camión con 17 indocumentados." May 29, 2003, 7A.

———. "Hallan en el desierto a 35 migrantes sin agua." August 2, 2004, 1C.

El Mexicano. "México, 'Patio trasero de E.U.'" November 12, 2003, 1C.

————. "Mueren tres migrantes en Arizona." May 30, 2003, 2C.

————. "Murieron cinco migrantes en enero." February 9, 2004, 6C.

————. "Pemex no se vende." May 13, 2003, 1C.

————. "Rescataron a mas de 100 ilegales en Arizona." February 20, 2004.

————. "Retienen en Arizona a cinco niños mexicanos." May 21, 2003, 4C.

Meyer, Leonard. *Emotion and Meaning in Music.* Chicago: University of Chicago Press, 1961.

Mohar, Gustavo, and María Elena Alcaraz. "U.S. Border Controls: A Mexican Perspective." In *The Wall around the West,* edited by Peter Andreas and Timothy Snyder, 139–50. Lanham, Md.: Rowman & Littlefield, 2000.

Molotov. *Dance and Dense Denso.* Mexico City: Universal, 2003.

————. "Four Latin Grammy Award Nominations for Molotov." July 2003. http://www.molotov.com.mx/ (accessed May 15, 2004).

Mooney, Margarita. "Migrants' Social Capital and Investing Remittances in Mexico." In *Crossing the Border: Research from the Mexican Migration Project,* edited by Jorge Durand and Douglas Massey, 45–62. New York: Russell Sage Foundation, 2004.

Moran, Chris. "Volunteers Begin Border Watch: Group's Message Aimed at Feds." *San Diego Union-Tribune,* October 2, 2005, B2.

Murillo, Samuel. "Mueren 4 migrantes en Valle Imperial." *Frontera,* September 30, 2003, 1.

Nevins, Joseph. *Operation Gatekeeper.* New York: Routledge, 2002.

New York Times. "Traces of Terror: Gas Masks Being Stockpiled on Capitol Hill." June 26, 2002, 19.

North, David S., and Marion F. Houstoun. *The Characteristics and Role of Illegal Aliens in the U.S. Labor Market: An Exploratory Study.* Washington, D.C.: Employment Training Administration, U.S. Department of Labor, 1976.

Oktavec, Eileen. *Answered Prayers: Miracles and Milagros along the Border.* Tucson: University of Arizona Press, 1995.

La Opinión. "Destacan auxilio fronterizo." January 5, 2004, 4A.

Orozco, Graciela, Esther González, and Roger Díaz de Cossio. *Las organizaciones mexicano-americanas: Hispanas y mexicanas en Estados Unidos.* 2nd ed. Mexico City: Centro de Estudios Migratorios del Instituto Nacional de Migración, 2003.

Orrenius, Pia. "The Effect of U.S. Border Enforcement on the Crossing Behavior of Migrants." In *Crossing the Border: Research from the Mexican Migration Project,* edited by Jorge Durand and Douglas Massey, 281–98. New York: Russell Sage Foundation, 2004.

Ortiz, Mercedes. "Migrantes hacen sudar a patrulleros." *Frontera,* June 27, 2004, 15.

Pacini Hernandez, Deborah. "Race, Ethnicity and the Production of Latin/o Popular Music." In *Global Repertoires: Popular Music within and beyond the Transnational Music Industry*, edited by Andreas Gebesmair and Alfred Smudits, 57–72. Hants, U.K.: Ashgate, 2001.

Pérez, Ramon. *Diary of an Undocumented Migrant*. Translated by Dick Reavis. Houston: Arte Publico Press, 1989.

Preston, Julia. "Fewer Mexican Immigrants Are Sending Money Back Home, Bank Says." *New York Times*, August 9, 2007, A10.

Prieto, Monica. 2004. "Un corrido de reflexión para Juárez." Univision Communications. http://www.univision.com/ (accessed May 17, 2004).

Quintana, Enrique. "¿Abrir Pemex a la inversion?" *El Imparcial*, May 12, 2003, 15A.

Reichart, Joshua. "A Town Divided: Economic Stratification and Social Relations in a Mexican Community." Social Problems 29, no. 4 (1982): 411–23.

Reuters. "2 More Illegal Aliens Found Dead in Desert." *Ottawa Sun*, May 25, 2001, 26.

Revelli, Philippe. "Mexico: Devourer of Migrants." *Le Monde Diplomatique* (English edition), July 2003. http://www.mondediplo.com/2003/07/09revelli/ (accessed July 9, 2003).

Rich, Paul, and Guillermo De Los Reyes. "Mexican Caricature and the Politics of Popular Culture." *Journal of Popular Culture* 30, no. 1 (1996): 133–45.

Ríos Navarrete, Humberto. "En Tijuana un grito creativo." *Milenio*, May 10, 2004, 74–77.

Rodríguez, Mariángela. *Mito, identidad y rito*. Mexico City: Centro de Investigaciones y Estudios Superiores en Antropología Social, 1998.

Roe, Keith, and Gust de Meyer. "One Planet—One Music? MTV and Globalization." In *Global Repertoires: Popular Music within and Beyond the Transnational Music Industry*, edited by Andreas Gebesmair and Alfred Smudits, 33–44. Hants, U.K.: Ashgate, 2001.

Rohter, Larry. "Brazilians Streaming into U.S. through Mexican Border." *New York Times*, June 30, 2005, A3.

Rozemberg, Hernán. 2002. "Border Patrol Keeps Tabs on Group's Migrant Aid." *Arizona Republic*. http://www.azcentral.com/specials/special03/articles/0722azsamaritan22.html/(accessed July 22, 2002).

San, Luis Adolfo. "Calvario de niños migrantes." *El Vigia*, March 21, 2004, 6.

———. "Ilegar a E.U. . . . a como de lugar." *Frontera*, June 27, 2004, 11.

Sánchez Zambrano, Eneida. "Pegueros: Pueblo de migrantes, pueblo 'californiano.'" *El Vigia*, April 27, 2004, 6.

Santibáñez Romellón, Jorge. "La guerra y la frontera." *Frontera*, March 21, 2003, 13.

Schele, Linda, and Mary Miller. *The Blood of Kings: Dynasty and Ritual in Maya Art*. New York: George Braziller, 1986.

Schmitt, Eric, and Julia Preston. "Threats and Responses: Washington, U.S. Ready to Back New U.N. Measure on Iraq, Bush Says." *New York Times*, February 7, 2003, A1.

Schwarz, Bill. "Conservatism, Nationalism and Imperialism." In *Politics and Ideology: A Reader*, edited by James Donald and Stuart Hall, 154–86. Milton Keynes, Pa.: Open University Press, 1986.

Secretaría de Relaciones Exteriores. "Guía del migrante mexicano." http://www.sre.gob.mx/tramites/guiamigrante/pagel.htm/ (accessed January 20, 2006).

Siegrist, Michael, Carmen Keller, and Henk Kiers. "A New Look at the Psychometric Paradigm of Perception of Hazards." *Risk Analysis* 25, no. 1 (2005): 211–22.

Sifuentes, Edward. 2004. "Experts, Advocates Criticize Gatekeeper at 10th Anniversary." *North County Times*. http://www.nctimes.com/articles/20Q4/10/03/news/top stories/17 25 4010 2 04.txt/(accessed October 5, 2004).

Simonett, Helena. "Narcocorridos: An Emerging Micromusic of Nuevo LA." *Ethnomusicology* 45, no. 2 (2001): 315–37.

Smith, Claudia. "Border Enforcement: Deadlier Than Ever and Ineffective as Always." *Latino Studies* 2, no. 1 (2004): 111.

Smith, Jeffrey. "Rural Place Attachment in Hispano Urban Center." *Geographical Review* 92, no. 3 (2002): 432–52.

Sorell, Victor. "Telling Images Bracket the 'Broken-Promise(d) Land': The Culture of Immigration and the Immigration of Culture across Borders." In *Culture across Borders: Mexican Immigration and Popular Culture*, edited by David Maciel and María Herrera Sobek, 99–148. Tucson: University of Arizona Press, 1998.

Spellman, Francis, ed. *Holy Bible*. New York: Douay Bible House, 1953.

Spener, David. "Controlling the Border in El Paso del Norte: Operation Blockade or Charade?" In *Ethnography at the Border*, edited by Pablo Vila, 182–98. Minneapolis: University of Minnesota Press, 2003.

Stalker, Peter. *The No-Nonsense Guide to International Migration*. Oxford: New Internationalist, 2001.

Sterngold, James. "Rights Groups Urge Change in Border Policy." *New York Times*, May 26, 2001, 10.

Strauss, Anselm, and Juliet Corbin. "Grounded Theory Methodology: An Overview." In *Handbook of Qualitative Research*, edited by Norman Denzin and Yvonna Lincoln. Thousand Oaks, Calif.: Sage, 1994.

Strickland, Daryl, and Scott Gold. "17 Found Dead at Texas Truck Stop." *Los Angeles Times*, May 14, 2003, A2.

Taplin, Dana, Suzanne Scheld, and Setha Low. "Rapid Ethnographic Assessment in Urban Parks: A Case Study of Independence National Historic Park." *Human Organization* 61, no. 1 (2002): 80–94.

Taylor, Steven, and Robert Bogdan. *Introduction to Qualitative Research Methods: A Guidebook and Resource*. New York: Wiley, 1998.

Thompson, Ginger. "Littlest Immigrants, Left in Hands of Smugglers." *New York Times*, November 3, 2003, A1.

———. "Mexican Leader Condemns U.S. for Migrant Bill Passed by House." *New York Times,* December 20, 2005, A6.

———. "Mexico's Migrants Profit from Dollars Sent Home." *New York Times,* February 23, 2005, A1.

———. "Mexico Worries about Its Own Southern Border." *New York Times,* February 3, 2006, A1.

Thompson, Mary, Dilek Onkal, Ali Avcioglu, and Paul Goodwin. "Aviation Risk Perception: A Comparison between Experts and Novices." *Risk Analysis* 24, no. 6 (2004): 1585–95.

Los Tigres del Norte. *Pacto de sangre.* Mexico City: Fonovisa-Univision, 2004.

Toma, Robin, and Jill Esbenshade. "Day Laborer Hiring Sites: Constructive Approaches to Community Conflict." Los Angeles: Commission on Human Relations, Los Angeles County, 2001.

Umphlett, Wiley Lee. *Mythmakers of the American Dream.* Cranbury, N.J.: Associated University Presses, 1983.

U.S. Commission on Immigration Reform and Secretaría de Relaciones Exteriores. *Binational Study: Migration between Mexico and the United States.* Mexico City, 1997.

U.S. Conference of Catholic Bishops. *Welcoming the Stranger among Us.* Washington, D.C., 2000.

Valenzuela, Javier. "El Programa Beta: La protección de los derechos humanos de los migrantes indocumentados desde una perspectiva policíaca no convencional." In *Migración y fronteras,* edited by Manuel Ángel Castillo, Alfredo Lattes, and Jorge Santibáñez, 463–73. Tijuana: El Colegio de la Frontera Norte, 1999.

Valenzuela Arce, José Manuel. "La música en la cultura popular." In *Encuentros: Los festivales internacionales de la raza,* edited by Amelia Malagamba Ansotegui, 27–66. Tijuana: El Colegio de la Frontera Norte, 1988.

———. *Nuestros piensos: Culturas populares en la frontera México–Estados Unidos.* Mexico City: Dirreción General de Cultures Populares, 1998.

Vann, Bill. "18 Migrant Workers Die in Texas." 2003. World Socialist Web site. http://www.wsws.org/ (accessed May 26, 2004).

Vásquez, Nancy. "Piden por los migrantes." *El Vigia,* January 22, 2004, 16.

Viana, Virginia, Rubén Ruiz, Alfredo Larreta, and Luis Adolfo San. "Sufren los niños por trevimiento." *Frontera,* February 3, 2004, 15.

El Vigia. "Arrestan torturador de indocumentados." October 2, 2003, 8.

———. "Campaña para indocumentados." August 18, 2004, 4.

———. "Más de 2 mil migrantes muertos." September 29, 2003, 3.

———. "Matan a inmigrantes." February 6, 2004, 4.

———. Mojados a terroristas." *Center for Latin American Studies: University of California* (Berkeley), September 11, 2003, 1.

———. "Mueren casi 2 mil migrantes." October 2, 2003, 9.

———. "Rescatan del frío a Nogales en S.D." February 25, 2004, 11.

Vila, Pablo. *Crossing Borders, Reinforcing Borders: Social Categories. Metaphors, and Narrative Identities.* Austin: University of Texas Press, 2000.

———. "Introduction: Border Ethnographies." In *Ethnography at the Border*, edited by Vila, ix–xxxv. Minneapolis: University of Minnesota Press, 2003.

———, ed. *Ethnography at the Border.* Minneapolis: University of Minnesota Press, 2003.

Villegas, Manuel. "Gritan los creativos." *Frontera*, April 21, 2004, 1.

Villoro, Juan. "Nothing to Declare: Welcome to Tijuana." In *Puro Border: Dispatches, Snapshots and Graffiti from La Frontera*, edited by Luis Humberto Crosthwaite, John William Byrd, and Bobby Byrd, 197–205. El Paso: Cinco Puntos Press, 2003.

Wall, Allan. 2003. "Molotov's *Frijolero*—Malicious Mexican Music on MTV," July 22, 2003. Center for American Unity. http://www.vdare.com/ (accessed May 15, 2004).

Washington Post. "Peso Crisis Spurs Migrants' Quest for Dollars." January 28, 1995, A1.

Wheaton, Sarah. "Huckabee Immigration Plan Emphasizes Security." *New York Times*, December 8, 2007, A13.

Wherry, Aaron. "Worldwide Short File Festival." *National Post*, May 14, 2004, B3.

Wiederhorn, Jon. 2003. "Molotov Explodes at MTV Latin Music Awards." http://www.MTV.com/ (accessed May 15, 2004).

Ybarra-Frausto, Tomas. "Arte Chicano: Images of a Community." In *Signs from the Heart: California Chicano Murals*, edited by Eva Cockcroft and Holly Barnet-Sanchez, 54–67. Albuquerque: University of New Mexico Press, 1999.

Index

About the Author

Lynnaire Maria Sheridan has a strong interest in community, social justice, environmental, and tourism issues, particularly relating to Latin America. Sheridan's passion for Latin America, and her Spanish language skills, developed during a yearlong student exchange to Argentina. She completed her Bachelor of Applied Science (Environmental Management and Tourism) at the University of Western Sydney before undertaking a comparative cultural analysis of visitor characteristics and behavior in the national parks of Australia and Argentina as her honors degree study. After working for the International Ecotourism Society in Vermont, she completed her doctorate on the unauthorized migration of Mexicans to the United States, also at the University of Western Sydney. A sociocultural researcher and adjunct senior lecturer with Edith Cowan University, Western Australia, she currently teaches and conducts research at the University of Wollongong, New South Wales.

2858